# The Nation across the World

# The Nation across the World
## Postcolonial Literary Representations

*Edited by*
Harish Trivedi, Meenakshi Mukherjee,
C. Vijayasree, T. Vijay Kumar

**OXFORD**
UNIVERSITY PRESS

# OXFORD
## UNIVERSITY PRESS

YMCA Library Building, Jai Singh Road, New Delhi 110 001

Oxford University Press is a department of the University of Oxford. It furthers the
University's objective of excellence in research, scholarship, and education
by publishing worldwide in

Oxford   New York

Auckland   Cape Town   Dar es Salaam   Hong Kong   Karachi   Kuala Lumpur
Madrid   Melbourne   Mexico City   Nairobi   New Delhi   Shanghai   Taipei   Toronto

With offices in

Argentina   Austria   Brazil   Chile   Czech Republic   France   Greece   Guatemala
Hungary   Italy   Japan   Poland   Portugal   Singapore   South Korea   Switzerland
Thailand   Turkey   Ukraine   Vietnam

Oxford is a registered trademark of Oxford University Press
in the UK and in certain other countries

Published in India by Oxford University Press, New Delhi

ISBN-13: 978-0-19-569024-8
ISBN-10: 0-19-569024-9

Typeset in Goudy Old Style by Mindways Design, New Delhi 110 032
Printed in India by De Unique, New Delhi 110 018
Published by Oxford University Press
YMCA Library Building, Jai Singh Road, New Delhi 110 001

# Contents

# Preface and Acknowledgements

The intense ongoing debate on the idea and the reality of the Nation has proved to be of central concern not only in the disciplines of political science and history but equally in postcolonial theory and literature. This was amply reflected in the XIIIth International Triennial Conference of the Association for Commonwealth Literature and Language Studies (ACLALS) on the theme 'Nation and Imagination: The Changing Commonwealth', held at Hyderabad, India, from 4 to 9 August 2004.

The present volume offers a selection from the over 200 papers presented at the conference by speakers from numerous nations of the Commonwealth, Europe, Latin America, and from the US. Two other volumes compiled by the same editors are being published separately.

The editors (who as office-bearers of ACLALS for the period 2001 to 2004 had the responsibility for planning and holding the conference) would like to thank the following organizations for their generous support: the Commonwealth Foundation; Foundation internationales des langue et litteratures modernes (F.I.L.L.M.); the British Council in India; the Australia-India Council; the Sahitya Akademi (the National Academy of Letters), New Delhi; Orient Longman; Penguin Books, India; the Oxford University Press, India; and Akshara, Hyderabad.

Following presentation at the conference, Bruce Bennett's essay has appeared in the *Journal of Commonwealth Literature* 40:3

(2005), and Priyamvada Gopal's essay has appeared as Chapter 1 of her book, *Literary Radicalism in India: Gender, Nation and the Transition to Independence* (London: Routledge 2005).

April 2007                                      The Editors

# The Nation and the World

## An Introduction

HARISH TRIVEDI

In the beginning was the World, whole and entire, but now it lies fragmented in narrow warring Nations. Though the nation was invented, or imagined into existence, only in the nineteenth century in Europe, it has since been the cause of untold conflict and misery, leading to two grotesquely wasteful World Wars (—so called, however, and not international wars). The harmful phenomenon of the nation has rapidly multiplied in the rest of the world, beyond the West, and it has there too aroused the worst of loyalties and passions. It has been responsible for tension, discord, armed conflict, partition, invasion, and occupation in all parts of the globe, in Ireland, in the Arab 'world', in India, Pakistan, Sri Lanka, in the divided Koreas and Vietnams, and in China and Japan as well. In many nations, it is the most reactionary and fascist strands of the polity which are labelled as nationalist, not only by others but by themselves too. Whether the state withers away or not, the nation as a divisive political category must therefore be neutralized and rendered obsolete before we can have world peace, harmony, and prosperity. Indeed, that is why various international and multinational organizations and globalizing economic and cultural forces are now beginning to sweep the world and a good thing too.

Such would seem to be, broadly speaking, the present state of opinion and wisdom on the subject of the Nation, especially in Theory. However, a reality check at the ground level discloses a rather different picture. As Anthony D. Smith, probably the most prolific and encyclopaedic of all contemporary scholars of the nation, wrote at the beginning of his earliest book on the subject:

In the world today, there are well over a hundred [nations], if thereby we mean the member states of the United Nations. Each possesses its own flag, anthem, administration, educational system, army, judicial system, legislature, citizenship rights, founding myth and constitution, coinage and capital. The nation-state is the norm of modern political organization; and it is as ubiquitous as it is recent. The nation-state is the almost undisputed foundation of world order, the main object of individual loyalties, the chief definer of a man's identity. It is far more significant for the individual and for world security than any previous type of political and social organization. It permeates our outlook so much that we hardly question its legitimacy today…. We tend to regard nations like skin-colour—as a 'natural' attribute of man. When we talk of 'society' today, we refer implicitly to 'nations'. (Smith 1971: 2–3)

This was in his *Theories of the Nation* and, notwithstanding that title, his blithe pre-Theory innocence is betrayed by his unself-conscious and unproblematized use of terms like 'man' and 'skin-colour'. Yet, that does not invalidate the verifiable pragmatic force of what he says.

Indeed, in the three decades and a half since the above paean to the nation was written, the idea of the nation has lost none of its appeal or charm but has instead gained further ground, so to say. The number of the member states of the United Nations, 'well over a hundred' when Smith wrote, was, to be more precise, 132 in 1971; it has since risen to 192 in 2006. It was 55 when the United Nations was founded in 1945, stood at 82 in 1958, but then leapt by another 50 members within fourteen years as the 'winds of change' swept colonialism away from Africa and the Caribbean islands. In a second major spurt which accompanied another world-shaking development of our times, the number of nations went up from 159 in 1990 to 184 in 1993, following the break-up of the Soviet Union and the new Balkanization set off as a chain reaction (United Nations 2007). Theory—meaning thereby mainly Marxist and/or postmodern/postcolonial theory—may do all it can to damn and deconstruct the nation, but popular will all over the world seems to continue to aspire to it and cherish it.

More than any other single work perhaps, Benedict Anderson's seminal book on 'the Origin and Spread of Nationalism' has set the terms of contemporary discourse on the subject, and its title, *Imagined Communities*, has prompted many readers (and non-readers) of that book to believe that the nation is, somehow, a less than real entity. It is, however seldom noticed that Anderson began his book by acknowledging that 'nation-ness is the most universally legitimate value in the political life of our time', even as he noted the rueful acknowledgement by another Marxist scholar Tom Nairn that '[t]he theory of nationalism represents Marxism's great historical failure' (Anderson 1983: 12, 13). Altogether, then, to adapt a dictum from Dr Johnson, all Theory may be against the Nation but all practice seems to be for it.

## I. Empire, Nation, and Culture

The view that the nation emerged in nineteenth-century Europe is counterpointed by the view that nations are 'in some sense "natural", "essential", "substantial" and "enduring", [...] a primordial element of nature, and intrinsic to the human condition' (Smith 2001: 9–10). Such a belief would not only give nations a hallowed ancient genealogy but would make their origin pre-historic; it would also allow that pre-modern nations were based on ethnic and cultural collectivity rather than on political organization and unity, for they were in any case much smaller territories than are now associated with nations.

The mere size of satrapies, duchies, and kingdoms did not stop them, however, from attempting constantly to encroach upon each other and to expand, as if such an impulse and endeavour were also a primordial element of nature. Perhaps the first formal recognition that this need not be the normal state of affairs came about through the Treaty of Westphalia in 1648, which brought to an end the Thirty Years' War as well as the Eighty Years' War. It is commonly agreed to have established the idea of the sovereign state, which would not as a norm intervene in the internal affairs of other sovereign states and thus ensure relative stability, and also guarantee its subjects some basic civic and secular rights including the right to adhere to a minority denomination.

Meanwhile, an alternative mode of ensuring stability and peace was for a feudal kingdom to grow so large as to turn into an empire, by having already conquered and assimilated most rival kingdoms that would or could have challenged it and warred with it. The Holy Roman Empire (which was a major player in the Treaty of Westphalia), the Ottoman Empire, the Mughal Empire, and the British Empire all imposed a kind of stability and peace in their respective domains, but it was a peace brought about not by mutual understanding and harmony but by brute force. Pax Romana and Pax Britannica, for example, were made possible by those mighty military machines having fought many wars professedly to end all wars and to enforce peace. The far-flung subjects of these vast empires often had not much more in common than that they were ruled by the same dynastic and despotic emperor and governed by broadly the same system of administration.

In contrast, when the nation-state finally emerged following the collapse of successive and various empires and consolidated itself as a universal political norm, it was as a rule seen to be a sovereign political entity on the outside which also had ethnic, linguistic, and cultural cohesion within. The hard shell, or the skeleton, or the infrastructure was the state, while the soft filling within, the flesh and blood, the superstructure was the nation. The shell was in a broad sense political; the content within, in an equally broad sense, cultural. If cultural nationalism remains perhaps the most vexed, the most problematic and therefore the most vigorously debated of all the forms of nationalism, it may be precisely because it represents the most intangible and yet the most hegemonic constituent of the nation-state. After conducting a scrupulous, even legalistic, even-handed arbitration of the claims of 'a liberal version of cultural nationalism', through the possible permutations and alternatives of 'ethical universalism', 'cultural cosmopolitanism', and 'distributive justice' within the frame of the nation-state, Chaim Gans concludes his book *The Limits of Nationalism* (2003) by wondering whether it has in the end been an argument against cultural nationalism or for it (Gans 148, 173)!

Terry Eagleton, in contrast, is quite certain of the centrality of culture to the debate on nationalism, and even reverses the priority between them by suggesting that the former is to be defined in terms of the latter and not the other way round: 'We owe our modern notions of culture in large part to nationalism and colonialism, along with the growth of an anthropology in the service of imperial power' (Eagleton 2000: 26). This serves to make one ask as to which the cart is and which the horse between culture and nationalism, and also goes a long way towards accounting for the fact that in many colonies in Asia and Africa, cultural nationalism substantially reinforced political movements for freedom and often predated and provided a major impulse for them. In a corresponding articulation of the triangulation between colony, nation, and culture, while Frantz Fanon insisted that anti-colonial liberation movements must not be merely national but must retain an international consciousness, he recognized at the same time, as Ali Behdad points out, that 'every culture is first and foremost national' (Behdad 2006: 72).

## II. Beyond the Western Nation

If the idea and practice of the nation is palpably different in the West from that in the rest of the world, it is so probably because while the rise of nationalism in the West led to colonization by it of other parts of the world, it was precisely this colonization that gave rise to nationalism in those other parts. But this would imply that nationalism in the colonies was not only a retort to nationalism in the West but also basically modelled on it. Partha Chatterjee has engaged with this intertwined and even paradoxically circular process in a more sustained and trenchant manner than perhaps any other non-Western scholar, by repeatedly countering, on a variety of grounds, the formulations of the foremost Western theorists of the subject. To cite only the most salient of such arguments from a vast and complex body of work, Chatterjee points out in his *Nationalist Thought and the Colonial World* (1986) that Western nationalism is, somewhat implausibly, predicated on a 'cultural essentialism' and on post-Enlightenment rationalism at the same time (Chatterjee 1986: 14, 17), and that the discourse of nationalism is caught up anyhow with the discourse of modernity, reform, and progress, and should therefore be regarded as only a part of a larger, allegedly 'derivative' discourse encompassing both nationalism and modernity (Chatterjee 1986: 22–6).

In *The Nation and its Fragments* (1993), he suggests that it was 'the collapse of Soviet socialism' that prompted the West to identify nationalism as the next major source of threat, as 'a dark, elemental, unpredictable force of primordial nature threatening the orderly calm of civilized life'. After the anti-colonial victories nationalism had won in Asia and Africa in the preceding decades, it was seen by the West to have safely exhausted its agenda, but then it seemed to be raising its ugly head again: 'Like drugs, terrorism and illegal immigration, it is one more product of the Third World that the West dislikes but is powerless to prohibit'. To Anderson's formulation of the nation as an 'imagined community' on the basis of evidence adduced by him almost entirely from the evolution of the nation in the West, Chatterjee said he had 'one central objection': if the nation had been thus imagined in the West already, what did the nationalisms outside the West 'have left to imagine?' (Chatterjee 1993: 3–5).

These are not only acute arguments; these are also splendid rhetorical flourishes in a radically postcolonial and broadly 'Left nationalist' (Chatterjee 1997: 8) cause, and like all rhetoric, they not only shoot the mark but perhaps also overshoot it. One could argue, for example, that the main objection to Anderson's argument is not that he does not allow that a national community could be imagined differently in other parts of the world, for he does recognize, however inadequately, the respective trajectories of nationalist formations in countries such as Indonesia, the Philippines, 'Siam', that is, Thailand, and fleetingly and erroneously, even India, where he is strong on Macaulay (cf. his barb, 'So far, so Macaulay') but gets the one nationalist leader he cites, Bipin Chandra Pal, grievously wrong, by depicting him as 'angry enough' in 1973, 'a quarter of a century after India became independent' (Anderson 88), whereas Pal had in fact died in 1932, fifteen years before independence was attained. Further, and more seriously, Anderson confuses Pal with the deracinated Anglophone Indians whom Pal had in fact severely criticized (Anderson 88–9, 109).

So, it is not that Anderson is not aware of several different forms of nationalism all over the world in their many phases, including what he calls the post-Second World War 'Last Wave' of liberationist nationalism in Asia and Africa and to which he devotes a chapter (104–28). Rather, the trouble with Anderson is that the decline of religion, the consolidation of a designated vernacular as a national language, and the dissemination in that language of a collective identity through print-capitalism, which he identifies as the three pillars of nationalism, are not then equally applied and tested by him on different grounds. The rise of nations in the Indian subcontinent alone is enough to provide substantial variations on each one of Anderson's tenets.

To start with, the partition of the colonial nation into two independent nation-states, India and Pakistan, in 1947 was brought about by the primacy of religion (see Jinnah 2007: 233–4) which Anderson regards (probably correctly enough in the European context) as a spent force which the nation comes to replace. While the subsequent dismembering of West Pakistan and East Pakistan/ Bangladesh seemed a triumph of the one language-one nation formula over the claims of a common religion, as endorsed by Anderson, that was so only from the point of view of Bangladesh (see Anisuzzaman 2007: 370–91), for what remained of Pakistan continued to function, without any further break-up, in at least five major languages: the official Urdu and also Panjabi, Sindhi,

Pushtu, and Balochi. Finally, in India, many religions and many more languages, including the eighteen inscribed in the Constitution as 'national languages', have coexisted within the same nation-state for six decades now, thus giving the lie not only to Anderson's theory but also to most other theories of nationalism. Moreover, in all these three nations, the rate of literacy is still 60 per cent or less, undermining seriously any claims to be made for print-capitalism as a key instrument of national formation. Given Anderson's parameters, it would be difficult to imagine that these three nations do actually exist. And this is not even to mention the bottom-line fact that anti-colonial nationalisms were not so much *imagined* through a common language and books and newspapers as they were forged in the smithy of blood, sweat, and prison cells. In the modern world, perhaps more people have suffered and laid down their lives in the cause of the nation than for the sake of religion or indeed in attempting armed revolutions.

Some other notable theorists of our times have been prevented by more explicitly ideological considerations from recognizing that a country, upon liberating itself from colonial rule, may be thought to have become a nation. They argue that decolonization by itself is not enough, and that the whole system by which a country is ruled needs to be revolutionized or at least radically altered before such a country can be called a nation. In a long chapter titled 'Disavowing Decolonization' in his book *Nationalism and Cultural Practice in the Postcolonial World*, Neil Lazarus cites numerous instances of what he calls 'First Worldist interpretations of nationalism' (Lazarus 1999: 68) in this regard as well as instances of writings from within the Third World, such as by Mahasweta Devi which show, according to Gayatri Chakravorty Spivak, that for the subaltern, there is no real difference between the empire and the nation (Lazarus 109–10). Nor is this a matter of economic justice alone, for Spivak has gone on to state that '[I]t was the eruption of Hindu nationalism in India in December 1992, resulting in the destruction of a mosque in Ayodhya, that taught us about the failure of decolonization in India', and then proceeded to identify such failure as 'the remote motor of the exodus of those of us who became the globe-trotting postcolonials' (Spivak 1999: 362–3). But this looks like post facto rationalization of postcolonial globe-trotting for, in this case as also in the cases of most other diasporic Indian critics and writers, the migration had taken place some decades before the mosque in Ayodhya was brought down. 'I would argue,' Spivak says more comprehensively, 'that ... nationalism in many ways is a displaced or reversed legitimation of colonialism'—and this despite the fact that by Spivak's own (apparently unironic) account, Mahasweta Devi has also narrated stories of 'subaltern freedom in the new nation' and of the possibility of 'action within the postcolonial new nation' (Spivak 141–2).

As Robert Young has scrupulously recounted in his *Postcolonialism: An Historical Introduction*, the Communist Party line on anti-colonial national struggles, as debated and adopted at successive Congresses of the Comintern (with notable contributions by 'the great Indian Marxist' M.N. Roy), kept shifting on whether or not to set up a United Front with bourgeois nationalist movements in colonies where revolution did not seem to be an immediate possibility. In the process, Gandhi was denounced in 1928 as 'a prime agent of British imperialism', the Communist Party of Great Britain was asked to take charge of the Communist Party of India which had no more than 150 members by 1934, and at the outbreak of the Second World War, the Party in India exhorted the people to rally behind Britain, whereas Gandhi in 1942 asked the British to quit India forthwith (Young 2001: 125, 145–50; 115–81 *passim*).

Following decolonization, achieved without anything approaching revolution in the vast majority of the colonies of Asia and Africa, many of these newly independent nations adopted in any case an avowedly socialist agenda of development, vigorously opposed neocolonialism, and even showed a 'capacity to generate a class-conscious, critical analysis of nationalist elites ... [and an] ability to envision and attempt liberatory government and wealth distribution', as Laura Chrisman has pointed out (Chrisman 2004: 188). It may be useful to distinguish here, as Terry Eagleton does, between a 'revolutionary nationalism in the Third World' which 'faltered in the 1970s', and a '"post-revolutionary"' phase which came to be dominated by 'the power of the transnational corporations' (Eagleton 1996: 205). As proof of this radical pudding, one may point to the substantial, even spectacular, economic development of many of these postcolonial nation-states through redistribution of land, various subsidies to the poorer sections of the population, and positive discrimination made obligatory by law to help put members of the backward communities on a fast track in terms of education and employment. It was precisely such unmistakable socialist orientation that led to the geopolitical fact that, throughout the decolonized decades which coincided with the Cold War, the First World, and especially the US had many more 'enemies' among the nations of the Third World than it had friends.

## III. Na(rra)tion, DissemiNation, Allegory

When Anderson used the term 'imagined' in formulating his notion of a national community, in the sense of 'created' (rather than 'invented'), he also conceded at the very outset that not only the nation but '[i]n fact, all communities larger than the primordial villages of face-to-face contact (and perhaps even these) are imagined' (Anderson 15). Nevertheless, his book (or at least its arresting title) has fired the imagination of numerous subsequent scholars into speaking of the nation as if it were not a material-historical but a merely verbal and fanciful category. This impression has been reinforced and extended by the unforgettably titled *Nation and Narration* (1990), a collection of sixteen essays edited by Homi K. Bhabha, including one by himself titled 'DissemiNation' which seemed to have undercut the nation ludically with a reiterated negative: 'dis' and 'semi'. What had convinced Bhabha of 'the need for a volume of this nature' was a seminar he had taught at the University of Sussex which had been titled plainly enough 'Novel and Nation' (Bhabha 1990: ix).

Now, however, Bhabha not only quoted Anderson on the first page of his 'Introduction' but went on to declare that 'the project of *Nation and Narration* [was] to explore the Janus-faced ambivalence of language itself in the construction of the Janus-faced discourse of the nation' (Bhabha 1990: 3). This doubly double-faced (de)constructionist procedure was a clear advance on the last page of Anderson's book which had cited a rather less ambivalent face, from Walter Benjamin's description of the Angel of History: 'His face is turned towards the past' (cited in Anderson 147). The seductive alliteration of Bhabha's title here—which could be said to have as much reason as rhyme—was matched perhaps by his own beguiling felicitous phrasing in his later book, *The Location of Culture* (1994), where he spoke of the nation largely in terms of migration from one's unhomed nation to an alien other, and of the nation as located 'within a growing transnational culture'; such migration, he added, was a form of 'cultural translation', indeed of 'the transnational as the translational'—in the etymological sense of the word 'translation' (Bhabha 1994: 173–4). This was as effective a way as any of cutting the ground beneath the feet of the historical location of the nation.

Are nations then imagined and narrated as a primary precondition of their existence? In a broadly post-structuralist sense reinforced by 'the linguistic turn', they necessarily must be—but then so must everything else at the same time. As Anderson clarified, not only the nation but all communities—including what other scholars in different contexts have called 'organic' and 'knowable' communities—are equally imagined. As for narration, the rise of the nation—like the rise of the middle classes or of the bourgeoisie—in many parts of Europe may have broadly coincided with the rise of the novel there, but must it follow that it did so equally everywhere? In India, for example, the middle classes are finally seen to have risen within the last decade or two, together with the advent of liberalization and globalization, but the novel in India had by all accounts already risen more than a century beforehand. The title of a conference organized by the Sahitya Akademi (the 'National Academy of Letters' in India, so called in English, though the word 'national' does not occur in the official name in Hindi as perhaps it does not need to) in New Delhi in 1999 was

'The Novel in Search of the Nation', but as more than one speaker pointed out, it might as well have been 'The Nation in Search of the Novel'. In Hindi, for example, which was already acclaimed as the national language of a yet-to-be-independent India by Gandhi in 1918 and incorporated into the freedom movement as a vital plank of nationalism, many of the major nationalist novels—the epics of the nation—were written in the wake of the rise of Gandhi and his movement and not before it. The nation and nationalism came first; the narration afterwards or at least alongside.

Another kind of theoretical correlation between the nation and the novel concerns not when and how novels are narrated but instead just how and where they are read. The major statement here is by Fredric Jameson, which was promptly followed by a major counter-statement by Aijaz Ahmad, two theorists who share radical convictions but are separated, apparently even divided, by their location in the First World and the Third World respectively and by what Ahmad in his rejoinder called 'Jameson's Rhetoric of Otherness' (Ahmad 1994: chapter title). The key formulation by Jameson here is not to the effect that '"All third-world texts are necessarily …"' national allegories (as cited in Ahmad 96), which is what Ahmad directs most of his fire-power against, but something more qualified and complex, as finally quoted in full by Ahmad several pages later:

All third-world texts are necessarily, I want to argue, allegorical and in a very specific way: they are to be read as what I will call *national allegories*, even when or perhaps I should say particularly when their forms develop out of predominantly western machineries of representation such as the novel (cited in Ahmad 109).

In Jameson's formulation, then, Third World texts are not consciously produced as national allegories, as Ahmad takes him to mean; they are only to be read as such, clearly and necessarily by readers outside the Third World, especially in the present 'Era of Multinational Capital'. In Jameson's acute if cryptic rider, this becomes even more necessary, paradoxically, when the mode of literary representation is not indigenous but markedly contaminated by a Western genre such as the novel—possibly for the reason that the adaptation of the Western form to non-Western content may involve a kind of double-coding. In any case, it is clear that Jameson is not belittling such texts through his suggested procedure of reading them as either national or allegorical; instead, he is recognizing them to be more pervasively and complexly political.

Further, one may ask, are not nearly all novels implicitly taken, by readers from a different nation or 'world', as standing in for the reality of their native countries, and do not Third World readers in their turn quite often read works not only by Dickens and Balzac but also, to a considerable degree, by say even Proust and Woolf as sources of primary if mediated information about England and France, as 'representations' not only of fictionally free-floating individual characters but of the social ground on which such characters are located, and indeed as novels narrating those nations in their own direct or elliptical ways? Besides, as Imre Szeman has pointed out in his elaborate rescue of Jameson's essay, Jameson had also used the term 'national allegory' earlier with reference to a First World novel with an international cast set in Paris, *Tarr* (1918) by Wyndham Lewis; he means by 'allegory' not a 'morality' tale but rather an exceptionally complex text which requires of the reader 'a kind of translation mechanism'; and that Jameson's discussion ultimately helps us in 'decolonizing' the concept of the nation by positing it as a valid category of interpretation and as a differently formulated 'theoretical problematic' (Szeman 2003: 56, 57, 60–62).

Though the 'nation' is perceived to be a derogatory enough category when applied to the space where one is located, it is worth noting that Ahmad had taken even greater umbrage at Jameson's use of 'Third World', a discriminatory term Ahmad has historicized in order to excoriate in other contexts as well (Ahmad 96, 43–71). Whereas all nations can be referred to equally as nations, the division of the globe into the so called Three Worlds is clearly arranged in a descending order, besides the fact that a 'World' is far more homogenizing and flattening than a nation, however large, ever could be. Other terms in currency in this broad context include 'multinational' and 'transnational', both with globalizing and exploitative economic connotations rather than with any substantial political signification.

## IV. Nation, Cosmopolitanism, and Diaspora

In some recent discussions, the term 'cosmopolitan' has come to stand for the opposite of all that is culturally narrow and limiting in the nation. In his book-length discussion of Salman Rushdie's *Midnight's Children*, a text that apparently began crying out to be read as a national allegory as soon as it was born (or as soon as its hero was born, on its opening page, precisely at the moment India became a free nation), Neil ten Kortenaar in conclusion offers a judiciously nuanced arbitration between the nationalist and the cosmopolitan impulses that have shaped that canonical postcolonial text as well as its readings. Though himself a self-confessedly cosmopolitan admirer of Rushdie, Kortenaar readily grants the assumption 'that national writers are somehow superior or more authentic'—on the grounds that Rushdie too '*feels the same way* (or else why would he hide his errors behind Saleems' unreliability?). Rushdie the cosmopolitan wants some of the authority that belongs properly to nationalists' (Kortenaar 241; emphasis in the original). Indeed, Rushdie seems to claim such authority wholesale through his apparently limitless magical omniscience and presumed expertise on all matters Indian, for if he could not demonstrate that he is first of all an authentic insider, he would not be an ostensibly cosmopolitan author; he would be a merely metropolitan one.

The distinction between the cosmopolitan and the national is more often formulated in postcolonial discourse as that between the diaspora on the one hand, and (as the diasporic Rushdie himself has put it) 'imaginary homelands, Indias of the mind' on the other (Rushdie 1991: 10). Indeed, migration, exile, diaspora, and hybridity have been among the most widely theorized issues in postcolonial theory. It is, however, the voluntary migration of the Third World postcolonial intellectual to the First World which has almost exclusively defined the parameters of this debate, with relatively little attention paid so far to the much larger and wider subaltern diaspora of indigent labourers and farm-workers, which the British Empire sponsored and coercively promoted throughout the nineteenth century and well into the twentieth to sustain its exploitative economic dominance. When a rare attempt is made to historicize this older diaspora, a view of the diasporic condition emerges that seems directly to contradict 'the late-modern celebratory argument on behalf of diasporas' commonly put forward by what Vijay Mishra has called 'romantic practitioners of diasporic theory'; indeed, the deeply diasporic Mishra begins his book by affirming: 'All diasporas are unhappy, but every diaspora is unhappy in its own way' (Mishra 2007: 1, 10).

Another related aspect of migration and diaspora that is hardly ever theorized is that even now in our dramatically shrunken global village, the overwhelmingly large majority of the population of any nation seems to show no wish to migrate but instead prefers to stay put where it belongs. The Indian diaspora, one of the biggest out of any nation, may seem to be visibly and prominently present all over the world, and yet it is estimated to be no more than 20 million persons in all, which is less than 2 per cent of the current population of India of 1.3 billion. Of those who do migrate, most are never fully accepted in their new locations, many cling to their old nationalities either out of an ineradicable emotional affiliation or because a new nationality turns out to be hardly the easiest thing to acquire, and many end up as refugees, as people without papers, rights, identity, and community.

In one of the most sensitive meditations on the condition of exile and its almost Manichean relationship with the nation, Edward Said suggested that 'the interplay between nationalism and exile is like Hegel's dialectic of servant and master, opposites informing and constituting each other' (Said 2001: 176). He also sought to counter the distortion introduced in our understanding of exile through an over-valorization of it in the literary sphere, by adducing the hard facts of a ground reality not often represented in literature: 'You must first set aside Joyce and Nabokov and think instead of

the uncountable masses for whom UN agencies have been created'
(Said 175). By its own statistics, the office of the United Nations
High Commissioner for Refugees had, since its inception in 1950,
helped more than 50 million persons, and was at the beginning of
the year 2006 assisting a further 20.8 million persons 'of concern'
to it (UNHCR 2007). These are lost souls, unsung and adrift in a
strange wide world from the moorings of their native nation-states
or, to put it differently, people fallen through the interstices of
diaspora as a shimmering object of desire.

## V. A Postnational World Order?

In many of the most influential historical studies of the nation, in
what may be called master narrations of the nation as an institution,
there may be found a desideratum to move beyond or even behind
the nation to some larger political sphere, and to assert instead
the ideological preferability of some form of internationalism. E.H.
Carr's somewhat optimistically titled book *Nationalism and After*
(1945), in Ernest Gellner's re-reading of it half a century later,
appeared to be a work which constantly placed the historical
evolution of nationalism constantly in the context of an
international world order: 'Strictly speaking, Carr's theme is the
fragmentation of a universal or international order, rather than
nationalism as such' (Gellner 24). E.J. Hobsbawm, in his survey
of nations and nationalism since 1780, made the paradoxical
assertion that more than half of all the nation-states in the world,
which had come into existence within the last four decades, had
done so not on the traditional basis of nationalism comprising
ethnicity, language, culture, etc., but on its 'opposite' premises
and were indeed not nationalist but '[i]n effect ...
*internationalist*'—for the reason that they were inspired by an
international people's movement for decolonization (Hobsbawm
1990: 171; emphasis in the original). However, it does not occur
to Hobsbawm to ask if an *internationalist* movement *for
nationalism* would not in fact be directly in contradiction of its
purported internationalism. The same unshakeable ideological

orientation makes him view nostalgically, indeed 'in melancholy retrospect', the break-up of the Soviet Union, that 'multinational country' as he calls it which, while it lasted, had to its credit 'the great achievement' of being able 'to limit the disastrous effects of nationalism' (Hobsbawm 173)—apparently by holding together the many separate nations which came tumbling out at the fall of the Soviet Union and in fact partly caused the Soviet Union to implode and burst at the seams.

In distinction, the focus of Jurgen Habermas's anxiety, in the face of 'the postnational constellation' that now seems to be arising, is how best to protect the 'civil solidarity' and 'the social welfare state' made possible by 'the democratic self-legislation of the citizens of a nation-state [and] the democratic self-steering of a national-state society' (Habermas 2001: 64, 65). It is this 'national-state institutionalization'—so far the repository and custodian of such democratic rights—which is now under 'increasing pressure from the force of globalization', for a global economy is 'a very largely unregulated (and many would argue unregulatable) domain' (Habermas 65, 67). Against such rampaging spread of globalization, in Habermas's view, the firmly grounded democratic nation-state constitutes a major possibility of resistance: 'In contrast to the territorial form of the nation-state, "globalization" conjures up images of overflowing rivers, washing away all the frontier checkpoints and controls, and ultimately the bulwark of the nation itself' (Habermas 67).

Though a global economy may seem only now to be assuming a dominant role, some powerful international economic institutions had already been put in place around the end of the Second World War, as Habermas notes (Habermas 70), in the form of the World Bank (1944), the International Monetary Fund (1945), and the General Agreement on Tariffs and Trade (1947). The most recent of these, born very much in the age of globalization and regarded by many as its ugly and reprehensible face, is the World Trade Organization (1995), whose official website feels the need to list '10 common misunderstandings about the WTO', of which the first goes as follows: 'Is it a dictatorial tool of the rich and powerful?

Does it destroy jobs? ...' / [Answer:] *'Emphatically no'* (WTO 2007; emphasis in the original).

Meanwhile, as these economic organizations have clearly gained in strength, the comparable political institution, the United Nations, after its tempestuous sessions in the early phases of the Cold War in the 1950s and the 1960s, especially with its oligarchic Security Council often at odds with its democratic General Assembly, has now become more and more ineffective, beating in the global moral void its sanctimonious wings in vain. There seems little doubt any more, especially keeping in mind the history of the 'Common Market' or the European Economic Union, that if a new world order were ever to emerge, it will be basically economic rather than political, and driven by markets and profits rather than by any vision of universal harmony and egalitarianism. In any case, imaginings of a single political order in the world, of a world government, or even of a supranational or transnational monolithic state, have so far all been frighteningly totalitarian and dystopic, as for example in *Brave New World* (1932) by Aldous Huxley or *Nineteen Eighty-four* (1949) by George Orwell. One may dearly wish to go beyond the institution of the nation to some more universal formation but the journey from the nation to the world is clearly not going to be a small step for mankind. The idea of the nation may be a much battered idea in theory, but the regime of the nation-state in popular practice looks likely to go on.

## VI. The Nation across the World

The 196 nations of the world perhaps show as many different ways of how a nation is imagined, conceived, born, narrated and constituted (literally, in terms of its Constitution), and how it actually functions and runs. The present volume offers only a very small sample of these diverse spaces and processes but a widely varied one. This is because the sixteen essays published here come out of a vast catchment area, an international conference at which over 210 papers were presented on the theme of 'Nation and Imagination'. The essays here also serve to illustrate how the same common theme can be located and interpreted on so many different sites and from so many different viewpoints. Therefore, these essays not only bear out the inexhaustible possibilities of thinking about the nation in our world but they also extend that range. It helps that nearly all our contributors have led international lives, with about two-thirds of them in fact living and working currently in a country other than that in which they were born—though one must hasten to add that this extreme diasporic condition is far from being the case in general of most members of even the (at least nominally) universal fraternity of university teachers worldwide.

The volume begins with not the keynote address of the conference but the keynote *conversation* instead, which was the livelier, more spontaneous, and more creative mode Vikram Seth preferred. Seth is an international novelist by acclaim and reputation but not in the usual sense of writing about the exchange and interaction between characters from different nations; in fact, he may be the only novelist ever to have published three consecutive novels set firmly and entirely in three different countries, with all the characters in each novel belonging to that particular country alone. It is interesting then to find him saying, *inter alia*, that he feels a novelist needs to have lived for two complete cycles of seasons in any country before writing creatively about it. The other novelist in this volume is Austin Clarke, a Canadian who was born in Barbados and has described his childhood and early education there in a memoir titled *Growing Up Stupid Under the Union Jack* (1980); he offers here an impassioned, and autobiographically embedded, account of how the narratorial voice in fiction has a defining tone and indeed colour which make it authentic.

In the first of the five essays in the section 'Nations in Black and White', Homi Bhabha in 'The Black Savant and the Dark Princess' discovers a whole web of interconnections between W.E.B. DuBois's novel *The Dark Princess,* which has for its eponymous protagonist an Indian princess (somewhat improbably) named Kautilya, and the writings of the contemporary Indian leader Lala Lajpat Rai, a fellow spirit of DuBois's who espoused Indian nationalism while also commenting acutely on the Black sub-nation in the US. Set against the background of the first Universal Races Congress held in 1911 in London, such 'internationalization of the color-line', Bhabha argues, pushed an aspiration for a 'national society' to its limits without 'eviscerating or erasing' it. John Scheckter explores international affiliations in his essay 'Borderless: Empire, Race, and the League of Nations' through his contextual reading of two novels by Frank Moorhouse set at the League of Nations in Geneva, in which the Australian-born heroine moves towards a borderless personal identity while still remaining colour-blind to the inter-racial composition of the League which Japan, acting as a spearhead, problematized.

In 'One Step on Australian Soil and You're History', Geoffrey V. Davis offers an account of Australian racism at home by following the figure of Egon Erwin Kisch, both in fictional representation and in real life, as an irrepressible German-speaking Jewish journalist born in Prague, who was refused entry into an absurdly racist White Australia because he failed a test in Scottish Gaelic though he could speak eleven other languages—a scenario stranger than fiction which '[e]ven Kafka in his darkest dreams couldn't have imagined'. Gerald Gaylard, in '*Disgrace*-ful Metafiction', shows how, despite its ostensible concern with 'realist socio-historical and national' issues, J.M. Coetzee's famous novel has for its primary intertext high European Romanticism, and the hero's deep enculturation in that literary matrix, especially with regard to his predatory sexuality, comes into conflict with a new postcolonial South Africa, which is no country for old [White] men with that kind of cosmopolitan hybridity. In 'Shoring Up Britain', John Clement Ball takes for his text a novel by the Guyanese British novelist David Dabydeen, *Disappearance*, in which the little island of Britain, in the middle of a post-imperial, multicultural redefinition of its national 'territory, culture, society, and identity', is faced with the danger of its cliffs near Hastings disappearing into the sea, until an immigrant, a West Indian engineer of African descent, undertakes to build a wall to protect that foundationally historic stretch of the coast.

The next section of five essays, 'Nations and Empires', comprises two essays on India, one on Sri Lanka, one on Britain as seen by an irreverent Australian, and one on an old outpost of the empire, Singapore. Sukeshi Kamra focuses on the critical moment of the Indian 'Mutiny' of 1857 to recover two contrasted modes of colonial records, the one authored by the British as official reports which comprise about 95 per cent of the surviving archive, and the other produced by the 'natives', often speaking under duress or in terms of fearful abjection which the British could readily assimilate into a 'rhetoric of loyalty'. With reference to the decade leading up to India's Independence in 1947, Priyamvada Gopal distinguishes between two kinds of nationalisms which in that period formed 'a historical conjuncture', the mainstream nationalism of Gandhi and Nehru, and a 'nationalitarian' project espoused by the Progressive Writers Association which represented a radical endeavour that was 'simultaneously flawed and visionary'. Chelva Kanaganayakam looks at the deeply torn Sri Lankan nation where 'the country continues to be both unified and divided [and] … two national imaginaries make up one nation'; he asserts that 'postcolonial literature has a deep investment in the idea of nation' though there is a hiatus between 'the literary world and the national imaginary' as also between diasporic writing in English and local writing in Tamil. Bruce Bennett examines the variegated career of the writer and TV journalist Clive James, who left Australia, 'a second-hand country', for Britain, the Mother Country, so as to move on from being a provincial to a self-styled metropolitan, and whose life-long fascination with 'the remains of empire' has perhaps inevitably led to 'a comic melancholy'. And Eddie Tay shows how the city-state of Singapore, one of the smallest nations in the world (with 187 nations larger than it), which is in some ways First World and in some ways Third, has attempted to construct a national identity for itself not only by inventing a huge mythic beast, the merlion, to illustrate the etymology of its Sanskrit-based name, but also by attempting to assemble the 'spare parts' of the many ethnicities washed up at this strategic harbour.

The last section, 'Nations at Play', contains three essays on how different nations are staged in theatrical and film representations while the fourth focuses on cricket, perhaps the most colonial of all sports. In his account of dramatic representations of national identity in Fiji, another very small country created by the colonizing British and deeply divided ethnically among indigenes and immigrants, Ian Gaskell considers plays written by both native Fijians and Indian-Fijians, in both English and in Fijian Hindi, to show how such partial representations may still both reinforce separateness and constitute an aggregative national identity. Poonam Trivedi recovers a history of the repeated tours of colonial India in the latter half of the nineteenth century by Dave Carson, who began by performing black-and-white minstrel shows but soon acquired huge popularity by localizing his comic-satirical act to exploit emerging Indian character types representative of a new colonial hybridity; in fact, his onstage satire even ruffled race relations off-stage. Focusing on films, which are now arguably a more popular and powerful medium of narrating nations than novels, Isabel Santaolalla brings together a set of comparable and even intertextual narratives which explore new forms of European identity especially in Spain and Britain, and involve ethnic and gendered 'crossings' between different segments of the nation, between different nations, and between the First and the Third Worlds too. And Kathleen Firth explores the impact of cricket, the English gentleman's game, on remote colonial lives in the West Indies, in particular on C.L.R. James, radical intellectual and one of the most influential historians and theorists of cricket, who argued that the game was a 'metaphor for colonialism' though he might also have endorsed the view of a younger West Indian writer, Caryl Phillips, that it was much more than a sport and exemplified 'all that is decent and positive in human achievement'.

Such are the paradoxes not only of colonialism but equally of the postcolonial nation. Incidentally, the processes of formation of postcolonial nations are interestingly illustrated in the case of 'the West Indies', which are not a single nation but were briefly, from 3 January 1958 to 31 May 1962, a political federation of several newly independent postcolonies, comprising 24 larger (but still not really large at all) islands including Jamaica, Trinidad, and Barbados (but not Bermuda, the Bahamas, or continental Guyana) as well as about 200 tinier islands. After the, perhaps predictable, break-up (as happened also between Malaysia and Singapore), 'the West Indies' survives as a unified entity mainly as a multinational cricket team (though Bermuda notably played as a separate 'minnow' team in its own right in the cricket World Cup 2007); it perhaps needs to be noted, however, that 'the West Indies' had in fact been playing international cricket under that collective or federational name right since the 1930s. There remains, besides, one other happy legacy of the brief cohabitation of the small nations in that region, a multinational multi-campus University of the West Indies, which actually offers an MA course in the history of West Indian cricket.

There are more nations and histories of national formations, in the world than this volume can even begin to encompass. But it may be hoped that it will provide a substantial and varied enough contribution to the vigorous ongoing debate on the numerous Nations in our one and only World.

## Works Cited

Ahmad, Aijaz. *In Theory: Classes, Nations, Literatures.* Delhi: Oxford University Press, 1992; rpt. 1994.

Anderson, Benedict. *Imagined Communities: Reflections on the Origin and Spread of Nationalism.* London: Verso, 1983.

Anisuzzaman. 'Towards a Redefinition of Identity: East Bengal, 1947–71', in *A South Asian Nationalism Reader.* Ed. Sayantan Dasgupta. Delhi: Worldview Publications, rpt. 2007.

Behdad, Ali. 'On Globalization, Again!', in *Postcolonial Studies and Beyond.* Eds Ania Loomba et al. Delhi: Permanent Black, 2006.

Bhabha, Homi K. (Ed.). *Nation and Narration.* London: Routledge, 1990.

———. *The Location of Culture.* London: Routledge, 1994.

Chatterjee, Partha. *The Partha Chatterjee Omnibus, comprising Nationalist Thought and the Colonial World* [1986], *The Nation and Its Fragments* [1993], *A Possible India* [1997]. New Delhi: Oxford University Press, 1999.

Chrisman, Laura. 'Nationalism and postcolonial studies', in *The Cambridge Companion to Postcolonial Studies,* Ed. Neil Lazarus. Cambridge: Cambridge University Press, 2004.

Eagleton, Terry. *Literary Theory: An Introduction*. Second Edn. New Delhi:
   Maya Blackwell, 1996; rpt. 2000.
————. *The Idea of Culture*. Oxford: Blackwell, 2000.
Gans, Chaim. *The Limits of Nationalism*. Cambridge: Cambridge University
   Press, 2003.
Gellner, Ernest. *Encounters with Nationalism*. Oxford: Blackwell, 1994.
Habermas, Jurgen. *The Postnational Constellation: Political Essays*. Trans. Max
   Pensky. Cambridge: Polity Press, 2001.
Hobsbawm, E. J. *Nations and nationalism since 1780: Programme, myth, reality*.
   Cambridge: Cambridge University Press, 1990.
Jinnah, Mohammad Ali. 'Hindus and Muslims: Two Separate Nations', in *A
   South Asian Nationalism Reader* Ed. Sayantan Dasgupta. Delhi: Worldview
   Publications, rpt. 2007.
Kortenaar, Neil ten. *Self, Nation, Text in Salman Rushdie's* Midnight's Children.
   Montreal: McGill-Queen's University Press, 2004.
Lazarus, Neil. *Nationalism and Cultural Practice in the Postcolonial World*.
   Cambridge: Cambridge University Press, 1999.
Mishra, Vijay. *The Literature of the Indian Diaspora: Theorizing the Diasporic
   Imaginary*. London: Routledge, 2007.
Rushdie, Salman. *Imaginary Homelands: Essays and Criticism 1981–1991*.
   London: Granta Books, 1991.
Said, Edward W. *Reflections on Exile and other Literary and Cultural Essays*.
   New Delhi: Penguin Books, 2001.
Smith, Anthony D. *Theories of Nationalism*. London: Duckworth, 1971.
————. 'Nations and History', in *Understanding Nationalism*. Eds Montserrat
   Guibernau and John Hutchinson. Cambridge: Polity Press, 2001.
Spivak, Gayatri Chakravorty. *A Critique of Postcolonial Reason: Towards a History
   of the Vanishing Present*. Cambridge, MA: Harvard University Press, 1999.
Szeman, Imre. *Zones of Instability: Literature, Postcolonialism, and the Nation*.
   Baltimore: The Johns Hopkins University Press, 2003.
United Nations (2007). http://www.un.org/members/growth.shtml. accessed
   27 March 2007.
UNHCR (2007). http://www.unhcr.org/basics.html. accessed 29 March 2007.
WTO (2007). http://www.wto.org/english/thewto_e/whatis_e/whatis_e.htm.
   accessed 29 March 2007.
Young, Robert J.C. *Postcolonialism: An Historical Introduction*. Oxford:
   Blackwell, 2001.

# PART ONE

## Nation and Creation

# Vikram Seth
## In Conversation with Meenakshi Mukherjee and Shirley Chew

**Shirley Chew:** I am delighted to be chairing this opening session of the XIIIth Triennial Conference of the Association for Commonwealth Literature and Language Studies (ACLALS) at Hyderabad. The keynote speaker is the internationally acclaimed poet and novelist, Vikram Seth—'the best writer', it has been said, 'of his generation', and the recipient of many literary awards.

Taking part in the session with Vikram Seth is Professor Meenakshi Mukherjee, a well-known critic, an academic of repute, and also currently Chairperson of the ACLALS International Executive.

You will have noticed from your programmes that the kind of opening session we are getting today is a little out of the ordinary—not the familiar hour-long Keynote Lecture, but a 'conversation'. The idea for this innovative venture has come from Vikram Seth and only someone like Meenakshi—unconventional spirit that she is—would have agreed to take on such a challenge. Needless to say, the 'conversation' we are about to listen in to will be true to the meaning of the word—an amiable exchange of ideas enlivened with spontaneous or calculated turns of thought and attitude. A 'conversation' which will stake out that 'shared ground with difference' (to borrow a phrase from the Canadian writer Daphne Marlatt) which is one of the aims of the Conference.

Vikram Seth was born in Calcutta, attended school at Dehra Dun, and went on to pursue higher studies in England and California. Beginning as an economist, he was, while embarked on his PhD candidature at Stanford University, overtaken by his passion for writing, and is today the author of a wonderfully varied and significant oeuvre: four books of poetry, including a *Collected Poems* (1995); a travel book, *From Heaven Lake: Travels through Sinkiang and Tibet* (1983); *The Golden Gate* (1986), a novel in verse comprising about 600 sonnets, which has been described by Gore Vidal as 'the Great Californian Novel'; a book of animal fables, *Beastly Tales from Here and There* (1992); *Three Chinese Poets* (1992), translations of poetry from the Tang dynasty; *Arion and the Dolphin* (1994), a libretto for an opera with music by Alec Roth, which was performed at the English National Opera; two novels, *A Suitable Boy* (1993) and *An Equal Music* (1999). [Since this conversation, a new work, which is discussed below near the end, has come out, entitled *Two Lives* (2005).]

Some of you will know Vikram Seth chiefly as the author of a novel which, by the time you got to page 1000, left you with another 349 pages before you arrived at what we conventionally term the ending. My first encounter with his work was with something far shorter: *The Humble Administrator's Garden* (1985), his second book of poems. For a Singaporean-Chinese like me who had developed a deep fondness for Indian literature (though admittedly it was Indian literature in English to begin with), the idea of a young Indian poet writing about his experiences in China was captivating. And just as the poet figure of the opening poem, 'A Little Night Music', is 'skein-drawn by the sound / of someone playing the erhu' somewhere among the alleys and 'beneath the wutong trees', so I became 'skein-drawn' by Seth's writing, as I moved from poems set in China to India to California—poems evoking hauntingly a sense of loss brought about by the precariousness of relationships, and the fugitive nature of time and beauty.

To speak in detail of Vikram Seth's achievements is clearly out of the question here. I shall mention in brief just three aspects of his work. First, as many of his reviewers and critics have noted, a distinctive quality of his writing is its musicality. Music is of course a subject Seth writes about, as in *A Suitable Boy* and, more particularly, *An Equal Music*. It is also something he *makes* out of his sensitive, disciplined, and versatile experiments with language and form. The appeal—directly, sensuously, and resonantly—is to our auditory imagination or, to borrow a phrase I first came across in Chinua Achebe, to our 'mind's ear'.

Another aspect of Vikram Seth's oeuvre is its variety. Within an extensive literary terrain many different narrative genres, settings, and characters can be found to be accommodated; and similarly many cultural encounters so that there is room for *ghazals* and *raags* as well as Schubert's songs, for Shakespeare's plays as well as the poetry of Ghalib and Mir, and for the modernist works of T.S. Eliot as well as the classical traditions of Li Bai and Du Fu. To a large extent this amplitude has to do with Seth's inbuilt resistance to borders, and *From Heaven Lake* is exemplary in this respect. An account of his hitch-hiking journey out of Sinkiang to Lhasa in Tibet, and from there into Nepal and thence to Delhi, it underscores his dogged refusal to fall in with the illogic of the boundary regulations imposed by the Chinese government and designed, it would seem, to prevent him from making his way back home to his family by the most direct route according to geography. Only 'a sound core of madness', as he called it, kept him going in the face of inclement weather and implacable officialdom. But there were lucky breaks, too, often in the form of chance meetings, as when spending some time with a troupe of local musicians in Turfan, and being compelled to sing, he found himself launching forth into the theme song from *Awara* (The Wanderer), 'a sentimental Indian movie from the 1950s that is astonishingly popular in China'.

Vikram Seth has been compared to Jane Austen, George Eliot, and Tolstoy. Among contemporary Indian novelists, he can be said to have some affinities with R.K. Narayan, a writer he deems 'probably the greatest' among those writing in English. All these writers have a strength in common—a vivid and concrete sense of place and history. It is a strength Vikram Seth also possesses. To read *A Suitable Boy*, for example, is to be inducted into the fictional world of Brahmpur, its big houses, lush gardens, and congested streets; its factories, government chambers, and law courts; its amazing range of characters and their complex relationships. It is to be inducted also into the heady, and expansive, and often confusing years following Independence, a retrospective account of the early 1950s which is at the same time a prefiguring of the tensions and conflicts of India forty years on, in the closing decades of the twentieth century, a narrative, in other words, of a nation in the process of being imagined.

Now, over to you, Meenakshi.

**Meenakshi Mukherjee:** Most of my questions will be brief. My job is merely to prompt you to express your ideas. Only the first question might be a little long because it relates to the broad theme of our conference: 'Nation and Imagination'.

How do you respond to the theme, Vikram? Is nation a concept that sustains the writer, anchoring him and providing him with a secure base from where to view the world, or does it restrict his freedom? Your views on this will be of special interest to us because there is a fluidity in your work that makes it difficult to put a national label on you as a writer. Your three novels are located in three different parts of the world: the Bay area of San Francisco in *The Golden Gate* and the Gangetic plain of North India in *A Suitable Boy. An Equal Music* is set mostly in London but also parts of Europe. Each of them evokes the social ethos of that region easily and unselfconsciously as if the author is an insider to that culture. Your early volume of poems, *The Humble Administrator's Garden*, has three sections bearing names of trees from three countries: *wutong* from China, *neem* from India, and *live oak* evoking North America. I could also cite examples from your other books of poems, where different cultures coexist and sometimes overlap. Is this a conscious choice for you—a deliberate erasure of national boundaries to go beyond the boxes that divide people, or is it a denial of your own historical and geographical origin?

**Vikram Seth:** Well, it's not the last. It's very difficult with a long question. I will have to work backwards to where you started. The fact was, right from the beginning, the reason why I thought it was best to have this—not particularly this format but a non-speech format—was that I get terribly nervous for months in advance if I have to give a lecture. I sweat over writing a speech for this kind of a learned audience. I'm not sure if speech is the genre of my choice at the moment. There are many hassles in preparing a written script beforehand. I would spend a lot of psychological energy on something which would not necessarily be better or worse than conversation. I think this is more interesting—two people talking to each other. When Meenakshi wanted to send the questions to me in advance, I said, 'Please don't. I would like to be surprised.' Particularly since you have asked me something trenchant like the last part of the question. It is not that I am not nervous now, but these lovely cups of tea you have given me make me feel better.

To get to the question itself, it is true that I have ranged in my novels from country to country and in my various other books from genre to genre as well. It has been more a matter of what inspired me at that moment rather than a deliberate plan to make myself a kind of international writer who can easily drift from one region to another. I do not always have the choice either. If I were asked to write the story of an Icelandic fisherman I couldn't do it. Also I do not have the experience of a country like Japan, for instance. The only countries that I feel I can write about are obviously those where I've had some personal experience, where I've lived for at least two complete changes of seasons, two complete cycles of the year, so that I can tell what is a fixed feature of the calendar from what happens in a particular year. That is the very minimum. I could write something like a travel book about China; I don't think I could write a novel about that country because I don't have the experience of a true insider that is necessary for a novel.

I do feel it's not good enough to write a novel that passes muster only with the critics, say, or only with some readers. It has to be acceptable to the people whose lives you are writing about. For instance, *The Golden Gate* was read in England and thought to be skilfully done, enjoyably written, and so on; and I believe people on the East coast of USA were also appreciative of the book. But unless people who live in California, especially in the Bay area, feel I have got it right, there is no point in writing it at all. It would be, to my mind, an artistic failure. So it is true that when I have lived and loved in a country, when I have friends there, when I am familiar with nature there, only then have I been inspired to create a story about it. A novel presupposes an intimacy with the place and the people, but it is also born of inspiration; in my case it is not at all related to a wish to chart my career in a certain way. Actually, if one thinks consciously of writing as a career, it might even be counter-productive to change tracks because once you have a niche audience with one kind of a book it is safer to satisfy them by writing similar books. If you do something different, it could be a problem. But I can write only when something motivates me to write. About your question about roots: it is not that I do not have roots—but I feel multi-rooted. I feel at home in many places.

**MM:** Did you say that if the people about whose lives a novelist writes don't feel interested in the book, then you know it has not succeeded? Is that always true?

**VS:** Not necessarily. People who read about what they are familiar with may say, 'What is he teaching us, we know all these things anyway.' But they can always tell when it does not ring true.

**MM:** But does it surprise you that a lot of people who are not familiar with the location or the context of your novels also read and appreciate them? It surprises me, I must confess, because when I read *A Suitable Boy* before publication—may I share with this audience the fact that you let me read one of your earlier drafts as you were writing it in Delhi?

**VS:** Will you also tell them what your family said about cluttering up the house with the numerous spiral-bound volumes?

**MM:** I don't dare.

**VS:** I'm grateful.

**MM:** I felt desolate when you finished the novel and the spiral-bound volumes stopped coming. I had become so involved in it, I wanted the story to go on and on forever. It was sad to part company with the characters and their interlinked lives. But at that time I did wonder secretly, I am ashamed to admit this today, I enjoyed it so much because I know this place, I know these people. I grew up in a North Indian town similar to Brahmpur—where the novel is set. Will those who do not know this world feel so totally engrossed? It has been a continuous source of surprise to me—and of delight—that the book became a success everywhere. You go to Australia, you go to the USA (I remember a woman taxi driver in Boston talking to me about *A Suitable Boy*, probably because I was from India), you go anywhere—even in Denmark I met somebody who said, 'Have you read this book called *A Suitable Boy*? It's the most wonderful book I have read.' He had no connection with India at all. Does this surprise you, Vikram?

**VS:** Yes, it does. Talking about the spiral-bound volumes coming to an end it is only conventionally ended. But it continues in various possible formats in my mind, it presumably does in other people's minds as well. I suppose the reason why the reception of the book surprises me is that it's not set at a period of great national turmoil. It's not set at the time of war with Pakistan or China; it's not set at the time of the assassination of a Prime Minister; it's not set at the time of the Emergency. It's set in 1951, a relatively stable time, and located in what might be seen as a backwater. I thought to myself—Okay, I'm going to write this book, I'm inspired by this material, I have to stay with this even if it runs to 500 pages, or 1000, or whatever. The first draft was even longer than the 1400 pages of the final version. I did not worry about what it was going to mean to anyone who did not live in North India, who had no experience of the range and the diversity of the area and the geography that provide the context of the novel.

My publishers in England and America suggested that I add a glossary to explain the details. But my feeling was—No. I have not tried deliberately to be obscure. Why should people not get used to words and worlds? For instance, the word *paan* could in no way be adequately explained in the glossary. Even if you could describe what it looks like and how it is consumed it is not possible to convey its variety, its subtle cultural nuances, and the resonances of offering a pan to someone. So I decided not to explain. I don't expect every reader to understand everything. But I did not expect it to be a hugely saleable book because of its length and its weight, and the obscure nature of the time and place of the narrative. People have liked the story—or so I've been told. For that I must thank the gods or chance.

**MM:** The location of *A Suitable Boy* is a fictional town called Brahmpur. In your other two novels they were real places on the map. Is there any reason that you needed to place the action of this novel in an imagined town? Does it have something to do with any special kind of realism that you were attempting in this novel?

**VS:** Brahmpur—why does it have to be a town of imagination rather than, say, a town like Lucknow, or Patna, or Allahabad? Let me first take up the question of imagination which is what is basic to a writer. Imagination is not limited to a place. Satendra Nandan, my old teacher in Doon School, taught us *Julius Caesar* and also directed the play in which we performed. Now you might say, what does the Roman world have to do with India? But it fascinated us. We were only twelve or thirteen years old and it opened up a world of the imagination—Julius Caesar, the troubles of the time, the fact that the character of Caesar came and disappeared in Act III, the curious battles, the politics and society of the Roman empire; all that acted on us. We were transported. Even what is not one's own world becomes real through the imagination—if it is based on universals such as characters and human relationships. I think that's what motivates readers and that is the kind of writing I aspire to. That is why R.K. Narayan is a supreme writer. I am moved by his characters, I laugh with them, love them. As I have often said, and I am saying it again, if he had written about North India, I would not have—I would not have dared to. So I think that above anything else, what would make me write a novel is because I'm moved by the story.

The other thing Meenakshi asked: Does Brahmpur have to be a city that is not actual but constructed? I am told that someone here, in this audience, a lady from Brazil, has actually drawn a map of Brahmpur piecing together information, like how far the race course is from the club, or how far the jail is from the university, and so on. It gratifies me because I wanted to imagine something that was really concrete. Well, I lived in Patna for ten years but I also wanted to introduce features of say Lucknow such as its Imambara, and Benares with its temples, and Kanpur with its leather industry, and Allahabad with its Kumbh Mela. Basically, Brahmpur was a composite city. The fact that I created the city gave me the flexibility to introduce elements from different cities. Now that is as far as the positive side is concerned. The negative side is I didn't want to be open to criticism for using or not using certain features. Introducing a particular character, for example a chief minister or a well-known public figure, would have been more difficult for me if I named an actual city or an actual state. I could create characters as well as use people whom I knew or knew about with a certain amount of freedom. I was able to play the game of the imagination with fewer constraints.

**MM:** While we are on the subject of *A Suitable Boy*, before passing on to other issues, I would like to ask a question about perspective. It is a polyphonic novel. There are characters from different communities, classes, and castes with their distinctive voices which are pitted against each other giving an impression of realistic representation. But a careful reader would see that one particular voice is privileged over the others: the modernist, secular voice. I was wondering if that has anything to do with the fact that you were writing the book in the late 1980s and the early 1990s when secularism was under some threat in India. In 1951–2— which is the period of your story, secularism was the accepted ideology in our country. Nobody challenged it. The fractures became visible only towards the end of the century. Do you think, because you have faith in secular India, that the threat perceived by you in *your* present affected the way you represented the debates of that earlier time?

**VS:** I think it is true, this is my viewpoint clearly. I think in this I may have privileged the views of Mahesh Kapoor, his impatience with religious obscurantism and so on. But it extends too much in Mahesh Kapoor's voice to an intolerance of religion. He is very hard on his wife, a deeply feeling genuine character rooted in her religion who lives in her world—and doesn't go anywhere. She does pooja everyday. She wanted the reading of Ramayana on certain days of the year. Only after her death did her husband agree to the recital of the Sundarkanda from the Ramayana in his house. She is a character who is close to my heart. I'm not particularly impressed by characters like the Raja of Marh who wants to tear down a mosque in order to have the linga installed mainly to hurt the people of other religions—I certainly do not feel any sympathy with him—but it is not for me as a writer to say that. I have to enter into each character as much as I can without bias, simply enter imaginatively into the spirit of someone, like Agatha Christie (yes!) or Shakespeare did. We have to believe that there is an aspect in which a character emerges in his own voice. I think you have to be a sort of judge where the author's sympathies lie. Now in a book like *An Equal Music* there's a problem. I speak in the voice of the central figure, a young man I'm not particularly sympathetic with. I think he is quite a wimp in a sense. He is so involved in his own problems that he does not understand other people including the women whom he has loved. But here again is the problem. I think the primary responsibility is to the inspiration of the book; the author cannot consciously voice his views.

As far as the Nehruvian vision of the early days of independence is concerned, it is very fortunate that our country had someone at the helm who for all his economic mistakes, fluffiness of policy, etc., never made any citizen of the country feel that he or she was any less important because of some accident of birth or religion. We are in a country today which is again quite relaxed in terms of identity. At least most of us are relaxed about having a Sikh as a prime minister, or a Christian as the leader of the majority party in the ruling coalition, and a Muslim president. We don't feel, Meenakshi, I don't think you feel threatened by this at all. You just feel this is part of India as a nation. Surely it must be in this manner, where we do not think, except for the purposes of explanation that I'm doing now, that people should be judged by anything other than the quality of their personality, of their merits, their qualifications.

**MM:** I think I will pass on to another kind of question. The fluidity that I mentioned in the beginning, about your national identity, I think extends to a fluidity of genre as well. All your readers know and Shirley has also pointed out that you have moved form poetry to travel book, back to poetry, a novel in verse, poetry again, and a novel in prose and a children's book, and a book of verse in between; and now from accounts in the media we know that you are writing a biography, a biography of a very unusual kind, a biography of two people together who come from two different parts of the world. You have constantly shifted from genre to genre. I would like you to talk about this a little bit and tell us what will happen when you have exhausted all the possible genres.

**VS:** I'd go round the racetrack once again, I think! This is difficult to explain. Let me talk about one well-known writer from the past, that is Pushkin. I don't think I would have been a novelist but for him. I read him in translation, a wonderful translation. Let me digress by saying how important translations are. I can't read Russian; I read Pushkin in a very good English translation. I was inspired by him. I stopped writing my Economics dissertation, which is why I am not Dr Seth today. I was inspired by the fact that Pushkin took up many different genres, whether it was a play or a short story, or pornographic poems which were not published in his lifetime, or children's stories, or a lyric, or an elegy. He did not let himself be bothered by the question of genre when he wrote. He was inspired by something; he wrote in whatever form came to him. Also he wrote the history of the Pugachev Rebellion and a biography of his grandfather who was a black African from Ethiopia—or was it his great-grandfather?—who became an engineer in St Petersburg. So in every case it was the inspiration that was paramount, and I think I took it from his example both in terms of the geography of what I have rendered and the genre. There's no point in trying to preempt your moods. It's such a lucky business to be tapped on the shoulder and told to go on and write. You can't just shut off and say I'm sorry I'm supposed to be an Indian writer, so I'm going to write only about India or I've lived in California for the last ten years so publishers and readers expect I should write about that. Similarly about genre; if I were told I was going to write only poetry for the rest of my life, I don't think I would be at all excited.

When I repeat myself or drift from genre to genre, it's almost a matter of irrelevance to me. So when the obvious genres are exhausted, there will be another genre I have not yet thought about, or I'll repeat a genre: *A Suitable Girl*, or *An Unsuitable Boy*, or *An Unsuitable Girl*. I hope it doesn't happen soon; it would consume the next ten years of my life. But if it happens that's what I'll do.

**MM:** You know you have mentioned two influences on you so far in your conversation. One is R.K. Narayan—you did not say you were influenced but you named him with some admiration— and you mentioned Pushkin. And that leads me to ask a question about politics and literature, since both of them seem to have stayed clear of that in a way, you know, or not been ideologically very obvious or polemical. I find that you take up a lot of contemporary issues—for example, in *The Golden Gate* you talked about nuclear disarmament, you talked about alternative sexuality—but you touch upon them all very lightly and without making an issue of them. Is this casualness something that the temper of that particular book necessitated or is it generally true of your own attitude to writing—not to be taking sides overtly on issues like these?

**VS:** If you take too obvious a stance in what seems to be a novel, that will be preaching to the converted and putting off the non-converted. Also, if I write about my views in a novel, that sort of precludes my writing an essay on a particular political issue or introducing in a speech what I feel honestly and deeply about. I would say that the responsibility of a writer is no greater or less than the responsibility of a citizen to deal with matters as and when he or she sees they require address. As far as Pushkin and R.K. Narayan are concerned, such excellent writers, I would say that for Pushkin there was the great problem of censorship. Anything he wrote had to pass the Russian censor and great chunks of *Eugene*

*Onegin* were not published because they were actually removed. There are stanzas, of which you could see the first four lines because the last ten lines had actually not been published. It was rather like during the Emergency in India when you saw blanked out pieces of the front page in the newspaper.

Now in the case of Narayan, it is very interesting. I mean *Swami and Friends* was published during British rule. The book incorporates a statue of a British administrator in Malgudi and hilarious things happened owing to the non-functioning of the governmental apparatus. It is a subtle medium between ironic comedy and a fairly direct commentary on what was going on at the time. This morning, at the inauguration of this conference, when we stood up, again thanks to the non-functioning of our sound system which was to play the national anthem, we all sang it together. Well, that song too provides an interesting example. It was written at the time of the durbar when the Prince of Wales was coming to India and was presumably addressed by Tagore to King George V. But it has never been very clear to whom it was in fact addressed because the very words about the leader of the destiny could as well be addressed to the Supreme Being. So, within the constraints of the system people interpret or write ambiguous texts to express, I think, their views about circumstances and situations that exist.

**Shirley Chew:** One of the pleasures I get out of your writing is this marvellous interplay with other writers and texts and with music. You have mentioned Pushkin and Narayan but you have mentioned Shakespeare also. The two Shakespeare plays that I find very central to the textual patterns of your writing are *Twelfth Night* and *The Winter's Tale*. *Twelfth Night* is clearly an intertext in *A Suitable Boy*. Does the late romance *The Winter's Tale* function similarly in *An Equal Music*?

**VS:** *The Winter's Tale*—that's a problem play. But perhaps *Midsummer Night's Dream* is the one that most entered my imagination from Shakespeare because there are stories within stories, plays within plays, and a mixture of tragedy and comedy which is again lightly touched upon.

**SC:** Would you like to say something about the impact of music on your work—specially of your relationship with Western music, particularly Schubert?

**VS:** When I was writing *A Suitable Boy* I often found that I wanted to learn Hindustani music. I was at home living with my parents and spent most of the time in my room writing. That was when I began learning music. Had it not been for my music and my parents (on whom I shamelessly depended for seven years) I don't think I would have completed the long book that *A Suitable Boy* turned out to be. Even though I had two MAs in Economics I had no income coming. Had they not supported me I could not have gone on. As for music, my father can't hold a tune. My mother, when I was a child, she used to sing to me a lullaby about Chanda Mama and so on. I would tell her, 'Mama, *tum mat gao, Koli mashi ayegi. Koli mashi gayegi.*' I was not tactful as a child. But still the fact is my parents had an enthusiasm for music—that helped me in some ways.

I had a friend who was in Delhi when I was writing my novel, a diplomat, who introduced me to Schubert's music. He said, 'Why don't you sing a little Schubert?' I said, 'I can't even easily read Western music, how can I possibly sing Schubert?' He said 'Why don't you do it in the Indian guru-*shishya* style: listen to it and just repeat it?' I listened to the CDs of what I liked and just sang them from memory.

**MM:** Tell me about what you are currently working on.

**VS:** A book about my mother's uncle and his German wife. He was born in Biswan in Uttar Pradesh in 1908 and he died in 1989 in London. He got his PhD from the University of Berlin, Germany, and could not get a job there, went to England, joined the army, had the right arm blown off during the war in Monte Cassino in Italy but continued to work as a dentist. He lived in England for forty years.

My great-aunt was also born in 1908 but in Berlin. She was a German Jew but escaped Hitler's concentration camp unlike some other members of her family. She managed to get out of Germany one month before the war because she got sponsorship from a

Professor of Arabic, A.J. Arberry, incidentally, the man whose wonderful translation of the Quran inspired me partially in the course of my writing *A Suitable Boy*. I had no knowledge of her connection to Arberry before researching her life. She died at the age of 80 when I was a student in England. My parents would never have allowed me to go to London had they not known that Shanti Uncle and his wife were there to take care of me, to provide me some sort of refuge against women, alcohol, and other temptations. My further discovery was of letters by my great-aunt and letters sent to her after the war when she was trying to find out what had happened to her sister and mother. Those letters triggered off my curiosity. So the story of these two interlinked lives is what I am working on now—which covers a good part of twentieth-century history.

*At the end of the formal conversation, some questions from the audience followed:*

**Question:** What is your preferred genre of writing—poetry or fiction?

**VS:** I take what I am given. I don't think I would have been a novelist but for *Eugene Onegin* by Pushkin, which is both a long poem and a novel. After reading it I found that I had the stamina for writing a work of fiction. When I came back home to India, I thought *A Suitable Boy* could be a limited comedy of manners of about 200 pages because I myself am not fond of reading long books. Writing prose and poetry are very different in their explication, or expression, or elusiveness. I think there is a different kind of satisfaction for both the writer and the reader in prose and in verse. With poetry there's a kind of finality which tells you: now it is a finished work. With prose you never really know whether a novelist has finished or just abandoned his task at some point. There's nothing really to tell you about the rhythm, the correct rhythm, of a prose text. But there is as much of a question of planning, of prodding, and of revising in prose. Sometimes there is as much elusiveness, not to mention allusiveness, in prose as there is in verse.

**Question:** A related question: don't you feel that your fiction has eclipsed your poetry?

**VS:** Probably yes. But that is the function I'd say partly of the market, partly of peoples' impatience with poetry.

**Question:** When you wrote the poem 'Rakhi' there is a human approach. Is that possible in a novel?

**VS:** Yes, 'Rakhi' is a poem which I wrote to my sister and there is a human approach in it. I would hope my fiction also carried something of the human approach. Again I see myself as a poet who has incidentally stumbled into fiction but enjoyed it greatly, and I am deeply grateful to my fiction which allowed me the economic freedom to have the time to write what I like.

**MM:** How do you feel when you are more often mentioned in the media for the amount of advances you have received rather than the kind of books you have written?

**VS:** That is a question I will leave unanswered.

# The Narrative that Defines Us

## AUSTIN CLARKE

A narrative is a tale, or a story. It may be a recital of facts. I think there is a small contradiction here: 'facts' narrated in the writing of 'fiction'. But the other definition of a narrative is that it is a story told in the first person, and it is this rendition in the first person that gives the narrative its currency, its historical and racial legitimacy.

The narrative I am concerned with, therefore, has a magnified significance, if it is a story about a social, and by extension, a moral condition that affects the narrator. It may not be oppressively burdened with 'facts'. But if the narrative is a tale about colonialism—or slavery; or any other kind of racial oppression—its significance and its value, must lie in the narrating of this experience by one who has lived through it. This emphasizes why a narrative about colonialism has got to be written in the first person. It gives, as I have said, legitimacy to the tale being told.

This is why *The Polished Hoe* is written in the first person, displaying the personality and character of the narrator Mary-Mathilda, validating the authenticity of the colonial experience. I do not couch this narrative of Mary-Mathilda, the main character in the novel, in a background of 'historical facts'. *The Polished Hoe* is not, and was not, intended as a historical novel. But my disavowal of that kind of authority does not take away from Mary-Mathilda's insistence, through her narrative, that her story of her own colonialization is not supreme, is not sacred, and more sanctified because it is being delivered precisely in her voice. Her voice is more reliable than any reporting, than any journalistic presentation, or reported speech, *oratio obliqua*, might provide.

I shall refer to two other examples of a narrative: the first in the novel *The Confessions of Nat Turner* (1967) by William Styron, a white native of Virginia, in the American South, in a town named Southampton, the place where the second example of a narrative was set. I am referring to the document, 'The Confessions of Nat Turner, Leader of the late Insurrection in Southampton, Virginia. *As Full and Voluntarily made to Thomas Gray, in prison where he was confined*' (1831). I have added the italics to the phrase, 'As Full and Voluntarily made to Thomas Gray, in prison where he was confined', since in this phrase lies the disqualification that the document is a narrative in the sense that *The Polished Hoe* is. Nat Turner, unlike Mary-Mathilda, was 'confined'. Nat Turner, like Mary-Mathilda, was colonized within the institution and condition of his slavery.

We are morally and intellectually permitted to ask ourselves some questions: If Nat Turner was questioned by Thomas Gray, an officer of the Court, what proof do we have that what is written down in these 'Confessions' in the third person, in *oratio oblique*, are really the words of Nat Turner, spoken in his voice—even if not his physical voice, spoken in his idiom, in his ethnic-racial language?

What realistically was the significant impetus, exerted through the presence of Mr Thomas Gray in the prison cell with Nat Turner, that worked inordinately against the narrating of 'facts' in the 'confession' that Nat Turner was providing? What are the 'facts' about the person whose 'confession' is being written?

Whose voice?

And whose narrative?

The 'Confessions of Nat Turner, as told to Mr Thomas Gray', are in *oratio oblique*—in indirect speech. They, presumably, were delivered by Nat Turner in *oratio recta*—in direct speech; and later transcribed or transliterated.

We may infer that a definition of narrative could realistically have the meaning that 'recta', in oratio recta, comes close to meaning 'right' or 'correct'. And that it is the 'right', or true voice of the person confessing. I wonder, therefore, if we might not substitute 'right' for 'facts'. I mentioned my concern at the fact that Nat Turner's narrative was delivered in oratio oblique, in a prison cell, in Southampton, Virginia, in the American South, in 1831. In 1831, the psychological as well as the geographical environment was the slave plantation, an 'unspeakable' condition of colonialism.

Of this kind of colonialism, Elizabeth Abbott, in *A History of Mistresses* (2003), talking specifically about the relationship between slave woman and slave master, cautions us that 'slave narratives need careful reading. They provide what few other sources can: the slave woman's perspective on her life and world, with details of personality and perception, time and place, and sequence of events.'

And to get a taste of the language of a slave narrative, here is Martha Spence Bunton giving us her ancestry.

When Mawster Burrows died, Mawster Spence bought fathaw, and he came on down to Texas. I was born on Mawster John Bell's cotton plantation at Murphfreesboro, Tennessee, dis was on 1 January 1856, right on New Year's day. We belonged to Mawster Bell, but he sold us to Joseph Spence. Dat's why later, I got the name ob Spence, Martha Spence.

Mary-Mathilda, in another corner of the world of colonialism, introduces herself with more self-assurance: 'My name is Mary. People in this village call me Mary-Mathilda.'

Frantz Fanon, the Martinique psychiatrist and author of *Black Skin, White Masks* (1952), writing in the chapter entitled, 'The Negro and Language' said that 'the fact of juxtaposition of the white and black races has created a massive psychoexistential complex.' The historical experience of Nat Turner on the plantation of his master, admitting to being 'the property of Benj. Turner' at birth, later owned by Putnam Moore, was certainly, according to Fanon, one of mutuality. The juxtaposition had already created its 'massive psychoexistential complex'.

We cannot take the liberty of believing that Mr Thomas Gray's reporting of Nat Turner's 'confessions' contains 'facts' of his life. Thomas Gray interposes his personal opinion of Nat Turner, in amongst his own narrative of Nat Turner's character, in these words: 'Mrs Nathaniel Francis, while concealed in a closet, heard their blows, and the shrieks of victims of these ruthless savages.' He goes farther. 'Few indeed, were those who escaped their work of death. But fortunate for society, the hand of retributive justice has overtaken them, and not one that was known to be concerned has escaped.'

How would Nat Turner have described this encounter in his own voice, in direct speech?

Mr Gray's 'psychoexistentialist' views do not end there. He shows his true colours, and gives his palette of colonialist complexes regarding Nat Turner's insurrection wider rein. 'It (the Nat Turner Insurrection) will be remembered in the annals of our country, and many a mother as she presses her infant darling to her bosom, will shudder at the recollection of Nat Turner, and his band of ferocious miscreants.'

In *Livy Book XXI*, which deals with Hannibal crossing the Alps and occupying parts of Italy, at the height of the Roman Empire, in 218 BC, we find whenever Roman nannies wanted to demand quiet and discipline from their charges they threatened them with these words, 'If you don't behave, I'll call Hannibal for you!'

During Kenya's struggle for liberation from British colonialism, white expatriate English nurse-maids achieved complete obedience of their children by frightening them into submissive discipline with the threat, 'Jomo Kenyatta and the Mau Mau are coming for you!' This was in 1953.

It is usually the white child who first is taught to draw a comparison between brightishness and blackness. In other words, the seed of this brand of phobia that has psycho-sexual implications is planted at an early age. In his book *Black Skin, White Masks*, Frantz Fanon says that it is 'implicit that to speak is to exist absolutely for the other'. The 'other' suggests the juxtaposition of the colonized and the colonizer in the same geographical and administrative environment.

I shall now introduce to you an example of colonialism in which Mary-Mathilda lived, namely the plantation on which she lives and its manager, Mr Bellfeels, who controls her life. The narrative that defines *The Polished Hoe* is not, as I have said, hinged on history. It is a story, a tale, told in the first person, by a woman whose life is the mirrored definition of colonialism itself. When Mary-Mathilda speaks, her narrative is the portrait of the 'facts' of her life; and she is determined to have these 'facts' understood at the very beginning of her narrative.

'This is my history in confession,' she tells the Sergeant, who like Thomas Gray, is an officer of the Court, and who is taking her statement, 'better late than never, which in your police work is a Statement. And I wonder, as I sit here this Sunday evening, why I am giving you this history of my personal life, and the history of this island of Bimshire, altogether, wrap-up in one?'

She goes farther, and challenges the established medium of authority and authentication, the local newspaper, the *Bimshire Daily Herald*, that previously had provided the facts of her life in the colony. Her rejection of the newspaper's ability to report the 'facts' of her life brings to mind the partiality and bias of Mr Thomas Gray's reporting of Nat Turner's 'confessions'. Mr Thomas Gray operates within the American culture of racial colonialism, and usurps Nat Turner's voice, giving us instead, not Turner's 'confession' in Turner's own words, but rather the sentiments of the 'other'— the colonizer's sentiments in the culture of colonialism.

It will thus appear, that whilst everything upon the surface of society wore a calm and peaceful aspect; whilst not a note of preparation was heard to warn the devoted inhabitants of woe and death, a gloomy fanatic was revolving in the recesses of his own dark, bewildered, and overwrought mind, schemes of indiscriminate massacre to the whites. Schemes too fearfully executed as far as his fiendish band proceeded in their desolating march. No cry for mercy penetrated their flinty bosoms. No acts of remembered kindness made the least impression upon these remorseless murders. Men and women and children, from hoar age to helpless infancy, were involved in the same cruel fate. Never did a band of savages do their work of death more unsparingly.

From the book *And Now the Dead Shall Rise: The Murder of Mary Phagan and the Lynching of Leon Frank by Steve Oney*, there is James Conley, a twenty-nine-year-old black sweeper at the National Pencil Co., who in 1913 was characterized by the defence as 'a plain, beastly, drunken, filthy, lying nigger ... fired with lust (for a white woman)'. The *New York Times*, covering the trial, referred to Conley as a 'drunken, low lived, utter worthless ... black human animal.'

The Prosecution said, 'Never in the history of the Anglo-Saxon race ... did an ignorant filthy negro accuse a white man of a crime and that man declined to face him.'

In contrast to this environment of racialistic colonialism, I opened the narrative of Mary-Mathilda's story in her own voice, expressing the dignity of defining herself by her own name, demonstrating the dignity of establishing immediate family, and extended family relationships, asserting her distinct relationship to place, and time, and history—asserting the importance of visibility in that personal definition.

My name is Mary. People in this village call me Mary-Mathilda. Or Tilda, for short. To my mother, I was Mary-girl. My other names I am christen with, are Mary Gertrude Mathilda, but I don't use Gertrude, because my maid has the same name. My surname that people 'bout-here uses, is either Paul, or Belfeels, depending who you speak to ...

Mary-Mathilda has escaped the more heinous aspects of the colonialism of slavery, and can breathe this veneer of distance and amelioration. Her mother's surname of Paul has been used too long for it to be remembered as the surname of her mother's historical master. And Bellfeels, though it is the name and the symbol of the existing plantation, is ironically Mary-Mathilda's surname, by virtue of the morganatic 'kip-miss' relationship, or common law marriage to Mr Bellfeels. Nat Turner had not, in his lifetime, been capable of escaping the colonialism of the Southampton plantation to the extent that he could identify himself outside the patrimony of that relationship.

Mary-Mathilda, in defining herself, has broken the racial and political restrictions associated with inferiority that her status in colonialism presupposed.

She states her name, her ancestry, her status within the colonialist institutions, summoning cultural and racial antecedents, and laying down a sense of tradition and of belonging, all of which she legitimately ascribes to memory, and not to history. In her mind and in her contention, this memory provides the greater, effective narrative.

Nat Turner, in the document 'the Confessions', is always simply Nat. Always a boy, in spite of his age. Without a past; without a family. Cut off from antecedents.

The Muslims in America, like certain members of the Black Panther Party, and like Stokeley Carmichael—all self-declared 'prisoners' in the Amerikan (spelled with a 'k') colonialism of the 1960s embraced a concept of homeland, a political-cultural association with land, and consequently adopted Africa, and thereby demonstrated, in dramatic manner, a new cultural identity with their remembered ancestral, cultural, and racial homeland, Mother Africa.

Malcom Little became Malcom X. Leroi Jones became Amiri Baraka, Stokeley Carmicheal became Kwame Toure. Regarding the Black Muslims' bragging usage of the 'X', the irony that ought to be noted is that this same 'X' was the symbol of illiteracy. But it is also a symbol of political enfranchisement. 'Mark your X' on the ballot of Miami and Georgie Bush.

'My names I am christen with,' the heroine of the *The Polished Hoe* asserts, 'are Mary Gertrude Mathilda.'

Defining his status, and introducing himself to us through his interrogator, ironically none other than the local representative of the system that institutionalized his status of slave and consequently established his colonization, Nat's definition of himself is the definition that slavery gave him. He has to admit to his colonization: '... I was born the property of Benj. Turner, of this country.' Nat ascribes to his slave master the cultural identification with land, that is in his political background, but that is not of his cultural background—the plantation, Jerusalem, Southampton, that Malcom X and Amiri Baraka could not, and did not, embrace culturally. They did not want to be associated politically or culturally, or in any other way, with Amerika. Nat Turner admits, in fact glorifies, his colonization in Jerusalem Southampton in equal proportion to the passion with which Mary-Mathilda expresses her rejection of the plantation, and the symbol of the plantation, Mr Bellfeels, in her narrative.

'I was born the property of ...,' Nat declares with the pride of the house slave, and with an implied superiority over the field slave.

'My name is Mary,' says Mary-Mathilda, formerly a field hand, and now not only a house 'slave' but the mistress of the symbol of power who inhabits the Great House; and her rejection is the more ironical, and therefore more hostile towards the plantation house (the property) but also towards the house slave, because those alleviating conditions—her social elevation within the plantocracy—did not ameliorate her instinctual anger. '... My surname that people 'bout-here uses, is either Paul, or Bellfeels, depending who you talk to ...'

Mary-Mathilda retains the choice and the nature of her association with the plantation, which is in itself an ironical admission of ambivalence. She is saying 'If I want to be, and depending upon who you should talk to, I am a Paul. Or, I could be a Bellfeels.'

But Bellfeels is the name and the symbol of colonialism: the metaphor of her own oppression and colonization. Her adopting this name, Bellfeels, is tantamount to claiming as her own the language of the slave master, the plantation, and arrogating to herself the image of the colonizer. But more than this, she is expressing independence, and at the same time, a repudiation of the image of inferiority which the plantation system erected as her statue and as her heritage.

We must remember Fanon's statement about the colonized person's imitation of the language of the colonizer, and the facility he achieves in that language, and is forced to perfect and practise if he is to function successfully in the society controlled by the colonizer: 'It is implicit that to speak is to exist absolutely for the other.' Such facility in the language of colonialism is synonymous with the inculcating not only of the language itself, but also the acceptance of the superior value of that culture, the colonizer's culture. In other words, as Fanon says, the colonized person turns white.

Mary-Mathilda rejects this cultural integration, this submission to a white cultural standard.

She and her maid, Gertrude, chastise Wilberforce for his European manners; for his rejection—perhaps his forgetting—of the culture of the island in which he was born, and educated— Bimshire. And they both remind him that all the things that he worships from Europe, are available, are growing in the fauna and plants—even the sugarcanes—right here, if he has eyes to see, in Bimshire, in a more beautiful if ordinary profusion. They educate him about colonialism which induces one to be blind to the natural cultural landscape in which one lives.

'Expresso!' Gertrude shouts, almost in awe, to Mary-Mathilda, the first morning. The reason for Gertrude's disbelief is that Wilberforce, Mary-Mathilda's only living child, a doctor of Tropical Medicine, educated in England, at Oxford and at Cambridge, has, all of a sudden forsaken the breakfast which she, his maid, had been making for him, for years: 'two fried pork chops, three strips of fried plantain, two flour bakes, sliced cucumber with lime juice, fresh parsley, white vinegar, salt and nigger peppers ... and two large cups of strong Jamaica Blue Mountain Coffee!'.

'Expresso?' Miss Mary-Mathilda asks, in equal wonder.

'Expresso!' Gertrude repeats to her mistress. 'A Eyetalian habit he say he pick up in Italy. And him, a big man, Miss Mary-Mathilda, and a doctor, to boot, who should know more better! ... and come—telling big people that he having a continental breakfast instead! Expresso, Mistress? And eating stanning-up!' This is the language of compromise, that pleads for redemption, a language of subservience, a language that seeks authority in God, the Bible for its telling and that ascribes a divine motivation, and a theological, if illogical, philosophy to justify his act of rebellion. 'The first shall be last', he is made to say, reiterating a theology that apparently bypassed the reality of life for American slaves! Added to this naivety is the ironical statement replete with double entendre ascribed to Nat Turner when giving the motive for his rebellion: 'For he who knoweth his Master's will, and doeth it not, shall be beaten with may stripes, and thus have I chastened you'.

To which 'Master' is Nat Turner referring? A heavenly or an earthly master? Is it Benj. Turner? Putnam Moore, dec'd? Or God in Heaven?

Mary-Mathilda rests her anger and explains her resort to violence upon the ground that her degradation by the hand of the plantation was irredeemable, even though she has gained some marginal reprieve from its heinousness. No master, religious or lay, was worthy of compassion. She did what she did, because she believed in restitution. Because of a natural impulse: not a religious urging.

She did it, because 'Mr Bellfeels put his riding crop under my chin, and raise my face to meet his face, using the riding crop; and when his eyes and my eyes made four, he passed the riding crop down my neck, right down the front of my dress, until it reach my waist. And then, he moved the riding crop right back up again, as if he was drawing something on my body...'

'And that is why I did!'

On the other hand, if Nat Turner's statement, presented in the words of Thomas Gray who usurped the narrative, can be relied upon to be Turner's voice, that the insurrection he led 'was not instigated by motives of revenge or sudden anger', but that it was 'the result of long deliberation, and a settled purpose of mind', Mary-Mathilda did not take so long to reach the same conclusion. But Nat himself, in the closest example one recognizes as accurate reported speech in his narrative, attributes his anger to 'the fertility of my mind' (hardly his own words!); and to his ability 'to see things that happened before my birth'.

Compare these two examples of narrative, from Nat Turner's 'Confessions'. The first one is:

'I sometimes got in sight in time to see the work of death completed, viewed the mangled bodies as they lay, in silent satisfaction, and immediately started in quest of other victims.'

And the second is:

'... the white families having fled, we found no more victims to gratify our thirst for blood ...'

Whose voice is telling this tale? This 'tale' sounds like a tale, as we use that term to suggest evidence of questionable veracity. Which captured murderer, a slave, interrogated by a white man, himself probably a slave owner, would clothe his confession in words of such clinical morphology? One can easily recognize the sentiments of the interrogator seeping in amongst the narrative of the prisoner's evidence. Nat Turner's thoughts on his insurrection, and his philosophy of violence are being spoken for him.

Fanon believes that there is in language, as there is in behaviour (Nat Turner's or Mary-Mathilda's) 'a dualism' towards the white man; or in other words, a dualism of attitude and sentiment towards colonialism. And he explains this dualism as 'a direct result of colonialist subjugation'. Expanding upon this thought, he says that '... to speak means to be in a position to use a certain syntax, to grasp the morphology of this or that language, but it means above all, to assume a culture, to support the weight of a civilization.' I might add: to support the weight of degradation that colonialism breeds.

Like Mary-Mathilda, every colonized woman has to face the problem of language; and in facing this problem, she has also, to face the demand of narrative, the concept of that language. The narrative has to devise a literary idiom through which to record her insights, the insights of the colonized woman, since 'the gentleman' (Mr Bellfeels in *The Polished Hoe*; or Mr Benj. Turner in *The Confession of Nat Turner*) and 'the colonized woman', or the slave (Mary-Mathilda, or Nat Turner) 'lack common language and experience'.

The lack of 'common language and experience' is dramatically illustrated in Thomas Gray's interrogation, which pretends to be the voice of a slave.

The language of colonialism, the narrative that describes colonialism, may also be written in dialect (in 'nation language', to use the more proper term, embraced by the Barbados poet,

Kamau Brathwaite) and when this 'language' becomes the narrative, we know then that 'every dialect is a way of thinking'.

The dialect or 'nation language' of Trinidad that Earl Lovelace and Samuel Selvon use is perhaps the best example of this kind of declaration of a way of thinking.

In the novel, Earl Lovelace writes:

And it wasn't just men alone. It had women there that was even more terrible. They had to ban them from talking. They had to ban them from walking, from raising up their dresstail and shaking their melodies backsides. They wasn't easy. The plantation people couldn't handle them: they beat them. They hold them down and turn them over and do them whatever wickedness they could manage; but they couldn't break them.

And from Samuel Selvon's novel, *The Lonely Londoners*:

'I would advice you to hustle a passage back from home to Trinidad, today,' Moses say, but I know you would never want to do that. So, what I will tell you is this: take it easy. It had a time when I was first here, when it had only a few West Indians in London, and things used to go good enough. These days, spades all over the place, and every shipload is big news, and the English People don't like the boys coming to England to work and live.

But these narratives express disapproval with the root of colonialism: white resentment of a black presence in a racialistic context that illustrates what Fanon calls a 'psychoexistential complex'. Mary-Mathilda is more than critical of her experience of colonialism. Her attitude attacks the very foundation of the civilization of the colonizer.

I have said elsewhere, in my essay 'The Music of Narrative' (in 'Prize Writing', a pamphlet that celebrates the tenth anniversary of the Giller Prize), that the narrative of *The Polished Hoe* had to be delivered in the first person. 'It would be spoken by a woman, not by a man. And it would have to be conveyed, in its language, in its etymology'—in what Fanon calls its 'morphology' (the study of the form of words)—and in its psychic peculiarity, either primarily in nation language (formerly referred to as dialect) 'or in deliberate fifty-fifty blend. In other words, I wanted to invent a new language for this novel, and to creolize Oxford English'.

Talking about the political and cultural aspects in the nation's character, as expressed in its folk tales, stories, and songs, K. Anthony Appiah (in a review of *Favourite African Folktales* edited by Nelson Mandela) adds to my point about the meaning of narrative. 'Even the literary work of individual writers depended on this oral reserve of literary genius: you could only achieve greatness if you were fully in touch with the spirit of your own language.'

As I have shown, Nat Turner's 'Confessions' are never in 'tune with the spirit' of his own language.

The traditional, or colonial, language in my case, English, did not have the cultural racial scope essential to bearing the weight of Mary-Mathilda's narrative, that is, her intellectual scope. Her thoughts encompassed sentiments and intention of vengeance and retribution—a kind of demanding plea for moral and physical reparation. 'To throw away one's dialect is evidence of a dislocation, a separation,' Fanon says.

This is why Mary-Mathilda insists upon a liberating voice to combat the colonialism that surrounds her on the plantation, like virulent fields of sugarcane. She finds agreement with her narrative aggressiveness, which in *The Polished Hoe* becomes a kind of theology of liberation, as in Jean-Paul Sartre's *Black Orpheus* (1948). Sartre is almost complementing the timbre of voice and of theme that alarms and alerts. In the narrative Mary-Mathilda says: 'What then did you expect when you unbound the gag that had muted these black mouths? That they would chant your praises? Did you think that when those heads that our fathers had forcibly bowed to the ground, were raised again, you would find adoration in their eyes?'

Frantz Fanon provides the answer: 'If I cry out, it will be a black cry.'

A slight change in the verb, and we feel Fanon means, 'Our cry has got to be a black cry.'

Unfortunately, Nat Turner's cry, in his 'Confessions', is not a black cry. But I do not think that what is needed is a black cry of an individualist nature, but rather, a cry of unselfish proportion, a cry on behalf of all women. A cry like Mary-Mathilda's. A cry of collective animosity towards colonialism.

Narrative is contained also in poetry and in music, especially in the Blues. Amiri Baraka, formerly Leroi Jones, and Miles Davis, in poetry and in song respectively, remind us that the narrative that tells about colonialism is more effective when spoken in a collective voice. And a free voice:

> We want a black poem. And a Black World
> Let the world be a Black Poem
> And Let All Black People Speak
> This Poem
> Silently
> or LOUD.

I shall not attempt to imitate the piercing thrusts of Miles Davis' muted trumpet, playing 'I Loves you, Porgy' but I can, through the narrative of the lyrics, introduce to you the genius of that kind of musical narrative, with the help of a few lines of this Blues number:

> I loves you, Porgy,
> Don't let him take me,
> If you can keep me,
> I want to stay here
> With you forever,
> And I'll be good
> Don't let him handle me,
> And drive me mad.
> Don't let him handle me
> With his hot hands …!

Reminiscent of Earl Lovelace? Of Mary-Mathilda's lament? Whose hands is this song being told a story about, in this lamentation, in this Blues number? Is Miles Davis' lamenting on muted trumpet piercing as a surgeon's scalpel that is seeking out the fornicator? And who is the fornicator?

Whose hands? Are the hands those of Thomas Thistlewood, a
Penkeeper of cattle, in 1750, on a slave plantation in Jamaica, who
later became the owner of his own plantation, Egypt, and of slaves,
a man who visited the barracoon, the slave quarters, and used the
index finger of both hands, as Bellfeels used his riding crop over
Mary-Mathilda's body, to pick out the slave woman he wanted to
foop that night—the woman he wanted to rape—and was going
to rape ... the woman without choice, who he was going to flog-
foop and flog on that Saturday night. But he did not always wait
for Saturdays to come around, to satisfy his rapinage.

Thomas Thistlewood kept his own narrative in a diary, quoting
Latin and using code, to leave back for history and later times his
inscrutable and indelible novel, an autobiography of his avaricious
fertility. He had them, in many places (his narrative sometimes is
written in Latin) and in many forms and many positions: Tup
(twice); Sup. Lect. (on the bed); Sup Terr. (on the ground); In Silva
(in the woods); In Mag or In Parv (In the great or small house); Illa
habet menses (she has her period). And according to Elizabeth
Abbott, in A History of Mistresses, 'sometimes, notably when his
gonorrhea was in an active phase, Sed non bene (but not well).'

Fooping and flogging, Thomas Thistlewood went his merry way
rejoicing and ejaculating in the cane fields of Egypt. It is said that
his prowess in the barracoon was measured in a statistic that ticked
off more than three hundred and sixty-five and a quarter foops, more
times than he had to turn the leaves in his calendar to knock off
one year!

'The Negroes having loitered very much time away, and not
coming till late, flogged them all.'

On 26 May 1756, Thomas Thistlewood wrote in his diary that
a slave was 'catched by Port Royal eating canes. Had him well flogged
and pickled, then made Hector shit in his mouth.'

Elizabeth Abbott tells us that 'this sadistic and degrading
punishment' seemed to appeal to Thomas Thistlewood, whose diary
on 24 of July 1756 says that the same Port Royal, now a runaway
slave, was 'taken and brought back home', and the diary adds: 'Gave
him moderate whipping, pickled him well, made Hector shit in

his mouth, immediately put in a gag whilst his mouth was full &
made him wear it for 4 or 5 hours.'

But this is more than degradation. It is also sexual rapture.

'When Leo Frank's body was finally cut down, a local
Atlantic citizen stomped repeatedly on his face....' Thousands
pushed their way into a front hall through the gloweringly hot
afternoon to behold Frank's body with its trampled face lying on
the bier.

Finally, I must refer to one other narrative, found in William
Styron's novel, *The Confessions of Nat Turner*, based, admittedly
upon the same document we have been discussing, 'The
Confessions of Nat Turner, as told to Thomas Gray'.

Styron, who was born and raised in Southampton, Virginia,
claims that he is 'a super expert on slavery'. He bases this specialized
knowledge apparently on the significance of geographical location.
From the narrative he writes in the *The Confessions of Nat Turner*,
we cannot agree with his boast of historical expertise or with his
declaration of superior expertise, after his admission that his novel
took him three and a-half years to write, and is based 'upon one
hour of research'.

The research he refers to is the time it took him to read the
document, 'The Confessions of Nat Turner, as told to Thomas Gray'.

There are two contentious points I should like to deal with here.
The first refers to the question of appropriation, based upon race
and the attitude born of race. Styron is a white Southerner. Nat
Turner is a black slave. The two of them operate culturally and
racially within Fanon's 'psychoexistential complex'. The second
point, of lesser emotional nature, is whether knowledge derived
through birthplace, and a short-term period of research, even on a
subject regarded as second nature through that place of birth, and
the geography of that place, are sufficient warrant to qualify a novel,
and the narrative contained in that novel, as a historical novel. From
the number of times Styron departs from 'facts' contained in the
document, 'The Confessions of Nat Turner' that Styron himself
'researched', we might very well conclude that Styron was neither
historical nor factual.

We have the authority for this assertion in the pages of a book that deals with the Negro in the American Revolution, published in 1867, and written by James Wells Brown, a Negro. Brown tells a different tale from Styron's who seems to be writing a novel of imagination, and not a novel based upon historical 'facts'. Not even Thomas Gray's prejudice against Nat Turner expressed in his reported narrative comes close to Styron's degrading portrayal of Nat Turner, even though based upon his self-acclaimed expertise on slavery and on his abbreviated research.

'There deserted of all save those two acting out their final tableau—tar-black man and the woman, bone-white, bone–rigid with fear beyond telling, pressed urgently together against the door in a simulacrum of shattered oneness and heartsick farewell …'

Fifty years earlier, Tom Watson, the editor of the newspaper the *Jeffersonian*, expressed similar bigotry when writing about the Leo Frank murder case: 'The poor little Gentile is dust in the grave, while the Sodomite who took her sweet yong life basks in the warmth … the be-flowered pet of a national solicitude promoted by millionaire Jews.'

It is no wonder that ten established American black writers felt a moral, political, and black nationalist obligation to respond to Styron's portrayal, fifty years later, in 1967. During those civil rights' days, the black slave hero, Nat Turner, had been elevated as icon and symbol and hero of black nationalist resistance to racial segregation in contemporary America.

I am not so concerned with the question of legitimacy in literary appropriation as I am with the answer to the question, 'Whose narrative is it, any way?' Is the narrative, voiced in the first person by a slave, or a woman with an experience and background of colonialism, to be regarded as more legitimate than the narrative written by someone of the same race and sentiment as the colonizer? Is the narrative in *The Polished Hoe* more correct from a literary point of view than the 'narrative' in the document, 'The Confessions of Nat Turner', or in the novel *The Confessions of Nat Turner*?

But I come back to the fundamental question, 'Whose narrative is it?'

Mike Thelwell, a West Indian who is a librarian, one of the ten, wrote in his essay, 'Back With the Wind: Mr Styron and the Reverend Turner', that 'If this book is important, it is not so because it tells much about the Negro experience during slavery, but because of the manner in which it demonstrates the persistence of white Southern myths, racial sterotypes, and literary clichés even in the best intentioned and most enlightened minds.'

Mike Thelwell concludes that Styron's narrative operates with 'a white language and a white consciousness'. Thelwell gives this example: 'I recall one of my former owners, Mr Thomas Moore, once saying that Negroes never committed suicide. I recollect the exact situation, hog–killing time … while I stood by listening. "Ever hear of a nigger killing hisself? No, I figure a darkey he might want to kill hisself, but he gets to thinkin' about it, and he keeps thinkin', and pretty soon he's gone off to sleep. Right, Nat?" The neighbour's laughter and my own anticipated, expected, and the question repeated—'Right, Nat?'—more insistent now, and my reply, with customary chuckling.

"Yes, sir, Marse Tom, that's right sure enough."'

The real language, the narrative of persons like Mary-Mathilda, and even Nat Turner, if he were given the ability to speak in his own voice, can be found in the Spiritual and the Blues. This language, though produced by oppression and colonialism, is one 'whose central impulse is survival and resistance'.

If the oral tradition, the narrative of the folk, defined the national character, how much more important it is that Mary-Mathilda's statement, her oralization of her history, be the official testament of evidence, not only of her life but also of her times—of Bimshire.

J.M.W. Turner, English painter of the nineteenth century, was regarded as a brilliant artist because of his ability to make you use your eyes and your imagination in his landscapes and his sea-scapes. Mary-Mathilda's narrative in the *The Polished Hoe* seeks to do this. It is a wide cultural and historical panorama of a narrative, filled with her imagination and yet riveted to the truth of reality.

Mary-Mathilda, giving us her narrative in colonialism, is more in command of her identity, and she does not leave it to her interrogator, the Sargeant (who is taking her Statement), nor ask his permission to interpret her narrative for her, nor clothe her narrative in the morphology of the Court, or of the plantation.

This makes her narrative a declaration of 'survival and of resistance'.

I would see her, my greatgran-mother, just before she passes away, bent almost in half; her face scenting the bushes; picking and picking, putting a leaf or a twig or a stem inside her mouth and chew on it, to test it; and then spitting it out; with her braided–up grey hair slipping out from underneat her white head–tie and hanging low to the ground, searching through worthless rocks and stones as if they were precious pearls and corals, and picking a twig from this bush, a twig from the next; and putting all of them in her apron, even when she was long-past working in people kitchens. She spent most of her life in the kitchen at the Aquatic Club. It's a wonder to me, knowing what she must have went through in them days, that she did'nt put a lil piece of the root from the wrong bush, or a stem of Poison Ivy, a lil-lil piece of the root, in the tureens of turtle soup those bastards liked her to cook for them! Yes.

My great gran. Her apron was like a badge of honour. In her apron, always white and starch–and ironed, and pleated in straight lines from her waist down to below her two ankles, she would put those bushes, sersey bush, Christmas bush, miraculous bush, lignum-vitae bush, soursop leaves and leaves from the puhpaw trees, tamarind tree leaves and sugar apple leaves … I don't remember the other bushes! But I know that the sersey bush is what did the trick. Sersey bush that Gran boiled thick-thick until it came like tar, bitter and black; and that poor girl, my ma, no more than seventeen or sixteen, was made to drink that tar-tea every morning at five o' clock, until Mr Bellfeels vim was worked out of her system. And at every six o' clock every morning. Gran put Ma in a bush-bath, and soaked her until all the sin, and the stain, and the mistake, came out in the form of blood! Yes!

It take three days and three nights, with Ma's gran mother sitting sleepless in a upright chair, for Ma to regain her salvation, and have release from the thing that Mr Bellfeels sowed inside her, inside Ma.

But blood was always in our lives. Blood and more blood … and that is why I do what I did. Yes!

# PART TWO

## Nations in Black and White

# The Black Savant and the Dark Princess

## HOMI K. BHABHA

The problem of a minority group in a world torn by old and new national and racial divisions was of enormous difficulty: it was idle for us to repeat the old slogans of democracy in an oligarchic world; no matter how strongly we, with all forward looking thinkers, might envisage a birth of democracy ... amid turmoil and contradiction, beclouded by a thousand irrelevancies and bedeviled by every art of selfishness, but nevertheless clearly in progress. My problem was—How can American Negroes join this [international] movement and intelligently reinforce it, for their own good and the good of all men.

*A Pageant in Seven Decades: 1868–1938*
from *Pamphlets and Leaflets*

W.E.B. DuBois's Bollywood-style *Bildungsroman, The Dark Princess*, presents a strange juxtaposition of the African-American race-man Mathew Towns, figure of forbearance, and his revolutionary leader and lover, Kautilya, the dark Princess of the Tibetan Kingdom of Bwodpur, 'princess of the wide, wide world'.[1] The race-man struggles with beauty and death in the treacherous folds of the Veil of the racial colour-line 'where the doer never sees the Deed, and the victim knows not the Victor'[2]; the high-caste Hindu Princess imperiously commands a patrician *posse* of cosmopolitan modernists with Bolshevist leanings, banded together in an anti-Imperialist Council of Darker Peoples. In this odd coupling, the celebrated 'twoness' of DuBois's double consciousness—an American and a Negro—seems to lose its predominantly national mooring; and strangely beside that tortured, unresolvable dialectic, there opens up a third space—more anti-colonial and global in character—represented by Kautilya, who emerges on the American scene with all the *Sturm und Drang* of the DuBoisian *dramatis persona* now culturally cross-dressed in silks, turbans, and sarees.

Such an allegorical configuration of characters, countries, and commitments prefigures a method of representing the *particularity* of racial antagonism and ambivalence that DuBois was to frame as the rule of 'juxtaposition'[3] in the elegiac encounters of *Darkwater* (DuBois 1920). The rule of juxtaposition (which has been unfairly overshadowed in DuBois studies by the concept of 'double consciousness') describes the spatial designation of structures of discriminatory power, regulated by the local and the national state, that create an enforced intimacy, an antagonistic proximity, as they establish the colour-line across the uncivil society of the nation—a nation segregated not only by race, but deeply marked by complex class affiliations and divisions. In the interwar years, the political economy of the black community in the Northeast and the Midwest was in a process of transition; the largely unorganized rural world of migrant labour was entering the carceral domain of an urban and sub-urban proletariat of the 'black metropolis', oppressed by the mendacious practices of racist housing and employment laws, discriminatory market regulations, and segregationist forms of municipal and public life. Lynching was now supplemented by gang assaults. For many African-Americans, as you are well aware, the domestic era of Reconstruction still continues, *e pluribus divisi*, despite the Empire's unbridled zeal for the democratic deconstruction of Iraq.

DuBois's rule of juxtaposition represents what is intolerable in the 'local' lifeworld of racial injustice and inequality, placed in a contradictory contiguity with those forms of beauty and equality that do not surmount Jim Crow, but make its existence more readily survivable, and subvertible, if viewed from a philosophical perspective. The world of American racial segregation is *juxtaposed* with 'extra-territorial' symbolic signs and deterritorializing social orders in order to deprive domestic norms of discrimination and despair of their naturalized, even nationalized, moral and political authority. The quality of visibility DuBois attributes to what he sees as the contradiction, or perhaps, even the aporia, of this form of coexistence is reminiscent of the visibility that Fanon attributes to the racial differential in the colonial context where 'the economic infrastructure is also a superstructure':

Here, then [writes DuBois], is beauty and ugliness, a wide vision of world-sacrifice, a fierce gleam of world-hate. Which is life and what is death and how shall we face so tantalizing a contradiction? Any explanation must necessarily be subtle and involved. No pert and easy word of encouragement, no merely dark despair, can lay hold of the roots of these things ... There is not in the world a more disgraceful denial of human brotherhood than the 'Jim-Crow' car of the southern United States; but, just as true, there is nothing more beautiful in the universe than sunset and moonlight on Montego Bay in far Jamaica. And both things are true and both belong to our world, and neither can be denied.[4]

These juxtaposed scenes of a double 'truth'—at times incommensurable, at others, almost unbearable—cannot be transcended or rendered whole. Like Fanon's Manichean *topoi,* they 'confront each other, but not in the service of a higher unity'.[5] DuBois's *rule of juxtaposition* is less incendiary than Fanon's compartmentalized world, but both of them, despite their differences, represent the groundwork of a counterfactual approach to political agency and aspiration. Fanon draws on the psycho-phenomenology of the 'dream-work'—'dreams of possession; every type of possession'—to describe the native's aspirational struggle to take the *place* of the colonizer but *not his status* (Fanon insists on the distinction); while DuBois resorts to an assertive ethic of forbearance that encourages the race-man to persist in his anti-segregationist political project despite the 'tantalizing contradiction' that constitutes its conditions of possibility and effectivity. This contradictory, yet contiguous, mode of coexistence requires us to acknowledge the importance of the 'counterfactual' in the realm of political discourse and the desire for freedom. *And both things are true and both belong to our world, and neither can be denied,* is a statement of neither passivity nor quietism. To make an imaginative appeal to freedom through *counterfactual* choice—the freedom *from* humiliation, suffering, racism, class, or gender exclusion—cannot be dismissed as mere rhetoric. Such a counterfactual discourse 'of freedom as an effective power to achieve what one *would* choose',[6] Amartya Sen writes in *Inequality Reexamined,* is an essential value of the language and idea of freedom. 'The role of counterfactual choice becomes relevant', he says, 'indeed central … in … being able to live as one *would* value, desire and choose, is a contribution to one's freedom [and agency] and not just to one's well-being or agency achievement, though it is also that.'[7] Counterfactual choice is crucial to the process of constructing a legitimate *claim* to national freedom.

What, then, is the task of the discovery of freedom as narrated in *Dark Princess?* Princess Kautilya describes the common mission of the anti-colonial confederation in terms familiar to any reader of DuBois's work. Their goal, she says, is '[the recognition of] democracy as a method of discovering real aristocracy. We looked frankly forward to raising not all the dead, sluggish, brutalized masses of men, but to discovering among them genius, gift and ability in far larger number than among the privileged and the ruling classes. Search, weed out, encourage; educate, train and open all doors! Democracy is not an end; it is a method of aristocracy….'[8]

A political and aesthetic education for democracy lies at the very heart of DuBois's controversial, elitist theory of the Talented Tenth and derives its aspirational activism from the call to forbearance. '*Entbehren sollst du. Sollst entbehren*'[9] (forbear you must, you must forbear). DuBois echoes Goethe's Faust (Part 1) in the Wings of Atlanta where he defines his aims of education against what he describes as the scattered, haphazard educational practices of Booker T. Washington. Democracy as a pedagogical method of seeking the aristocracy of talent is a phrase that resonates suggestively both with the Deweyan influence on DuBois, and the Arya Samaj movement mentioned in *Dark Princess*. DuBois's Indian friend Lala Lajpat Rai may well have had a large part to play in his choice of an Indian heroine—appropriately exoticized and eroticized—as the protagonist of progress and world sacrifice. DuBois sent Lajpat Rai the manuscript of *Dark Princess* for his editorial comments, and although I have been unable to locate Rai's response, the link between this text and the history of their friendship has not been adequately explored for the history of African-American literature. They may well have been introduced around 1911 by Felix Adler of the Ethical Society, one of the chief organizers of the Universal Races Congress in London, which provided DuBois with the conceptual *donnee* for his novel. Lajpat Rai singles out Adler for particular thanks in the preface to *The United States of America* (1916), a work that opens with DuBois as frontispiece and contains several quotations from his works and anecdotes of his life. DuBois and Rai shared a pedagogical style of nationalist instruction based on a doctrine expounded in *Young India* (first published in the US in 1916) that 'Indian nationalism is thus entering an international phase ... and Indian scholars should make it an item of their programme to open India ... and thus bring India into the vortex of world forces.'[10] DuBois's editorship of the *Crisis* was marked by a consistent attempt at placing the African-American struggle within an international, decolonizing frame of reference, and he often wrote the sections on the struggle for Indian independence himself. The disciplinary medium of what we might call an internationalist 'nationalism'—of which Har Dayal and Madame Cama were also exponents during this period—was often a combination of literary narrative, religious reform, sociological speculation ('Herbert Spencer' and 'Karl Marx: A Modern Rishi' [*Modern Review, March 1912*]) all cast in a socialist mould with elements of anarchistic tracts on terror and rebellion. The 'informational' *genre* played a crucial part in this international pedagogy of anti-colonialism. What might seem at times like an elite preoccupation was, in fact, a rousing response to the British government's comprehensive redefinition of sedition to include all forms of political meetings and assemblies, publications, and propaganda, as well as a tight control of the Press. The rushed roster of the Seditious Meetings Act, the Explosives Act, the Press Act, and the violation of *habeas corpus* with the reactivation of the East India Company's Regulation 111 of 1818—all within a handful of years in the first decade of the twentieth century created political exiles committed to a range of anti-colonial publications. As Lajpat Rai writes in *Young India*, 'Indian patriots ... seeking and getting the opportunities of meeting and conversing with nationalists of other countries ...' was an extremely significant activity:

American literature and American events are also playing their own part in the influences that are feeding Indian nationalism. [Lajpat Rai continues,] 'The leaders are and have ever been close students of American literature and the history of the American Federation. Asia, however, is playing a greater part in moulding and influencing Indian nationalism. The recognition of Japanese as a great power by the Concert of Europe is regarded by Young India as the potent factor in Indian nationalism ... Turkey's war with Italy, followed by her struggle with the Balkan States, has done wonders in nationalising the Indian Mohammedians.[11]

DuBois was undoubtedly drawn to what he saw as Lajpat Rai's ability to blend an elite worldliness or cosmopolitanism, with the progressive 'authority' of a received and reformed tradition, and the engagement of a radical anti-colonial programme. Long plagued by a sense of the provincialism of the African-American race-man, DuBois was determined to create wider circuits of communication. But there were other elements of Rai's writings that certainly influenced his crafting of the *Dark Princess,* and enabled DuBois to couple the Indian anti-colonialist and the African-American anti-segregationists in the vortex of world forces. In *USA,* Rai translates the colour-line into the language of caste, arguing, no doubt controversially, that the Sanskrit term for caste—*jat* or jat dharma, not varna—is an equivalent of the English word for colour. Over and above the 'political distinctions', he argues, the restrictions on inter-dining and inter-marriage, education, and justice, all suggest that 'the worst features of the code of Manu find their parallel in American life'.[12] What is most informative for DuBois's allegory is the intersection of the caste-colour line with issues of gender and class. The Indian dark princess Kautilya is shadowed in the 'Chicago' section of the book—which space does not permit me to explore here—by an extremely light-skinned aspiring African-American princess who manipulates the graft-politics of Chicago and the Pullman porter's strike to emerge into the political limelight. The colour-caste line, Rai suggests—and remember that colour-caste was also a term used by the early interwar school of race sociology at the University of Chicago—is a modern form of prejudicial subjection that emerges as a representational and regulative force when the 'submerged castes'—the victims of class prejudice and gender discrimination—attempt 'to claim political or civil equality'.[13] The Brahmins fell and misused their power, imprisoning the people in 'forged chains of intellectual bondage,' Rai concludes, 'But they did not establish a soul-killing industrial system such as the modern industrial Brahmins of the West ... I would at any time rather be ruled by Rabindranath Tagore than by a magnet of Wall Street.'[14]

DuBois certainly found Rai's speculations on the international phase of Indian nationalism important for his allegorical inquiry into the internationalization of the colour-line which is the overarching theme of *Dark Princess*. But who is this dark lady? Far be it from me to dispel the dream of faery shared by critics from Herbert Aptheker to Arnold Rampersad who have endorsed Mary White Ovington's account of her sighting of the dark lady:

I think I saw the dark Indian Princess in 1911 as she came down the steps of the ballroom at the last meeting of the First Universal Races Congress in London....And by the Princess's side was one of the most distinguished men at the Conference, Burghardt DuBois. They were talking earnestly, of course, of the race problem. Did this Indian Princess remain in the American Negro's memory to become the Titania of his Midsummer's Night's Dream?[15]

My recent researches, however, have turned up another source for the lingering memory of the Indian Princess in the mind and art of DuBois. In 1907, DuBois took a summer sojourn in England and Europe, cycling through the Lake District, and being entertained by the liberal, and radical, members of the European middle classes. In these weeks of respite from the lacerating colour-line of America, DuBois abandoned himself to a Europe 'of past beauty and present culture, fit as I fondly dreamed to realize a democracy in which me and my people could find a welcome place'.[16] Had he, perchance, heard tell that very summer of a diasporic Indian revolutionary, daughter of a well-to-do Parsi family from Bombay, Madame Bhikaji Cama, who had lived in exile in Europe since 1902, finally settling in a small pension in Paris? Madame Cama was a fervent and fearless radical in the cause of Indian Independence, but one who saw the horizon of freedom stopping at no national border or regional boundary. She was, beyond her Indian interests, the inspiring leader of a group of Asian revolutionary anti-colonialists who had gathered in Europe. In August 1907, while DuBois was in Europe, Madame Cama attended the International Socialist Congress in Stuttgart, where she famously unfurled the Indian National flag whose middle band 'bore emblems to represent the Hindus, Mohammedans, Buddhists and Parsis'[17]—emblems that echo the passage in which DuBois's Princess Kautilya gathers the many peoples of India, Africa, and the Americas around the symbol of the rice dish.

I and my Buddhist priest, a Mohammedan Mullah, and a Hindu leader of Swaraj, were India; … We came in every guise at my command when around the world I sent the symbol of the rice dish; we came as laborers, as cotton pickers, as peddlers, as fortune tellers, as travelers, as tourists … the Day has dawned, Matthew—the Great Plan is on its way …[18]

Madame Cama spoke out against 'the slavery of the fifth of the whole of the human race … The perfect social state demands that no people should be subject to any despotic or tyrannical forms of Government'.[19] The *Leipziger Zeitung* commented on the rousing impact of Madame Cama (Mrs Kramas) on the gathered delegates. Dressed in shimmering silken garments, she 'displayed a silken tricolour, the banner of the oppressed, then the cheers of the International would not end.' Later that very summer, on 21 September 1907, a group of anti-imperialist revolutionaries, Indians and Egyptians prominent amongst them, held a soirée at the Hotel Palais on the Champs Elysees. Madame Cama, the *dark princess* no less, was the centrepiece of this gathering.[20] Was this figure of romance and revolution the inspiration for the *allegorical avatar*? Had DuBois read of Madame Cama as he was travelling in Europe in the summer of 1907, turning frequently to German newspapers as was his wont when in Europe? Or was Madame Cama mentioned to him by her comrade and compatriot, DuBois's faithful friend, Lala Lajpat Rai? When Rai was suddenly arrested in Lahore and deported to Mandalay under Regulation 111, Madame Cama immediately published a letter in the June 1907 issue of Krishnavarma's *Indian Sociologist* saying: 'If Hindus, Muslims, Parsis and Christians would realize that they were as much Indians as Lajpat Rai, this would provide the unity we require.'[21] On this occasion Madame Cama first enunciated the policy of non-cooperation, which Gandhi was to adopt in November 1919, and the debt is gratefully acknowledged in his autobiography. Eight or ten weeks after the Stuttgart meeting Madame Cama took her message and her tricolour to New York, urging the people there to support the efforts of Indian nationalists in exile 'to teach the people their rights and to throw off despotism'.[22]

Quite apart from a marked resemblance between the figure of Madame Cama and the character of Kautilya, there is an uncanny echo between Madame Cama's gathering of anti-imperialist revolutionaries in the Hotel Palais in Paris, and DuBois's *mise en scéne* for his novel which focuses on a similar, clandestine gathering of revolutionaries, around an Indian woman, in a Berlin hotel. In fact, the most widely read and interpreted scene of *Dark Princess* occurs in the Berlin revolutionary *boite*; it is here that the conceptual and fictional *leitmotif* of the novel is first encountered: 'Suddenly now there loomed plain and clear the shadow of a colour line within a colour line, a prejudice within prejudice.'[23]

Having fled to Berlin to take refuge from segregation in America, Mathew Towns is enraptured by the modernist, cosmopolitan knowledge of these Pan-Asian and North African leaders. His mind turned by their conversational fluency and *savoir faire*—Kandinsky with the canapés and Schoenberg with socialism—Towns is persuaded that he is, at last, in the emancipatory embrace of the finest flower of the anti-racist representatives of the Culture Societies (as DuBois called the 'old world' in the early 1900s). To the gathered revolutionaries, however, Towns is quite literally a *bête noire*; his blood, his low caste, and his African-American origin are all anathema to their foundational racial belief. The Japanese member speaks for the group when he states: 'For us here and for the larger company we represent, there is a deeper question—that of the ability, qualifications, and real possibilities of the black race in Africa or elsewhere.'[24] The genealogy of such a discourse of natural aristocracy—'Superior races—the right to rule—born to command—the inferior breeds—the lower classes—the rabble',[25] to quote the book—is itself a rich *mélange* of the imperial racial imaginary. Elements of Freeman's mid-Victorian version of the Teutonic myth of 'the community of blood' mixed with a late nineteenth century 'anthropocentric' theme of the backward and advanced races, all of it staged on the Roman Imperial model turned into baroque kitsch that rationalized the imperial despotism of the late Victorian Raj.

The Princess protests at the emergent colour-line that seems to shadow the thinking of her revolutionary anti-colonial cohort. She has been told in Moscow that '[the Negroes of America] are a nation today, a modern nation worthy to stand beside any nation here'.[26] The Egyptian and Japanese desperately want to change the subject. They turn the conversation to Schoenberg's recent transcription of Bach's choral prelude *Komm Gott, Schoppfer*. Matthew, who has so far 'felt his lack of culture audible',[27] is gripped suddenly by the passionate memory of the sodden masses of men in Black Africa, the old log church in Virginia, the strong arm of his father conducting the church choir. Then, from the depths of oppression and obscurity, rises the resounding anthem, 'The Great Song of Freedom': *Go down Moses!*

What sounds, at times, like an 'opera bouffé' in Berlin—Wyndham Lewis calls the novel a film-farrago[28]—is, indeed, a primal scene of *Dark Princess*. Such scenes prepare us for the great theme of the novel, which is the betrayal of common purpose amongst minorities who share a common historic condition of racial oppression. How do we account for the 'shadow of the color-line within a color-line',[29] the stain of prejudice amongst those who have themselves been the victims of prejudice? Is this the negation of human and ethical solidarity, or the necessary negotiation of cultural differences in constructing our inter-national claims to human 'rights?' Critics who have historically located the intellectual kernel of *Dark Princess* in DuBois's participation in the Universal Races Congress in London in 1911 have failed to see the profound historical irony that DuBois performs in his novel, by radically altering, even inverting—for the purposes of a kind of counterfactual poetic justice—the fundamental assumptions and aspirations of the Congress.

The organizing committee asked its participants to reflect on the shared awakening of the East and the Negro:

Who then can say that the re-awakening East may not eclipse the now over-confident West in sublimity of discoveries and brilliance of inventions? Who, then, may assert that the Negro in America or Africa has no proud future similar to that of his brother of European descent ... In short, history, impartially viewed and reviewed, vindicates the essential likeness of most peoples.[30]

Reporting from London for the *Independent*, DuBois welcomed the message of the Congress, which represented, as he often remarked, a turning point in his understanding of the colour-line: 'Every anthropologist present laid chief stress on environment in explaining these [racial and cultural] differences. Lyde of Oxford, added that even colour, which is today made the greatest of racial barriers, is with little doubt "entirely a matter of climatic control".'[31] Indeed, nowhere amongst the Asiatics present at the Congress was there even the merest shadow of the prejudicial, discriminatory colour-line. For instance, the Japanese member of the Princess' Council, who DuBois casts as the most vehement spokesman for 'natural aristocracy' and the discourse of 'pure' blood—'although I fear that always blood must tell'—speaks, in the novel, quite out of historical character.[32] Between 1919 and 1931 the Japanese were seen as leaders in the international fight for coloured equality. It was the Japanese who insisted on the 'racial equality' clause in the charter of the League of Nations; and DuBois himself publicly announced in an editorial in the *Crisis* that the Japanese would be the intermediaries for black America before the League of Nations; where 'Resolutions passed ... contained principles of equality which Jews and Japanese demanded.'[33] Yet, in a manner explicitly opposed to the spirit of historic precedent and his mimetic model, DuBois provocatively introduces 'the colour-line within the colour-line, prejudice within prejudice' as the problematic of political representation and narrative progress at the very heart of *Dark Princess*.

DuBois prefigures, perhaps, one of the most significant issues that Fanon raises in *The Wretched of the Earth*—the problem of spontaneous solidarity. The irresponsibility of the bards of Negritude lay in their uncritical appropriation of universalism in order to make a claim to a continental African culture that 'could pit themselves against the narcissism and ostentation of the European'.[34] 'The black world came into being,' Fanon writes, 'and Busia from Ghana, Birago Diop from Senegal, Hampate Ba from Mali and Saint-Clair Drake from Chicago were quick to claim common ties and identical lines of thought.'[35] A 'legitimate claim to a nation' must abjure the 'quick fix' of such spontaneous solidarities. 'A national consciousness,' Fanon argues, 'which is not nationalism, is alone capable of giving us an international dimension'[36] is one in which the cultural element is always conceived of as a differential—'the outcome of tensions internal and external to society as a whole, and its multiple layers'[37]—the disjunctive layerings of asymmetrical sites of power that create sites of tension, antagonism, and transformation. By casting the shadow of the colour-line within the colour-line and providing a tantalizingly contradictory version of the Universal Races Congress in *Dark Princess*, DuBois performs both the passion and the problems of spontaneous solidarity amongst the anti-Imperialist Council of Darker Peoples.

The *Dark Princess* signifies, through her Orientalist affect, a political passion and charisma that both eroticize and aestheticise her progressive, quasi-materialist, or Marxist political opinions. It is, indeed, this engendering articulation between the deep inheritance of aristocracy, royal blood, Indian caste-hierarchy, and her profoundly 'high modernist' tastes for Picasso, Proust, Meyerhold, Kandinsky, Schoenberg—even Marx!—that turns her into an incandescent icon of world-service and inter-national emancipation. Archaic and avant-garde, all at once. An ideological or 'class' contradiction, a capitulation to oligarchy in the name of a patrician populism, is transformed by the 'rule of juxtaposition' into a wily and wise political message. Indeed, Matthew suggests that although it is hard for a stranger such as the cosmopolitan-Marxist Indian Princess to see beneath the 'unlovely surface of this racial tangle [of American segregation] ... somehow he had counted on this woman—on her subtlety and vision; on her knowledge of the colour-line.'[38] What could her specific knowledge of the colour-line be? How could she, as an anti-imperialist Asian woman, part of the Indian freedom movement, be counted upon to illuminate the struggle around and against the segregationist colour-line?

'It is dominating Europe which has flung this challenge of the colour-line and we cannot avoid it,'[39] a (Chinese) character in *Dark Princess* declares. The Princess is now entering the terrain of the DuBoisian minority: 'When a minority group is thus segregated and forced out of the nation, they can in reason do but one thing— take advantage of the disadvantage.'[40] To understand how the Asian anti-colonialists took advantage of disadvantage and dealt with the discriminatory class and culture divisions of imperial westernization and modernization gives us an intimation of the reasons why Matthew may find the Asiatics so compelling. If, from the outset, my argument has been exploring the DuBoisian theme of the 'rule of juxtaposition'—which has also provided a design for the progress of my lecture—then let me turn to another version of 'the rule of

juxtaposition' in the domain of anti-colonial nationalism as put
forth by Partha Chatterjee:

Anticolonial nationalism creates its own domain of sovereignty within colonial
society ... It does this by dividing the world of social institutions and practices
into two domains—the material and the spiritual. The material is the domain of
the 'outside,' of the economy and of statecraft, of science and technology, a
domain where the West had proved its superiority and the East had succumbed.
In this domain, then, Western superiority had to be acknowledged and its
accomplishments carefully studied and replicated. The spiritual, on the other
hand, is an 'inner' domain bearing the 'essential' marks of cultural identity. The
greater one's success in imitating Western skills in the material domain, therefore,
the greater the need to preserve the distinctness of one's spiritual culture. This
formula is, I think, a fundamental feature of anticolonial nationalisms in Asia
and Africa.[41]

The civilizing mission initiated a cultural project similar to what
DuBois once described as the anomaly of 'amalgamation' in a
segregationist context—the assumption is that you *want* to be white
or westernized or 'modern', which is then only partially or
selectively permitted, so that your own difference is 'normalized'
and your desire naturalized into majoritarian claims. The anti-
colonialist minority strategy, as Chatterjee describes it, mounts a
challenge to colonial polity by 'redividing' the majoritarian domains
of colour-line discrimination into the realms of the outside (material
institutions) and the inside (cultural identifications). The greater
the influence of westernization in the material sphere, the stronger
the resistance to it in the spiritual and cultural enclave. This
tantalizing contradiction of 'double aims' 'trumped' the colonizers'
exclusionary political and cultural binarisms—premodern/modern,
despotic/democratic—by introducing an exorbitant hyphenation
of westernization-*and*-indigeneity, the inter-national—*and*—the
national, the modern *and* the local (not the archaic or premodern).
The anti-colonial re-alignment of the material and the spiritual,
the inner and outer, mimics the colonialist's colour-line of archaism
and modernity, but only up to a point. Beyond that point of

identification, there is a resistance to 'amalgamation' or cultural appropriation and dependence. And in this emergent vortex of the world Young India and Black America meet again and echo each other. In an essay entitled 'India and the World Movement' (1913) which deeply influenced Lajpat Rai's speculations on the same subject in 1916, Har Dayal speaks in a voice that will be recognizable to anyone who recalls the end of DuBois's *The Souls of Black Folk*. 'The world-force stands around India today, and it says,—"Assimilate me, or I will eat thee up." And new India should answer: "I know thee, O Time-Spirit, I will not only assimilate thee: I will control and guide and conquer thee." '[42]

In keeping with the DuBoisian structure of juxtaposition, this double mimesis involved in the anti-colonial strategy translates across the colour-and-culture line, allowing the African-American race-man, like Towns, to envisage a coevality of cultural 'difference', to strive for a right to an equality-in-difference. It is not that he transcends his twoness; he learns to negotiate another 'limit' between being an American and a Negro than the *nationalized* colour-line allows. The Asian strategy *as elaborated in the DuBoisian allegory* allows him a way of trying to resolve the 'ever present twoness' of being a Negro and an American without the transcendent hope 'of merging himself into a better and truer self'.[43] Having interleaved the anti-segregationist and anti-colonialist perspectives into a double consciousness that could now be described as 'Asian and African-American', we can proceed towards the novel's 'great synthesis', its transformative vision. DuBois projects a mode of nationhood that interestingly decentres the sovereignty of the 'state' by locating it in a region, the Midwest, and localizing it in a city, Chicago, and from there he traces an international routing of the Black Belt, careful not to homogenize, or harmonize *a la negritude,* the spontaneous solidarity of state or region. New York is a province of England; Virginia, Charleston, and New Orleans are 'memories ... California is just beyond the world ... Chicago is the American world and the modern world, and the worst of it. We Americans are caught here in our own machinery.'[44] Six years earlier than *Dark Princess,* DuBois had ventured this very vision of a synthetic, minoritarian nation in a condemnation of British imperialism and the cultural hegemony of the East Coast. In *Americanization* (1922) he made an appeal to the Midwest of the nation to envision a democracy that goes beyond the 'Englishmen or New Englander ... The great alliance then between the darker people the world over, between disadvantaged groups like the Irish and the Jew, and between the working classes everywhere.'[45] This 'quasi-colonial' alliance displaces the national perspective onto a local regional focus—the Midwest, the 'finer flower of democracy'. The alliance constitutes a community of minorities, racialized populations, workers, women, and the unwaged. Almost twenty years after the publication of *Dark Princess* and *Americanization*, the concept of the 'quasi-colonial' emerged in 1945 to remind us that the moral strains of racism and oppression had not passed; that the poetics of forbearance requires us to live and work within the contradiction of double aims. We must both follow and fight the rule of juxtaposition. DuBois's concept of the quasi-colonial, with its metaphoricity and its moral fervour, has lost none of its demographic and democratic relevance a half-century later:

We must conceive of colonies in the 19th & 20th centuries as [part of] the local problems of London, Paris and New York. [Here in America] in the organized and dominant states of the world, there are groups of people who occupy the quasi-colonial status: laborers who are settled in the slums of great cities; groups like Negroes in the United States who are segregated physically and discriminated spiritually in law and custom ... All these people occupy what is really a colonial status and make the kernel and substance of the problem of minorities.[46]

It is the mission of the quasi-colonial to take on the challenge of the 'contradiction of double aims', to use DuBois's canonical phrase, and struggle to produce a world-open message through the aesthetic and political rule of juxtaposition. For DuBois, minoritarian agency is envisaged as a process of political action and enunciation—the slave or the colonized represent their community in the very act of political poesis. The burden of the minoritarian 'message' is not merely the demand for the respect and recognition of cultural or political differences. This very act of communication or narration is also an ethical-political practice that 'is complete not in opening to the spectacle of or the recognition of the other, but in becoming a responsibility for him/her'.[47] The responsibility of the minoritarian agent lies in creating a world-open forum of communication in which 'the crankiest, humblest and poorest ... people must be the real key to the consent of the governed.'[48]

DuBois's central insight lies in emphasizing the 'contiguous' and contingent nature of the making of minorities, where solidarity depends on surpassing autonomy or sovereignty in favour of an inter-cultural articulation of differences. This is a dynamic and dialectical concept of the minority as a *process of affiliation,* an ongoing translation of aims and interests through which minorities emerge to communicate their messages *adjacently* across communities. This enunciative concept of minoritization is much in advance of the anthropological concept of the minority that is in place in Article 27 of the International Convention on Civil and Political Rights. For Article 27, minorities, in the main, are groups that have existed in a state before becoming beneficiaries of protection. It is their 'cohesion' as a minority that has to be protected for 'minorities have been conceived [in the article] as social entities wholly sustainable by their separateness'.[49] Immigrants and women, for example, have had problems in being recognized by Article 27 because, it is argued, they do not closely approximate to a 'jural order with institutions shared by the whole category', and they do not demand the right to sustain their culture 'as a fundamental group quality sought to be maintained as an end in itself'.[50] Such a strong preference for cultural 'holism' prevents Article 27 from envisaging, or providing protection for, new and affiliative forms of minoritarian agents and institutions that do not necessarily choose to signify their lifeworlds in the *political forms of nation-ness and nationalisms.*

DuBois stands, with the ethical minorities of his aspirational imagination, at the limits of national society without eviscerating or erasing its presence, adjacent to both the white and the black worlds, sending his double-aimed message in an 'inter-national'[51] or quasi-colonial direction (to use DuBois' concepts of 'enduring hyphenation'[52]). "It is not possible in a modern world to separate people by vertical partitions,' W.E.B. DuBois wrote in 1929, 'Who was it that made such group and racial separation impossible under modern methods? Who brought fifteen million black folk overseas? ... The world has come together in an organization which you can no more unscramble than you can unscramble eggs.'[53] As any good cook knows, and we have no reason to believe that DuBois was anything less, scrambling eggs is one of the great challenges to the enduring problem of integration: how do you get the right balance between the competing demands of egginess, the egg whites, the yellow yoke, the black pepper, in order to create a sublime consistency? How do we arrive at the right consistency and constituency for the labour of freedom?

There is a less obvious reading of the parable of the scrambled eggs, which hinges more directly on DuBois's critique of the modern nation and its 'organization' of majorities and minorities. In his statement from 1929, we see the anticipatory traces of a wider critique of the nation-state from the minoritarian perspective that DuBois was to launch much later, in 1944, against the resolutions of the Dunbarton Oaks Conference, where he represented the National Association for the Advancement of Colored People (NAACP). He argued that the Conference's 'emphasis on nations and states and the indifference to races, groups or organizations indicate that the welfare and protection of colonial peoples are beyond the jurisdiction of the conference's proposed governments'.[54] DuBois's 'challenge to the idea that human beings had rights and agency only as citizens of a nation-state'[55] was taken up at the United Nations in 1946–7, as Penny von Eschen notes, by an alliance of black Americans, Indians and black South Africans, and the Government of India. It was with such doubts about the 'statist' representation of the rights of minorities in mind that in a speech in New York on Human Rights, DuBois called for a transnational gathering of the 'quasi-colonial' not as a racial or ethnic community but as a 'community of *condition*',[56] to borrow a beautiful phrase from Albert Memmi.

DuBois's enduring doubts about the protection and representation of minorities by the nation-state were to echo menacingly more than half a century later, at the United Nations World Conference on Racism in Durban (28 August–7 September 2001). The chambers were decked out with smoke and mirrors when the cabals and collusions of sovereign nations cynically trumped the cause of persecuted and discriminated minorities. The unseemly rush, on the part of many major States, to run from their historical pasts, like Lady Macbeth fleeing the bed-chamber, was only matched by those great stalwarts of international democracy who stormed out of the Conference at the very mention of the deep divisions and discriminations that survive in their societies. As the *New York Times* reported it, 'India successfully lobbied fellow nations to prevent mention of caste and discrimination. Before walking out of the conference over criticism of Israel, the US objected to any discussion of reparations for the descendants of African slaves. Others refused to consider gays as victims of discrimination.'[57]

To ensure that 'no human group is so small as to deserve to be ignored *as a part*, and as a respected and integral part, of the mass of men …' in DuBois's words, is also to say that in the narrative of global history there is no mode of historical 'time and development'—that is, culture—that is so small or insignificant that it can be dismissed from democratic representation on the grounds of its lack of power, or its refusal to share the 'same desire to be *alike*'.[58] DuBois's combination of praxis and poesis—of *advocacy and aspiration*—places his work at the centre of some of the most urgent global, democratic dilemmas of our time. He gives us courage and hope because he takes the measure of existence from its most melancholic metaphors—the colour-line, the shadow of the Veil, the divided self, and enduring hyphenation. We know these things as we know the frail and fragile survival of life itself. It is from the fine adjustments of everyday alienations and agonies, everyday epiphanies and visions, that DuBois makes us part of the community of those 'gifted' with second *sight* in this 'American world'.

## Notes

1. DuBois, W.E.B. *Dark Princess*. Jackson: Banner Books, 1995, 307.
2. ———. *Darkwater: Voices from Within the Veil*. New York: Harcourt, Brace and Howe, 1920, 246.
3. ———. *Darkwater: Voices from Within the Veil*. Millwood, New York: Kraus-Thomson Organization Limited, 1975, 88–233.
4. Ibid., 225–30.
5. Fanon, Frantz. *The Wretched of the Earth*. Trans. Richard Philcox. Grove Press: New York, 2004, 4–179.
6. Sen, Amartya. *Inequality Reexamined*. Cambridge, MA: Harvard University Press, 1992, 69.
7. Ibid., 68.
8. DuBois, W.E.B. *Dark Princess*, 225.
9. ———. *The Souls of Black Folk*. New York: Penguin, 1989, 69.
10. Rai, Lala Lajpat. *Young India: An Interpretation and a History of the Nationalist Movement from Within*. Delhi: Publications Division, 1965, 222–3.
11. Ibid., 222.
12. Rai, Lala Lajpat. *The United States of America: A Hindu's Impression and a Study*. Calcutta: R. Chatterjee, 1916, 390.
13. Ibid., 389
14. Ibid., 398–9.
15. Mary White Ovington quoted in Arnold Rampersad, 'DuBois' Passage to India: Dark Princess', in *W.E.B. DuBois on Race and Culture: Philosophy, Politics, and Poetics*. Eds Bernard W. Bell, Emily Grosholz, and James B. Stewart. New York and London: Routledge, 1996, 165.
16. Lewis, David Levering. *W.E.B. DuBois: Biography of a Race, 1868–1919*. New York: H. Holt, 2000, 371–2.
17. Saha, Panchanan. *Madam Cama (Bhikaji Rustom K.R.), Mother of Indian Revolution*. Manisha Granthalaya: Bombay, 1975, 17–19.
18. *Dark Princess*, 297–8.
19. Saha. *Cama*, 17.
20. The details of the gathering are all from Panchanan Saha. *Cama*, 19–20.
21. Brown, Emily. *Har Dayal: Hindu Revolutionary and Rationalist*. India: Manohar, 1975, 33.

22. ——. 69.
23. Ibid., 22.
24. Ibid., 21.
25. Ibid., 24.
26. Ibid., 22.
27. *Dark Princess*, 24.
28. Lewis, Wyndham. *Paleface: The Philosophy of the Melting-Pot*. London: Chatto and Windus, 1929, 41.
29. *Dark Princess*, 22.
30. *International* Conciliation 'The First Universal Races Congress' (New York, May 1911).
31. Quoted in Lewis, David Levering. *W.E.B. DuBois: A Reader*. New York: Holt and Co., 1995, 46.
32. *Dark Princess*, 23.
33. Kearney, Reginald. *African American Views of the Japanese: Solidarity or Sedition?* Albany: State University of New York Press, 1998, 58.
34. Fanon, Frantz. *The Wretched of the Earth*, 153.
35. Ibid., 151.
36. Ibid., 179.
37. Ibid., 177.
38. *Dark Princess*, 59.
39. Ibid., 21.
40. *Darkwater*, 233.
41. Chatterjee, Partha. *The Nation and Its Fragments: Colonial and Postcolonial Histories*. Princeton, New Jersey: Princeton University Press, 1993, 6.
42. Dayal, Lala Har. 'India and the World Movement', in *the Modern Review* (Feb. 1913), 188.
43. DuBois. *Souls of Black Folk*. New York: Fawcett Publications, 1961, 5.
44. *Dark Princess*, 284.
45. DuBois, W.E.B. 'Americanization', in *The Oxford W.E.B. DuBois Reader*. Ed. Eric J. Sundquist. New York: Oxford University Press, 1996, 384.
46. ——. 'Human Rights for All Minorities', in *W.E.B. DuBois Speaks: Speeches and Addresses, 1920–1963*. Ed. Philip S. Foner. Pathfinder Press: New York, 1972, 183–4.
47. Levinas, Emmanuel. *Levinas Reader*. Trans. Sean Hand. Oxford: Blackwell Publishers, 1989, 108.
48. *Darkwater*, 153.

49. Ramaga, Philip Vuciri. 'The Group Concept in Minority Protection', in *Human Rights Quarterly,* Vol. 15, 1993, 581.

50. Ibid., 581.

51. 'international' always appears hyphenated in DuBois in order to emphasize his notion of a minoritarian global alliance rather than one based on national or nationalist populations. I have therefore adhered to his usage throughout the chapter.

52. 'Enduring hyphenation' is David Levering Lewis's resonant summation of the 'permanent tension' embedded in the racial dialectic of *The Souls of Black Folk* (Lewis, David Levering. *W.E.B. DuBois: Biography of a Race 1868–1919,* 281.)

53. DuBois, W.E.B. 'Report of Debate Conducted by the Chicago Forum: Shall the Negro Be Encouraged to Seek Cultural Equality', in *Pamphlets and Leaflets.* Ed. Herbert Aptheker. Kraus-Thomson Organization Limited: New York, 1986, 229.

54. Eschen, Penny Von. *Race against Empire: Black Americans and Anticolonialism, 1937–1957.* Ithaca, New York: Cornell University Press, 1997, 75.

55. Ibid.

56. Memmi, Albert. *Dominated Man: Notes Towards a Portrait.* New York: Orion, 1968, 38.

57. Swarns, Rachel L. 'After the Race Conference: Relief and Doubt Over Whether It Will Matter', in the *New York Times,* 10 September 2001.

58. *Darkwater,* 154.

# Borderless

## Empire, Race, and the League of Nations

JOHN SCHECKTER

By now, almost six decades after its collapse in 1946, the League of Nations is generally discredited and laughable, the embodiment of toothless diplomacy. In the face of subsequent history, the organization now seems as irrelevant and quaint as the top hats and high collars on the diplomats signing the Versailles Treaty in 1919: there, they would establish the League of Nations as part of a peace initiative so limited that it would almost guarantee the rearmament of Germany and bring a century of instability to the former Ottoman Empire. Yet the intentions of the League of Nations were not ill-founded, and despite the mistakes and lost opportunities that ultimately doomed it, the League of Nations attracted the efforts of thousands of people from every part of the world, and created a conceptual legacy of globalism that has far outlasted its formal existence. The Australian novelist Frank Moorhouse illustrates the attraction of the League in a sequence of two novels; examining *Grand Days* (1993) and *Dark Palace* (2000), this essay follows the emotional trajectory of the League itself, beginning in optimism and ending in despair.

Moorhouse's working title for *Grand Days* was *Borderless* (personal interview), an apt description of the League's early hope for redefining, and in some cases erasing, the basic concept of nation. It was widely acknowledged that nationalism, defined *circa* 1914, had led to disaster of a new type, the world war; nationalism had corrupted the very idea of modernization. In 1919, however, the only existing model of supranational organization was an imperialism rendered unworkable not on political or moral grounds but through lack of enforceability: the surviving empires of Europe had endured such heavy losses that they were ill-prepared for assertive action, and the upstarts, the US and Japan, were not yet prepared to move themselves forward. Through this default, the peace presented a crisis different from war, one that looked for resolution in projects of global cooperation rather than in schemes for national advantage. Cooperation among a large number of nations had already been demonstrated in limited venues, such as the International Postal Union, the Geneva Conventions for the Treatment of Prisoners of War, and a variety of world fairs and trade expositions at the turn of the century; international gatherings of non-governmental organizations or quasi-official delegations, such as the Universal Races Conference of 1911, which occurred with sufficient frequency to bolster the vision of a League that would serve as the permanent, sustained institution of good faith. Most immediately, the end of the war required a vast re-allotment of territory and resources. The collapse of Russia and Austria-Hungary left immense areas of Europe untenanted by government, along with 4 to 5 million stateless refugees (Hobsbawm 1996: 51); the difficult Ottoman lands had oil, which was gaining strategic value; and the former German colonies in Africa and the Pacific needed management under international mandate. Additionally, new technologies made national borders seem unenforceable: aircraft, submarines, and radio required new thinking about nations and armies while the pandemic of influenza which followed the war made the ineffectiveness of borders a scientific issue.

No single government or existing alliance could handle so much change at once, let alone grasp the tremendous opportunities apparent in supranational cooperation. It was clear, for a most pressing example, that an autonomous Poland would emerge from the wreckage of Russia and Germany, but no one quite knew what 'Poland' meant any more: 'by mid-1919, Poland was only two thirds Polish from the ethnic point of view—its population now included four million Ukrainians, three million Jews and one million Germans' (Mazower 1998: 52–3). The new Poland might follow a number of directions, leading toward liberal democracy, ethnic dictatorship, or civil war. The most urgent charge of the League of Nations was to forestall German or Russian intervention on behalf of its beleaguered respective minority in Poland; secondarily, the League might speak up for those 3 million Jews—though this did not happen to any great effect, and the lack of official interest helped to impel their doom.

Into this scene, enter Edith Campbell Berry. Moorhouse's protagonist arrives at the League headquarters in Geneva in 1926, and the two novels will span her twenty years there. Edith grew up as a modern Australian. In fact, she *is* twentieth-century Australia—her experience measures the nation itself. She is exactly as old as the century, which means that she was born at the time of Australian federation and in the midst of the intense cultural nationalism that fostered the writings of Henry Lawson, Joseph Furphy, and Miles Franklin, but also entrenched the White Australia Policy. Edith grew up in a small up-country town (a core site of Australian self-image), took a degree in science at Sydney (the most cosmopolitan choice of the time), and served an internship with a progressive politician. Edith's arrival in Europe both signals her entry into an expansive phase of personal development and embodies the modern reversal of European colonization—here, the strong child of empire comes to the aid of the ailing parent. She will return to Australia only once, but she will not see herself as an expatriate. Rather, Australia serves as a springboard beyond national identity, into a new form of being; national identity, then, is not birth-determined as it was before 1914, and would become in Germany and elsewhere in the 1930s, but can undergo amendment and transcendence.

The atmosphere of Geneva in the 1920s is palpably exciting, and Moorhouse describes the League of Nations as 'a college where the world went to learn new forms of cooperation and diplomacy' (personal interview). Edith daily moves among thousands of people, many of them her age, in the global community of the League administration and the adjacent national missions, interest groups, and news media. Politically and personally, they discard precedent and invent new relationships on the spot, in a hothouse community that often resembles interwar Paris or Berlin. Edith does not want to think as an Australian, and her role in Geneva is something entirely new: she is an 'international civil servant', whose duty is to the League of Nations and not to any national identity or policy. This is a state of mind different from the cultural cringe of colonial inferiority:

It wasn't that Australia was not a 'real' place, full of real people doing real things … It was that she needed now in her life to put herself in a position which made her productively *nervous*. Even if it was a bit uncomfortable at times. She had to be where she didn't know quite what was happening next, to be living precipitously (*Grand Days* 223).

Edith welcomes this borderless identity, for among other things, the League gives her official authority at a time when no national diplomatic corps would employ women above the clerical level. As novels of public activity, *Grand Days* and *Dark Palace* focus upon Edith's movement toward the centre of power and her relationship with the high secretariat. As a protocol officer, she is more concerned with managing negotiations inside the League than with the issues that national delegations must resolve. Her initial triumphs involve seating arrangements and physical facilities, but she rises as an organizer and has an important role in the World Disarmament Conference of 1932. This kind of activity, fostering the concept of global dialogue within a neutral higher body, is the best development of the League of Nations and its best legacy; by placing Edith within the sometimes mundane area of protocol, Moorhouse in fact sets her in the most innovative sphere of activity. Eventually, Edith outgrows the limits of job description, becoming a confidential aide within the highest echelon of the League executive. Diplomats are not often revolutionaries, and Moorhouse is careful not to characterize Edith as having attitudes at the forefront of social advancement. For all her pleasure in personal risk, Edith's political beliefs are fairly conservative. Although she organizes the Disarmament Conference, she herself favours armed *detente* and supports, at times, a proposal to create a military branch of the League. She owns a pistol. Earlier, her conservatism underscores her moment of greatest courage, when she and a few other women defend the League headquarters against rioters following the execution of Sacco and Vanzetti in 1927. For Americans, the murder conviction of these two Italian-born anarchists resulted from the most polarizing political trial of the twentieth century; only the O. J. Simpson trial of 1995 came close to recalling Edmund Wilson's assertion that the Sacco and Vanzetti case 'raised almost every fundamental question of our political and social system' (D'Attilio 2004). While the execution sparked demonstrations throughout Europe as well as the US, Edith generally feels that anarchists and communists are 'out of step with history' (*Grand Days* 343), and she 'had refused to sign a petition protesting their conviction, which she still believed to be a correct stand'. Her protection of the League building is genuine—she is wounded by smashing glass and her life is clearly in danger—but there is more to it.

Anarchists and communists, along with international labour movements, present supranational ideologies of their own, but these call for radical social reorganization. In contrast, the League of Nations depends upon the stability of its members, which are governments and not societies. The priority of nation over individual remains unchallenged. Edith may despair of the narrowness of nationalism, finding that 'national interest is a lazy formulation' (*Dark Palace* 327). Nonetheless, the League has no mandate to interfere in a nation's self-defined interests or in its internal matters, and has no means to influence the structure of member governments. Nor, as Mark Mazower (1998: x–xi) notes, is it at all certain between the wars that enlightened liberal democracy is the preferred arrangement; Moorhouse is accurate in portraying the wide approval of Mussolini and Hitler and the perceived utopian possibilities of totalitarian rule. That popular appeal was extensive: for example, between 1928 and 1937 the American car company Studebaker produced, along with its President and Commander models, an automobile called the Dictator.

While the League of Nations reflects continual tension between idealism and *realpolitik*, Edith's personal thinking is conditioned by the same borderless contest among rationalized behaviour, challenge to convention, and allowance for personal preference. For example, she prepares for marriage by having herself fitted for a diaphragm; in the context of the times, this is a bold and modern move. In fact, Edith likes her body: she likes good underwear, autoeroticism, and the effect of her beauty upon others. This self-awareness, largely unsupported by her training, flourishes at the same time as *Ulysses* and *Lady Chatterley* are banned and American law classifies birth control information as 'obscene material'. For Moorhouse to construct such a characterization without anachronistic liberation, but also with some erotic interest, is a remarkable feat—especially since he also shows the deep conflicts in Edith's attitudes. While cherishing her sensual and sexual awareness, Edith the international civil servant is terrifically embarrassed by public discussions of birth control; she cannot stand Margaret Sanger and is relieved when the League chooses to overlook the World Population Conference of 1931. Characteristically, Edith distances herself from the subject by classifying the argument as a political lesson in constituent interests within the League secretariat.

Edith tries to push her defensive distancing even farther. The consideration of birth control leads Edith to think about eugenics, a matter of debate in terms of both public health and national definition. Edith's view of eugenics in the early 1930s is generally favourable, reflecting her sharp sense of class and her belief that high culture emanates from north-western Europe; Australia for her is a British dominion in all senses—again, a highly credible attitude at the time. But the more she tries to avoid the collision, the more her personal and professional lives coincide, and Edith realizes that birth control and eugenics are in fact issues the League should take up (this recognition will also be discussed later, as it embeds a response to the Stolen Generations in Australia). Of course, there is a vast space between Edith's taste in French lingerie and Moorhouse's implication of Aboriginal issues, but surely the mind—and a pair of five-hundred-page novels—can be asked to embrace such a range.

Allowing a conflation of personal and professional identities is not easy for Edith: 'She saw that her primordial, or whatever, feelings were not impressed by her talk of scientific progress' (*Grand Days* 525). Again, such vocabulary—'primordial or whatever'—reflects authentically available discourse at a time when Freud and Jung dictate the discussion. Edith's self-analysis is pressing and complex, for her personal life is unconventional in many ways. She is married for a few years to an English reporter, a garden-variety cynical journalist, whose real love is reporting war—and the 1930s, of course, provide him with plenty of work. Before and after this attempt at conventional unhappiness, Edith lives with a truly odd character, Ambrose Westwood. By day, Major Westwood, formerly of the Medical Corps and the Foreign Office, wears indubitable suits and his regimental necktie. At night, he wears women's clothes. Thus, for Edith, who accepts the 'primordial' roles of womanliness, the perceived borders of gender and sexuality are transgressed even more actively than the so-called similar instincts of nationality. Ambrose introduces Edith to the Molly Club, an underground gathering of transvestite men, and she gains acceptance as a sort of honorary member. The meanings of that identity are almost hopelessly entangled. Edith is the 'real' woman among men who dress as women, forcing her to redefine their masculinity and her femininity. In a place where cross-dressing is the rule, Edith is the pretender, especially since there are few other types of female transgression to be seen. When the Molly Club is invaded by local fascists, Edith rises to protect her companions. And again, the multiplicity of roles is complicated by conservative self-contradictions: even in matching outfits, Edith and Ambrose are conventionally monogamous lovers in a long and stable relationship.

The League's hands-off policies toward the treatment of individuals within nations and Edith's sharp circumscription of her personal life combine as Moorhouse demonstrates the limitations of borderless cooperation. We know that the thugs who molest the Molly Club are precursors of horror, even as Edith is somewhat attracted to the fascists' claims of moral clarity. When the first hints of Nazi exterminations arrive in Geneva, the public Edith lacks the means to mention them within League protocol; the bearer of this news, a deserter from Heinrich Himmler's personal staff, is taken to the Molly Club and never comes to the attention of the League. Their private interests lead Edith and Ambrose to focus on the threats to homosexuals, and more or less dismiss the fate of the Jews and other targeted groups. Suppressing information, lacking direction, stymied by internal dissention, the League cannot respond to what will become the Holocaust—and here begins the foreshadowed descent into despair.

Edith has shown such narrowness before, the same close pattern of interests which she decries elsewhere as the worst fault of nationalism: thus her odd response to news that the Czech writer Stephen Lux has shot himself to death on the floor of the League Assembly. Lux's suicide note declares that he cannot 'find any other way to reach the hearts of men ... to pierce the inhuman indifference of the world' (*Dark Palace* 366). Edith asks Ambrose 'indifference to what?', and he answers, 'The treatment of the Jewish people. He said the world had to face that Hitler was preparing for war.'

'He was Jewish?'

'Oh yes.'

'How is it that I am the only one who never knows when someone is Jewish?'

'It's not a failing, dear' (*Dark Palace* 366).

The displacement, however, certainly *is* a failing: the too-quick, defensive reduction of Lux's horrifying message to a matter of social protocol, as if she were a headwaiter facing a difficult seating arrangement. In fact, whether Moorhouse meant this or not, *Grand Days* and *Dark Palace* are remarkable in reproducing the failures of the League of Nations as limitations of their fictional scope. For example, Moorhouse barely touches upon the refusal of the United States to enter the League that its own president so championed— a rejection which many observers claim 'deprived it of any real meaning' (Hobsbawm 1996: 34). Perhaps this gap is justified in the fiction because Edith is primarily concerned with daily workings of the organization and not its larger policies, but the effect emphasizes the inability of the League to embrace a truly global vision, and thus the slide into despair becomes steeper.

The trajectory of Edith's fictional career confirms a common accusation that the League was intended to reinforce the power of Great Britain and France. Despite the global membership of the League, the Geneva of Moorhouse's fiction is almost exclusively white: both of Edith's long-term partners are Englishmen who had been officers in the war, her friends are French and Canadian, all of her diplomatic mentors are European, and the two women who make sexual propositions to her are American and French. Moorhouse includes one Indian character—a malaria specialist— and a pair of cardboard Azerbaijanis, but draws no continuing character from outside Europe, North America, and Australia. On a visit to Paris, Edith has a drunken sexual encounter with a jazz musician, the only black character in a thousand pages; she recalls the adventure as evidence of borderless sexuality, but it is tucked away in memory and never developed, let alone repeated.

The League of Nations never managed to champion equality in any national, cultural, or ethnic sense. Non-European nations eagerly embraced the League Charter, with its promise of recognition, but the fictional Edith simply does not see the multitudes of South Americans, Asians, and Africans who work at the Palais des Nations. At the Charter Conference of 1919, Japan proposed an amendment to guarantee racial equality in the League covenant; their most vocal opponent was the Australian Prime Minister, Billy Hughes (MacMillan 2002: 319). The Great Powers were relieved: Lloyd George was content to let the White Australia policy speak for the Empire, and Woodrow Wilson needed the support of segregationists in the US Congress, which he never received anyway. The issue gained momentum as the Japanese proposal came to represent the aspirations of the non-white world as a whole and Hughes' rhetoric became increasingly crude and personally insulting. As Margaret MacMillan describes it, 'The Japanese delegates insisted on a vote. When a majority voted for the amendment, Wilson … announced that because there were strong objections to the amendment it could not carry' (320). For their part, of course, the Japanese would remember the insult, abandoning the League in 1933 and hardening their vision of national dignity into militarist aggression (321). Later, too, it would be clear that Billy Hughes' invective contributed to the brutal treatment of Australian prisoners in World War II.

The lack of diversity in Edith's professional life, and its inscription by Moorhouse as a limitation of fictional scope, reflect the multiple tiers of status within the League. Some nations simply matter more than others. Once this stratification is accepted procedurally, supranational idealism collapses into imperialism by another name, while smaller nations and minority enclaves return to muteness. In *Grand Days*, we first see this disturbing reversion in response to the Japanese invasion of Manchuria in 1931. At that point, Edith is still optimistic, but 'Deep in her heart, she also knew that Manchuria was, for Europe and the Americans, a problem too far.… All too far away from the busy life of the world's capitals. Because it was militarily impossible, she did not really consider Manchuria a fair test of the League' (*Dark Palace* 56). South America is too far, as well, and Moorhouse does not even mention the tepid response of the League to the Chaco War, a vicious and incompetent border war between Bolivia and Paraguay that killed 100,000 people between 1932 and 1935. The contest that really matters within the stratified scheme of national worth is the Italian invasion of Ethiopia in 1935. Italy is not too far—it is too close. As a common ancestor of European culture, as a wartime ally of Britain and France, and as a modern industrial power, Italy appeals to implicit and nearly undisputed hierarchies of evaluation; claims of equality among League members vanish as Italian invasion is recast as a defence of civilization and Ethiopian resistance is labelled barbaric insurgency. The weakness of the League's response is noted carefully by Germany, which no longer bothers to conceal its rearmament; after that, Poland and Czechoslovakia do not stand a chance.

Early in her career, Edith learns the diplomatic theory of *rebus sic stantibus*, which in part maintains that treaties and international relations depend not upon agreed terms but upon the will of the parties to continue their relations; otherwise, treaties would collapse the moment any signatory sensed an advantage. In the long run, *rebus sic stantibus* is a way of accommodating change through negotiation and mutual recognition. The League of Nations failed in this process, because it was unable to substantiate changes in the nationalism it was intended to supercede. In acquiescing from the beginning to a hierarchy of nations, and in legitimating the imperialism of Great Britain and France, the League left itself unable to oppose the expansionism of Italy, Japan, and Germany (Hobsbawm 1996: 37). Thus, its legacy is mixed: necessary changes in the idea of nation would come only with the decolonizing movements that followed the Second World War. This would be too late to save the League of Nations, but the League did establish a basis for supranational discussion by its successors, the United Nations and the World Courts. Personally, as this legacy is measured in Moorhouse's fiction, the result is mixed as well. As the League collapses, Ambrose consoles Edith, telling her she has '*lived fully*' (*Dark Palace* 657) in dedication and love. He is right in many ways. His consolation, however, invokes the shadow of the Stolen Generations of Aboriginal Australia, previously implied in the discussion of eugenics.

Issues of Aboriginal recognition and historical responsibility occupied a powerful forefront in Australian public discussion at the time Moorhouse wrote *Grand Days* and *Dark Palace*. While they are not set in Australia, and while Moorhouse has lived abroad for extended periods, the novels acknowledge that discussion, particularly with regard to *rebus sic stantibus* as a mechanism to ensure that all parties remain at the table, despite the recognition that all interpretations of historical precedent and contemporary context are liable to critical limitations of the same kind. Thus, constructing a fictional *zeitgeist* is much like diplomacy itself: a framework is produced in which some kinds of discussion are encouraged and others are silenced. It is true, and Frank Moorhouse does us the great service of acknowledging, that many attitudes that we now deplore were actually produced by enlightened liberalism. However, while Edith and many others saw Europe as the centre of all civilization, and measured the eugenic progress of non-Europeans by their assimilation of those values, it is nonetheless the case that dissenting voices were raised at the time. The discussion was not quite as limited as Moorhouse makes it. The consolation that Ambrose offers to Edith, that they tried with all their might, would be more convincing if the novels had shown their efforts against a wider background of the many possibilities for discussion that were actually available in Geneva at the time. Edith has a brilliant career—she is a magnificent character—but *Grand Days* and *Dark Palace* would be stronger if we could see more directly what Edith does not see, the borderless depth and variety that were truly the promise of the League of Nations.

## WORKS CITED

D'Attilio, Robert. 'The Sacco-Vanzetti Case'. http://www.writing.upenn.edu/~afilreis/ 88/sacvan.html. 25 July 2004.

Hobsbawm, Eric. *The Age of Extremes: A History of the World, 1914–1991.* New York: Vintage, 1996.

MacMillan, Margaret. *Paris 1919: Six Months that Changed the World.* New York: Random House, 2002.

Mazower, Mark. *Dark Continent: Europe's Twentieth Century.* London: Penguin, 1998.

Moorhouse, Frank. *Dark Palace.* Sydney: Random House, 2000.

———*Grand Days.* Sydney: Macmillan, 1993.

———Personal interview. 1 November 2002.

# 'One Step on Australian Soil and You're History'
## *Our Man K.* and the White Australia Policy

It may not be a particularly wise idea, but let me begin by quoting some splendidly bad—but in this case intentionally bad—verse by the Australian poet, C.J. Dennis:

> If you'd said to me a month ago, 'Who is this Kisch?'
> I should have answered, 'Please don't plague me so—
> Maybe you wish
> With some catch question to confound me quite
> Well, you poor fish
> Indulge your childish mind, come on I'll bite
> Who is this Kisch?
> [...]
> I don't know Kisch
>
> Or aught concerning him, so why get hot
> And feverish?
> He's a peace apostle or he's not

Just as you wish.
But now I'm all upset about the Kisch case
He has swum into my orbit like a star,
And the clamor and the cackle of the Kisch case
Has irked me till I dunno where I are.[1]

Had I penned that piece of doggerel verse myself—which God forbid!—I should have had to begin not with 'If you'd said to me a month ago' but with 'If you'd said to me thirty years ago ...', for that was when the discovery that some acquaintances of mine in East Berlin had spent part of their exile from Hitler's Germany in Mexico in the company of Egon Erwin Kisch first aroused my interest in the writer.

The Australian author Nicholas Hasluck apparently first came across the name Kisch when he noticed it on a plaque on a wall in Prague some ten years ago. The name rang a bell, excited his curiosity and eventually led to his writing a novel about Kisch, which, if nothing else, shows that Hasluck, legal mind that he is, was just as 'irked' by the Kisch case as had been Dennis so many years earlier.

The novel Hasluck wrote is entitled *Our Man K.*—and it is one of the relatively few works in postcolonial English literature which derive their inspiration from the works of German-language authors and where the intertexts are consequently German. For someone like me who has worked in the fields of both English and German literature, it thus constitutes a fascinating and almost irresistible challenge.

✧

There are no doubt many ways of getting into Australia. One of the more unusual—and certainly least advisable—was that chosen by Egon Erwin Kisch on 13 November 1934. As the liner which had brought him out from Marseille, the P & O vessel *Strathaird*, was moving away from the quay at Port Melbourne, Kisch jumped ship—literally. He leapt down some 18 feet to the dockside, breaking his leg in the process. This athletic feat was to provide the inventive journalist with the inspiration not only for an eye-catchingly appropriate title for the book he would later write about his Australian adventures—or, rather, misadventures—in English called *Australian Landfall* and in German *Landung in Australien*[2] but also for the memorable one-liner with which, having released himself from Sydney Hospital, he opened the first political address he gave in the country: 'My English is broken, my leg is broken, but my heart is not broken because I am able to fulfil my mission and deliver my message of peace to the people of Australia,'[3] Thereafter, wittily sidestepping allegations that he may well call himself a writer but no one in Australia had actually ever heard of him or read any of his books, Kisch would sign autographs for the many sympathizers who sought them: 'Egon Erwin Kisch, famous jumper'.

So who was Kisch? Although in 1934 certainly unknown to most Australians,[4] Kisch enjoyed a considerable reputation in Europe. Born in Prague, German-speaking and Jewish, his Czech citizenship had enabled his country's ambassador to extricate him from Spandau prison in Berlin, where he had been incarcerated after the burning of the Reichstag in 1933. He had served in the First World War, which had cost the life of his brother, and this traumatic experience recorded in his book *Schreib das auf, Kisch!* determined his own radical pacifism for ever afterwards. Before the Second World War he travelled the world visiting the US, the Soviet Union, and China, writing all the time. He fought in the Spanish Civil War and when Hitler came to power in Germany went into exile first in France and then in Mexico. He regarded exile not so much as a regrettable state of affairs to be endured for as long as necessary, but more as an opportunity for intensified activism—and the target of his truly unrelenting activity was, of course, Nazi Germany, which had burnt his books, deprived him of his readers, and was threatening world peace. In the Paris of the mid-1930s he became what his biographer has aptly described as 'a coordinator of intellectual resistance, an initiator of political alliances, an organizer of literary life, a militant publicist and speaker, and a charming diplomat'.[5] He was also, it would seem, quite indefatigable.

Kisch was a pioneer of what today we would call investigative journalism—a figure whose personal experience and political and social involvement served to authenticate his writing rather in the manner of an Orwell or a Günther Wallraff. In Germany he is credited with inventing a form of literary journalism which became known as 'reportage'. He delighted in casting himself as 'der rasende Reporter' ('the rampaging reporter') and certainly the titles of a number of his books did seem to offer more than a hint of the possibly sensational nature of their contents, *Marktplatz der Sensationen* (1942)[6] of course, but also *Hetzjagd durch die Zeit* (1926),[7] *Schreib das auf, Kisch!* (1930),[8] *China geheim* (1933),[9] *Eintritt verboten* (1934),[10] *Abenteuer in fünf Kontinenten* (1948),[11] and so on. But the titles were deceptive; Kisch was anything but rampaging and his books tackled issues far too serious to be regarded as sensational. Indeed, German critics, among them Ernst Bloch and Hans-Albert Walter, have paid tribute to the meticulous care which he lavished on the composition of each of his texts.

Nevertheless, his literary reputation has been uneven, the appreciation accorded his work often being determined—especially before the reunification of Germany—by the reader's sympathy or otherwise with his radical political views. For Kisch was, it appears, in spite of his repeated denials not to mention his propensity for deftly sidestepping the question, a member of the Communist Party, first in Austria, then in Germany, and later in Czechoslovakia. There is, however, apparently, no record of any activity of his on behalf of the German Communist Party during his exile.[12] His biographer terms him a 'communist curiosity'—an apposite enough description in the light of the many failed attempts to pin him down ideologically. For Kisch never bothered to define what he considered Communism to be; he was undisciplined; he had no schooling in Marxism and he never paid any attention to the cultural politics of the party.[13] Those who sought to attach the label 'Communist' to him—and this would include some in Australia—often found it difficult to square the politics and the man. No matter what they thought of his politics, few could resist the charm—and what Hasluck repeatedly terms 'the ebullience'[14]—of the man. Arthur Koestler spoke for many when he described Kisch as 'one of those irrepressible personalities to whom everything is forgiven'.[15] Even the narrator of Hasluck's novel would—as one Australian reviewer wryly remarked—'like to dislike Kisch, but fails'.[16]

Those unfamiliar with the story of Kisch's trip to Australia will be wondering why he should choose to endanger life and limb by electing to enter the country in such an unorthodox fashion.

His journey had been occasioned by an anti-war conference being held in Melbourne and timed to coincide with the Centennial celebrations of the State of Victoria. Kisch was to attend as a delegate of the European peace movement, specifically the World Committee against War and Fascism to which such luminaries as Henri Barbusse, Romain Rolland, and Bernard Shaw belonged. Having obtained a visa from the British consulate in Paris, Kisch arrived in Fremantle only to find himself refused entry. In Hasluck's novel this is formulated in the curt words of a customs official, which I have quoted in my title: 'One step on Australian soil, and you're history' (198). And the same scene would be re-enacted at each further port-of-call as the *Strathaird* proceeded around the Australian coast. Friends and well-wishers promptly sought legal redress, setting in chain a seemingly interminable series of proceedings designed to secure entry for Kisch against what turned out to be a most determined effort on the part of the Australian authorities to keep him out. A fruitless effort, it should be said, because the result was the opposite of what was intended: the legal proceedings served only to gain Kisch entry, to prolong his stay longer than he had planned and, thus, to accord him more political exposure than he could ever otherwise have hoped for. The legal process was rich in memorable scenes, lacking neither drama nor farce: Kisch's supporters racing to Sydney by sports car to present the legal documents for an appeal while the writer himself proceeded around the coast at a more leisurely pace, confined to the ship's hospital with his leg in plaster; the spectacle of Kisch still in his hospital pyjamas being transported into court on a stretcher and being laid out on the floor because the poor man could no longer stand up; the judge granting bail on the entirely reasonable grounds that a man with a broken leg was hardly likely to run away; Kisch hobbling around Australia on crutches to give fiery political speeches at peace rallies; but above all, the hilarious saga of the dictation test to which the authorities—in considerable desperation—resorted.

In terms of the Immigration Restriction Act of 1901, which was the main legal instrument used to enforce the so-called 'White Australia policy' and had been originally and primarily introduced to prevent the immigration of cheap Asian labour, a dictation test consisting of fifty words 'in any European language' could be imposed on a potentially undesirable immigrant. Failure to pass the test meant deportation after a six-month jail sentence, and such exclusion could, of course, be virtually guaranteed if a language was chosen for the test which the would-be immigrant did not speak.[17] This tactic had been successfully applied when the Irish had been tested in Swedish and the Germans in Greek.[18] But what was to be done about a well-educated and well-travelled Central European like Kisch who reputedly spoke eleven languages and who—as an anonymous wit put it in the *Bulletin*—

French like a native of Paris [could] speak
And [could] give you the dative
of 'crayfish' in Greek.[19]

Kisch's co-invitee to the conference, Gerald Griffin, a New Zealander born in Ireland, had just been failed and deported for his lack of knowledge of Dutch. Kisch, himself, was failed because he did not know Scottish Gaelic—but nor, as one commentator quipped, did Jesus Christ, who would doubtless have been excluded from Australia on the same grounds![20]

Kisch's failing the dictation test entailed several further episodes in the legal saga, whose deliberations would later provide Hasluck with some of his most amusing pages.[21] For now the legal plea was entered that Scottish Gaelic, being spoken by a mere fraction of the Scottish population and by a fairly remote one at that, could hardly be regarded as a European 'language' at all, at least not in terms of the Australian Immigration Act. This view was rejected in the first instance—which meant that Kisch was found guilty and sentenced to six months hard labour prior to deportation—but it was then accepted on appeal by the High Court, which promptly released him. The height of absurdity was reached when the counsel for Kisch argued that the police constable who administered the test was himself not proficient in the language, while the 'expert' witness called upon later proved incapable of translating a passage from a Gaelic text, even though on closer inspection it turned out to be the Lord's Prayer.[22]

The view of the Australian High Court judge that Gaelic 'is not the recognized speech of a community organized politically, socially, or on any other basis [and that] it might [only] excite the interest of scholars and perhaps the enthusiasm of the descendants of the Gauls'[23] got Kisch off the hook, but it caused a furore as irate Scotsmen flooded the press with protests abounding in satire and parody—and some of it in verse. By publishing some of the more controversial contributions to the debate while the case was still pending the *Sydney Morning Herald* placed itself in contempt of court and soon found itself in the uncomfortable position of having to admit that some of the articles it had published were 'inaccurate, intemperate, and unfortunately offensive'—a climb-down by a conservative newspaper that must have pleased Kisch and many on the Left in Australia.

The 'Kisch case' became the subject of acrimonious debate in the Australian parliament too, since the government in the person of the then Attorney-General Robert Menzies was called upon to justify its action in refusing the writer permission to land in the first place. Here the problem was that the government claimed that in pursuance of the Immigration Act it was empowered to exclude

Kisch on the grounds of information received from the government of the United Kingdom. And that such information with regard to subversive activities carried on by Kisch had in fact been received—which it then refused to specify. The awkwardness of this position for the government and the reason why it seemed hardly credible to the opposition was that it was, of course, the British through their embassy in Paris who had granted Kisch a visa to enter Australia in the first place. The fact that the nature of the subversive activity the British alleged Kisch was involved in has never been made known contributes to the mystery still surrounding the episode.

Kisch himself gave an account of his visit to Australia in a memoir entitled, in the English and Australian editions, *Australian Landfall*.[24] There also exists a sympathetic report under the title *On the Pacific Front: The Adventures of Egon Kisch in Australia* published under the pseudonym Julian Smith,[25] which came out in Australia before Kisch's own book appeared in Europe. In writing his book[26] Hasluck drew freely on Kisch's text, following his chronology and often quoting him verbatim, especially in his account of the successive court cases. Unlike Hasluck, however, Kisch does not waste words; he has a highly focused, fast-moving style; he disposes of details in a few words which Hasluck will devote whole pages to or elaborate into chapters. To heighten the satirical effect and to emphasize the dramaturgy of the self he is constructing, Kisch writes of himself in the third person, as 'our man'. That usage Hasluck incorporates into the title of his novel, of course, but he adds to it the initial 'K', intending thereby to generate thematic and symbolic associations with Kafka's novel *Der Prozeß* (*The Trial*) and his short story *In der Strafkolonie* (*In the Penal Colony*) and to evoke such Kafkaesque themes as the relationship between guilt and innocence and the effects of suspicion on behaviour. These associations are expressed not only through the reiteration—in slightly emended form—of the famous opening line of that novel—'Someone must have been telling lies about K, for one fine morning, without having done anything, he was arrested'—but also through the pervasive representation of the Australian legal system as an impenetrable bureaucratic labyrinth. Typically we read:

Even Kafka in his darkest dreams couldn't have imagined such a frightening scenario, an arrest fraught with xenophobia, red tape, and all the other vagaries afflicting a former penal colony at the bottom of the world—a place bedevilled by its convict past, rattled by recent crises, haunted by glimpses of the future' (251).

The sequence of events in the Kisch case, it is several times pointed out, was a nightmare more worthy of Kafka (257), the practice of the law in Australia was one that would have excited his interest (205). Not for nothing is Kisch's actual lawyer, Piddington, compared to the advocate in *The Trial*. Not for nothing do references to the 'former penal colony' take on overtones of Kafka's *Strafkolonie*.

While Kafka and Kisch may provide the major intertexts of Hasluck's novel, there are others—and even that 'K' in the title is rendered potentially more ambivalent through the author's propensity for giving other characters names beginning with the same initial: Kaub, the narrator; Kivaldy, the Hungarian count; Karl, the Habsburg Emperor (the one recently beatified by the late Pope John Paul II); and so on. As these names already indicate, Hasluck is proposing to do more than simply give us a fictionalized version of the Kisch story I have just outlined. Viewing the novel, as he tells us, as 'a means of re-imagining and thus more fully understanding the vagaries of the past',[27] as '[a]n opportunity to know the apparently larger-than-life figures of history completely, through the fiction writer's omniscient familiarity with the characters' inner lives',[28] Hasluck finds in the very lack of clarity about the Kisch case 'a space to be occupied by the novelist'.[29]

Since Hasluck evidently also regards the story as what he terms 'a golden opportunity to comment upon various contemporary issues' among which he lists—as the lawyer and judge he has been—'protracted litigation, denunciations of the High Court, Centenary celebrations [and] the move towards an Australian republic',[30] it is clear that he must situate Kisch on a wider historical canvas than that provided solely by his presence in Australia. He therefore weaves a second strand into the plot of the novel. Beginning in 1919, fifteen years before Kisch's visit, he focuses on the period of the peace negotiations after the First World War, on the subsequent demise of the Habsburg Empire and on the vain attempts of the last royal couple of that dynasty to restore the monarchy and thus prevent the establishment of a republic in Austro-Hungary—to all of which Kisch and his friends are witnesses. Although 'this glimpse of history in the making'[31] is one which, as Hasluck would have us believe, 'may have a resonance for Australians at the end of the twentieth century as we edge towards a new republican regime', it is not one that is particularly easy to integrate with the story of Kisch's visit to Australia.

In this novel, Hasluck tells us, 'getting the mix [of fact and fiction] right gave him more trouble than [with] any of his previous books.'[32] His solution to what thus constituted a structural as well as a thematic problem was to introduce the figure of a narrator in the person of one Robert Kaub, a 'footloose' young Australian poet, whose somewhat improbable biography is constructed—with some artifice, one may feel—to encompass the disparate elements in this, by now, much more complex story. Kaub's peripatetic career has thus seen him distinguish himself as a poet by composing a 'Federation Ode' recited at the ceremony to mark the inauguration of the Commonwealth of Australia, survive the trenches of the First World War, attend the Versailles Peace Conference, accompany the last Habsburg Emperor on both his forays into Hungary to regain the throne, execute a daring leap from a moving train in much the same manner as Kisch will later do from aboard ship, become the familiar figure of many of the writers acquainted with Kafka and Kisch in Prague and Berlin, and finally join Kisch on the voyage to Australia.

It is through the eyes of this fictional narrator that we follow events and it is through the development in his attitude to Kisch that Hasluck seeks to focalize the reader's own. Kaub proceeds from moral disapproval of Kisch's behaviour through scepticism about his political convictions to a certain grudging respect for his commitment. But his professed 'desire to find out what Kisch represented' is never satisfied; the questions he poses—Was Kisch something more than a journalist? Was he guilty of subversive activity? Was he a Communist? Was he working for the Comintern?—are never answered. The character of Kisch finally remains as elusive as did Gatsby for Nick Carraway. And some critics—in the *Bulletin*, for instance—thought it did for Hasluck too.

By the very nature of its theme, *Our Man K.* raises more questions than it can answer. And since, for this short presentation I have had to disregard so many questions I should have answered, let me wind up with the narrator's own conclusion as Kisch embarks for Europe:

After months of turmoil Egon Erwin Kisch was going back to where he had come from but without anyone being much the wiser as to why he had made the journey, or why those with an interest in the matter, the 'powers that be' in Canberra, decided to exclude him. Perhaps the crucial facts would never be known. Nonetheless, there could be little doubt that the place he had come to would never be quite the same.[33]

## Notes

1. Dennis, C.J. 'A Plea for Peace' originally published in the *Herald* (Melbourne); quoted from Smith, Julian. *On the Pacific Front: The Adventures of Egon Kisch in Australia.* Sydney: Australian Book Services, 1936, 208–9.
2. Kisch, Egon Erwin. *Landung in Australien.* Amsterdam: Allert de Lange, 1937; *Australian Landfall.* Trans. John Fisher and Irene and Kevin Fitzgerald. London: Martin Secker and Warburg, 1937; and Sydney: Macmillan, 1969. The Australian edition has a foreword by A.T. Yarwood.
3. *On the Pacific Front*, 51 and *Australian Landfall*, 87.
4. Hasluck reports this in his article 'Waiting for Ulrich: The Kisch and Clinton Cases', in *Quadrant*, April 1999, 28–33; here 29. He uses the idea in *Our Man K.*, 296.
5. Patka, Marcus G. *Egon Erwin Kisch. Stationen im Leben eines streitbaren Autors.* Wien: Böhlau Verlag, 1997, 165.

6.   Kisch. *Marktplatz der Sensationen.* Mexico D.F.: El libro libre, 1942; (English version, *Sensation Fair.* New York: Modern Age, 1941).

7.   ———. *Hetzjagd durch die Zeit.* Berlin: Erich Reiss Verlag, 1926.

8.   ———. *Schreib das auf, Kisch!* Berlin: Erich Reiss Verlag, 1930.

9.   ———. *China geheim* Berlin: Erich Reiss Verlag, 1933 (English version, *Secret China.* London: John Lane, 1935).

10.   ———. *Eintritt verboten.* Paris: Editions du Carrefour, 1934.

11.   ———. *Abenteuer in fünf Kontinenten.* Wien: Globus, 1948.

12.   *Egon Erwin Kisch,* 169.

13.   Ibid., 14, 16.

14.   For example, Hasluck. 'The Kisch Case Revisited', in *Overland* 159 (2000): 120.

15.   For example, Patka. *Egon Erwin Kisch,* 170.

16.   Max Watts, 'Kisch, Kosmos, Konspiracy', in *Overland* 157 (1999): 99.

17.   Yarwood, Alexander T. 'The Dictation Test—Historical Survey', the *Australian Quarterly,* June 1958, 24. Cf. particularly the lines: 'By the time the Bill passed to the Senate, the following points had emerged: [...] 2. The Customs Officer would select a language with which the intending undesired immigrant was unfamiliar. If any further assurance were needed on the second point, it was given when the Senate rejected (by 22:3) a motion that the test should be in a language known to the immigrant.'

18.   Ibid., 27–18.

19.   'The No-Balling of the Gaelic', by T. the R, from the *Bulletin;* quoted (see 61, 62) from Julian Smith, *On the Pacific Front,* 210.

20.   The aged Rev. Arthur Rivett just before his death. Kisch, *Australian Landfall,* 86.

21.   As it did for the Australian dramatist Mona Brand in her play 'Here Comes Kisch' (Montmorency, VIC: Yackandandah Playscripts, 1983), which uses some of *Australian Landfall* verbatim and gives the ship's captain the wonderful line: 'A man who can speak eleven languages, even without Gaelic, is a nuisance on any ship ... or, I should think, in any gaol...' (39).

22.   *On the Pacific Front,* 62.

23.   *Egon Erwin Kisch,* 248.

24.   *Australian Landfall.*

25.   *On the Pacific Front.*

26.   Hasluck, Nicholas. *Our Man K.* Ringwood, Vic: Penguin, 1999. Page references in the text are to this edition.

27. ———. 'Writing Ourselves: History and Creative Imagination', 2–3, www.nla.gov.au/events/history/papers/Nicholas_Hasluck.html.
28. ———. 'Writing Ourselves', 2.
29. ———. 'The Kisch Case Revisited', in *Overland*. 159 (2000), 121.
30. ———. 'Writing Ourselves', 3.
31. Ibid.
32. Rolfe, Patricia. 'A Man of Substance', in *Bulletin*, 15 June 1999, 117.
33. *Our Man K.*, 345.

# *Disgrace*-ful Metafiction
## Intertextuality in the Postcolony

### GERALD GAYLARD

*OED*—Disgrace—n—loss of favour or respect, downfall from position of honour, ignominy, shame, (is in disgrace); thing or person involving dishonour, cause of reproach.
Disgrace—v—Dismiss from favour, degrade from position of honour; bring shame or discredit on, be a disgrace to.

$M$y aim in this essay is to examine the relationship between nation and imagination via an analysis of the meaning of intertextuality in postcolonialism, or what the valency of postmodernism in postcolonial fiction is today. Perhaps the first thing to establish is the notion of intertextuality. Prior to Kristeva's theoretical intervention which established intertextuality as the notion of the radical interconnectedness of all texts, intertextuality tended to be understood via the ideas of imitation and allusion. Imitation implied the conscious use of prior texts or textuality, a learning from prior masters that was advocated by classical thinkers such as Aristotle, Cicero, and Horace and prevailed into the eighteenth century,[1] whilst allusion was a form of implicit reference. Kristeva's

'Revolution in Poetic Language' took these ideas further by suggesting that literariness was actually an interwoven universe, and hence that dependence upon other texts was a profound interdependence. Indeed, postmodernism generally sees intertextuality as a form of equality or democracy; unlike in Modernism, there is little hierarchy of intertexts, but rather the sense of a field of textuality.

My question is what this intertextuality means in postcolonialism, particularly given that postcoloniality is occuring in the time of globalization and increasing flows of information. My avenue into this examination is J.M. Coetzee's use of intertextuality in the novel *Disgrace*,[2] partly because many commentators have said something about some of the intertexts utilized in the novel, but nobody has made an attempt at a thoroughgoing analysis. Moreover, in analysing the intertextuality in the novel I want to make the claim against those who see *Disgrace* as primarily a realist text that merely provides an avenue into discussing sociological issues in South Africa today[3] that to read it in this way is to do a disservice to the novel and to reading generally, but also specifically to Coetzee's views on the value of literature and literariness. *Disgrace* ostensibly consists of a chain of provocations that tempt the reader into realist socio-historical and national interpretations, but a more careful reading of the novel shows how metafictional it is, and how subtle its analysis of cultural history is. This metafictional component then begs the question that Coetzee has been grappling within his entire oeuvre, namely the question of complexity within socio-historical circumstances and mindsets, particularly within South Africa, that tend to reduce complexity, sometimes to the extent of viewing it as an indulgence or extravagance.

So there is a strong temptation to read *Disgrace* as a realist text, indeed it might be said that the novel invites this kind of reading, and I want to link this to the issue of Coetzee's oeuvre, and particularly his style. It seems that with *Disgrace* Coetzee is unfolding a natural progression that was evident from his first novel, but perhaps most apparent in *Age of Iron*, towards an evermore terse realist style. So the question arises of what has happened to the other, the sublime, the unconscious that was more characteristic of his earlier and more experimental works with their slightly more gnomic prose and moments of defamiliarization? I am thinking of the hyperbolic and destabilizing repetition and the exorbitant airships with which Klein Anna is fascinated in *In The Heart of the Country*; the enigmatic person of Michael K and Friday in *The Life and Times of Michael K* and *Foe* respectively; the magistrate's encounters with the 'barbarians' in *Waiting for the Barbarians*; the complex intertextuality and enigmatic metafictionality of *Foe* and *The Master of Petersburg*. On the surface of it, the terse minimalism of *Disgrace* seems to have little alterity, or the sublime, or exorbitant in it, and if we read the text as realist we are bound to conclude that it is depressing and pessimistic, as a number of readers have done. However, I want to suggest that we can find the sublime, albeit an ameliorated sublime that might not merit the appellation, in the novel within the narrative trajectory of the story itself, and further I want to suggest that Coetzee is moving towards embodying rupture in narrative, as opposed to in style (although there is clearly no neat dividing line between the two). So although the prose is terse and spare, the narrative is punctuated and shaped by a number of shocking, even sensational, events: prostitution, the initial unwelcome scandalous seduction, the 'not quite rape', the expulsion, violence in the countryside, the dying fall of the ending; and, more importantly, these events are given meaning by intertextual clues (I count over twenty intertexts in the novel, from Blake to Kafka), primarily Romantic, and it is by following these clues that we can come closer to reading the text within its context, rather than reading the text as subordinate to its context.

Coetzee establishes this context within the first line of the novel. The first sentence, rapidly becoming infamous, if not already so, is 'For a man of his age, fifty-two, divorced, he has, to his mind, solved the problem of sex rather well' (1). The perfective tense of the sentence suggests closure but is interrupted by the modifier 'to his mind', signalling that Lurie's solution is not as final as he imagines it, and creating the sense of illusion and consequent doom that will dog our protagonist. Moreover, this sentence obviously begs the question: why is sex a problem? The answer to this question is two-pronged.

First, sex is a problem for Lurie because of his subjectivity; he is something of a roue, a lothario, and this is not merely an idiosyncracy, but is something that derives from his culture which is Western, romantic, erotic. So the first major intertext within the novel is implicit within the first sentence and it is Western Romanticism. This Romanticism is embodied in a particular form by Lurie and this form is thoroughly critiqued in the novel. Lurie has made a study of Western Romanticism on which he has written three books: one on the '*genesis*' (italics mine) of Mephistopheles (via Boito's *Faust*), one on 'vision as eros', the third on '*Wordsworth and the Burden of the Past*' (4). Notice that all of these tracts centre on the devil in the past in that they all deal with past Western Romantic masters. Satan has a number of faces, as we might expect. As Lucifer, he is a fallen favourite, fallenness being the narrative trajectory of the novel. He is also the snake, significantly called 'serpent' (16), David Lurie's 'totem', an image of venomous seduction, danger, corruption, and cunning, but also of change, growth, and spirituality. Lurie describes his sexual 'temperament' under this totem as 'lengthy, absorbed, but rather abstract, rather dry, even at its hottest' (3). Furthermore, Lurie's ambition is to write an opulent Gluck-like opera, *Byron in Italy*, which again suggests Romantic eroticism via notorious seduction, for a chamber opera triumph will return eros, and hence himself, to society. This operatic ambition will be severely attenuated in the narrative trajectory of the novel.

Lurie's emphasis upon a Romantically devilish sensuality is arguably macho and diosyncratic; but as Michael Williams points out in relation to Byron's poem 'Lara': 'In the 1940s, the 1950s and the early 1960s, explorations of the satanic were central to the study of such texts as *Lara*. Needless to say, this is the period when David Lurie—and incidentally his creator J.M. Coetzee—would have been encountering Byron in their university studies for the first time'[4]. Nevertheless, Lurie's emphasis is developed beyond this when Lurie teaches Byron's 'Lara' to his class (32–3). Lurie's reading of 'Lara' interprets the protagonist as 'Lucifer, the dark angel', which resonates with both Lurie himself and with the 'bravo' boyfriend of Melanie Isaacs, the student he seduces, who at that moment has muscled his way into Lurie's class. According to Lurie's interpretation, the identity and sexuality of Lucifer, Lara, Byron, himself, and presumably Melanie's boyfriend, is that of the alienated modern individual, rather like Hamlet, who 'will be condemned to solitude' (34), a chillingly prophetic image of Lurie's fate and a critique of Romantic identity, for Lurie says of his Romantic 'masters' that 'They all died young. Or dried up. Or went mad and were locked away' (15). Thus Romantic sexuality is not merely a metaphysical or humanist issue of evil, which is explored at some length in *Elizabeth Costello*,[5] but is also an issue of modernity.

Hence it would be wrong to assume that Romanticism is written off by the text as an anachronistic cultural embarrassment that can only lead to isolation and eventual disgraceful exile. Romanticism's ability to critique early modernity is never questioned; Romanticism seems to be the primary intertext of the novel because it was and is opposed to 'Newton's sleep of reason' with its emphasis upon spontaneous feeling and corporeal sympathy, particularly the love of nature. Moreover, we do not usually think of Romanticism as a culture that espouses the middle path, it appears too Dionysian for that, but that Romanticism can provide a link between spirit and body, between vision and manifestation, is apparent in Lurie's class on Wordsworth's 'The Prelude' in which he makes it clear that balance is necessary:

… we cannot live our daily lives in a realm of pure ideas, cocooned from sense-experience. The question is not, How can we keep the imagination pure, protected from the onslaughts of reality? The question has to be, Can we find a way for the two to coexist? (22)

It is appropriate that Wordsworth should be the exemplar of balance rather than Byron, but perhaps if we are going to critique Lurie without lapsing into specious judgement, then it should be in terms of his own professed ideal of balance and coexistence. Lurie is unable to live up to an ideal of balance because he is so enraptured with his Romanticism, maybe because it allows him to escape from his context. Lurie himself points out how unromantic reality can be when he asks, 'But now, do you truly wish to see the beloved in the cold clarity of the visual apparatus? It may be in your better interest to throw a veil over the gaze, so as to keep her alive in her archetypal, goddesslike form' (22).

Lurie is so possessed by archetypal images, so enculturated, that he falls into the trap of keeping his vision 'turned toward the great archetypes of the imagination we carry within us' (23): in the 'not quite rape' scene when he forces himself upon Melanie Isaacs he sees her as 'from the quiver of Aphrodite, goddess of the foaming waves, no doubt about that' (25); Lurie thinks '*I was a servant of Eros ... It was a god who acted through me*' (89). Lurie is unable to live up to his own Wordsworthian ideal of a balance between archetype and reality, between vision and objects, because he is rapt in his own ecstasy with Romantic archetype and vision. This is graphically illustrated by his need to take Melanie, to make her conform to his transcendental rapture by ignoring the fact that 'She opens the door wearing a crumpled T-shirt, cycling shorts, slippers in the shape of comic-book gophers which he finds silly, tasteless' (24). Moreover, his rapture with transcendent mythical imagery prevents him from seeing that his drives are partly motivated by the mundane dynamics of aging; he cannot see the links between rapist and father. So Romanticism has been part of Lurie's problem because it both fills up the void in his soul with art, but also creates that void since no physical manifestation or person can fulfil such a lofty artistic ideal. Romanticism all-too-often risks loss of balance; its emphasis upon rapture, ecstasy, the sublime opens it up to indulgence, egotism, loss of control, and indiscipline. Yet what other discourse opposes an instrumental rationality so rigorously or foregrounds what Lurie calls the 'rights. of desire...the god who makes even the small bird quiver' (89)?

So I hope it is clear that the first aspect of Lurie's dilemma is his rather predatory sexual identity which is at least partially a result of a particular Western Romantic enculturation. Perhaps the text is suggesting that the problem of sexuality is not only physical, but is also due to the repression or sublimation of erotic energy that modernity and a certain type and interpretation of Western culture involves? However, David Lurie's problem with sex is not merely his own subjectivity and his enculturation, but the clash between this and the particular postcolonial context within which he exists, and this forms the second horn of his dilemma. In other words, it is not Romanticism per se that is the problem, but a decontextualized and elitist Romanticism. Lurie, despite being an expert in Romanticism, appears blind to the fact that both Romanticism and 'the new South Africa' are post-revolutionary historical moments and therefore might be usefully compared; Lurie's Romanticism is decontextualized to the extent that it is ahistorical and lacking in agency. Further, Coetzee suggests that this problem is exacerbated by colonization and especially by globalization which institutes an 'emasculation' (4). So the question is not merely why sex is a problem, but also how David Lurie could possibly make his sexuality, intellect, and vision coincide with the new global capitalist dispensation?[6] That he can only achieve some such coincidence via the reduced role of celibate caregiver to dying and dead dogs speaks volumes not only about himself but also about the context in which he finds himself.

Notice that the one course in Romantic literature that Lurie is allowed per annum as a sop to 'morale' echoes the ninety minutes of sex he allows himself per week. So there is a link between Lurie's compartmentalized solution to the 'problem of sex' and the 'great rationalisation' (3) that characterizes 'the new South Africa' and the new global capitalist dispensation. Passion and commitment are giving way to organization and efficiency in this new world order, accompanied by an increase in puritanical surveillance and moralistic denunciation; instrumental empiricism has been conflated with an easy judgemental ethics. The new globalized state is characterized by a narrow political correctness and a functionalist technicism that is most apparent in Lurie's wonderfully graphic description of the form that he has to fill out for the disciplinary hearing resulting from his 'abuse' of his student:

There is a form to fill in. The form is placed before them, and a pen. A hand takes up the pen, a hand he has kissed, a hand he knows intimately. First the name of the plaintiff: MELANIE ISAACS, in careful block letters. Down the column of boxes wavers the hand, searching for the one to tick. *There*, points the nicotine-stained finger of her father. The hand slows, settles, makes its X, its cross of righteousness: *J'accuse*. Then a space for the name of the accused. DAVID LURIE, writes the hand: PROFESSOR. Finally, at the foot of the page, the date and her signature: the arabesque of the *M*, the *l* with its bold upper loop, the downward gash of the *I*, the flourish of the final *s*.

The deed is done. Two names on the page, his and hers, side by side. Two in a bed, lovers no longer but foes (39–40).

The contrast between the instrumental vertical and horizontal lines of the form and the italicized arabesque 'flourish' of the signature is stark, conveying the contrast between lovers in a bed together and the formalized conflict within which they are now caught. *Rapprochement* is virtually impossible within such a starkly polarized grid format which attempts to fit human beings into straight lines and boxes. Moreover, this new regime is not only schematic and instrumentalist but it is also womanist,[7] so that Lurie wonders if he is viewed as 'A shark among the helpless little fishies? Or does she have another vision: of a great thick-boned male bearing down upon a girl-child, a huge hand stifling her cries?' (53). Such womanism is most graphically signalled in the poster of 'Superman hanging his head as he is berated by Lois Lane' (177) adorning the wall of the office of young Dr Otto who has replaced Lurie; this satirizes not only the Romantic/Nietzschean hero, but also what this superman has been reduced to. This political correctness is unconvincing to Lurie; as he disparagingly comments of his students: 'Post-Christian, posthistorical, postliterate, they might as well have been hatched from eggs yesterday' (32). Whilst it is easy enough to justify the historical reasons behind contemporary womanism and to dismiss Lurie's condescending image of reptilian, even alien, birth, it is less easy to debunk his sense of the judgementalism of the new regime of globalizing rationality which he describes as a politics of 'blame' (44): 'The community of the righteous, holding their sessions in corners, over the telephone, behind closed doors. Gleeful whispers. *Schadenfreude*. First the sentence, then the trial' (42); as his ex-wife thunders at him: 'No sympathy, no mercy, not in this day and age' (43). Despite Lurie's melodramatic hyperbole in these passages, it is difficult to argue with his sense that 'These are puritanical times. Private life is public business. Prurience is respectable, prurience and sentiment. They wanted a spectacle: breast-beating, remorse, tears if possible. A TV show, in fact' (66).

This leads me to the primary point that I want to advance, which is that given a present which is governed by an instrumental and reductionist version of rationality, Coetzee returns to an earlier phase of opposition to that rationality in order to examine the possibilities for opposition today. That earlier phase was Romanticism, which was arguably the earliest and most powerful rebellion against the newly emergent industrial phase of Modernity. Moreover, European nationalism arose during the Romantic period, and it is highly appropriate that this cultural movement and period should be revisited when South Africa is undergoing nation-building, particularly as the rhetoric of such is 'the rainbow nation'. Thus Coetzee's metafictional intertextuality is highly politicized and relevant; any accusation of idiosyncracy and tangentiality in the novel would seem to miss this point. Thus intertextuality for the postcolonial artist, or Coetzee at any rate, seems to involve a reframing in which both intertext, text, and context pressurize each other, not necessarily creating a hybrid amalgam but at least recontextualizing and modifying. There is no fidelity to an original prior world or text, rather a deliberate contrapuntal recontextualization and/or hybridization forces the reader to reconsider both the intertext and the text in a comparative and political light, instantiating literary criticism within the fictional text. So intertextuality in postcolonialism would seem to consist simultaneously of both a contextually-specific and obliquely politically committed pastiche and parody.

From Lurie's perspective at least, postcolonial modernity is characterized by the myth that the past was dark and unenlightened in order to give us the feeling that we are evolved and progressive now, a myth that Foucault pointed out in *The History of Sexuality*: 'there may be another reason that makes it so gratifying for us to define the relationship between sex and power in terms of repression: something that one might call the speaker's benefit' (6).[8] Little does Lurie realize that the 'new' South Africa has also revolutionized labour relations, but he will come to realize that 'It is a new world they live in, he and Lucy and Petrus. Petrus knows it, and he knows it, and Petrus knows that he knows it' (116). Nor does he yet understand that there is no room for animals in this new 'humanist' dispensation; his daughter Lucy tells him that 'On the list of the nation's priorities, animals come nowhere' (73). So Lurie might be a roue, but he is also an anachronistic and de-historicized Lear figure, which is as much a judgement upon contemporary globalization as upon Quixotic Romanticism.

So much for modernity in the city, but what happens when this complex intertextuality enters the heart of the country? Of course, Romanticism has always been associated with nature and the pastoral, and in particular with the sublime epiphany that nature potentially offers to the attuned sensibility. We should perhaps keep in mind that it was during the Romantic period that South Africa was colonized, and that a minor Scottish Romantic poet Thomas Pringle, a year younger than Byron, would prove to be a major South African writer. These facts should alert us to Coetzee's awareness that nature is a particularly mediated and constructed concept in South Africa, something he points out in settler art: 'it is not oversimplification to say that landscape and art and landscape writing from the beginning of the nineteenth century to the middle of the twentieth revolve around the question of finding a language to fit Africa, a language that will be authentically African ... The quest for an authentic language is pursued within a framework in which language, consciousness and landscape are all related.'[9] So the landscape around Grahamstown to which Lurie escapes after his disgrace in the city is pictured in Romantic terms:

The wind drops. There is a moment of utter stillness which he would wish prolonged for ever: the gentle sun, the stillness of mid-afternoon, bees busy in a field of flowers; and at the centre of the picture a young woman, *das ewig Weibliche*, lightly pregnant, in a straw sunhat. A scene ready-made for a Sargent or a Bonnard. City boys like him; but even city boys can recognize beauty when they see it, can have their breath taken away.

The truth is, he has never had much of an eye for rural life, despite all his reading in Wordsworth (218).

The mention of Wordsworth conjures up the pastoral, and in particular via his Lucy poems which picture nature as a benevolent Gaia who gathers up her melancholy innocent maid to her breast, leaving her lover plangently bereft. This image of the nurturing innocent eternal feminine is echoed in '*Das Ewige-Weibliche/Zieht uns hinan*' from the chorus at the end of Goethe's *Faust II*[10] which adds the suggestion of the redemptive powers of the eternal feminine. Just so is Lucy's innocence lost/raped in *Disgrace*, but her being 'Rolled round in earth's diurnal course,/With Rocks, and stones, and trees'[11] does not involve her physical death, but the death of her, and her father's, pride in the compromising accommodation with Petrus which is an inversion of Apartheid power structures. The implication here I think is that despite Romanticism's utility as an ongoing critique of modernity and modernization, its axioms are far too luridly melodramatic to be appropriate metaphors for post-apartheid South Africa which requires an altogether more steely stoicism in order to survive its vicissitudes. Where redemption is available, it is not in terms of the pastoral enclosure of women, confining them to masochistic chaste purity, nor in terms of cymbal-clash transcendentalism, but in terms of a grinding endurance.

This 'grounding' of Romanticism, if I may call it that, is emphasized in the name of the village in the Eastern Cape near Grahamstown to which Lurie flees: Salem, the etymology of which is 'shalom' and 'salaam' meaning peace, and it is also a shortened form of Jerusalem and referred to Methodist chapels. Salem was one of the first towns to be settled by the English who managed to avert a Xhosa battle there by negotiation; hence it suggests the triumph of liberal rationality, a suggestion that Coetzee is to overturn in the novel. Salem also conjures up the puritan frontier of Nathaniel Hawthorne's *The Scarlet Letter* with the disgracing of women and the witch trials of Cotton Mather. Just like seventeenth-century America, South Africa has been puritanical, though in a Calvinist sense, and the parallel is not direct but inverted by having a male in disgrace. Perhaps Coetzee is suggesting that scapegoating, far from being redundant, will operate whenever and wherever any regime of correctness is reigning. Having said this, it must be pointed out that Hester Prynne's shaming in *The Scarlet Letter* is perhaps more marked than that of Lurie's in *Disgrace* for, after all, Lurie may be exiled, assaulted and burnt, but he is not branded with a sigil and he is not literally raped, a cruelty reserved for his daughter. Salem also conjures up Arthur Miller's *The Crucible* and McCarthyist censorship in the 1950s. Coetzee chose the name of Salem appositely, considering his essay on Noël Mostert's *Frontiers* which traces the violent history of racial conflict in the Eastern Cape (*Stranger Shores*).[12]

So as far as Lurie goes, his 'not quite rape' of the 'black' girl in the city is neatly inverted in the rape of Lucy by the black men in the country, giving a diptych structure to the novel. This diptych is part of his 'fall' and forces him to reflect upon his own complicity in the exploitation of women, the limits of his imagination, and the inappropriateness of European Romanticism: 'He thinks of Byron. Among the legions of countesses and kitchenmaids Byron pushed himself into there were no doubt those who called it rape. But none surely had cause to fear that the session would end with her throat being slit. From where he stands, from where Lucy stands, Byron looks very old fashioned indeed' (160). He may be making a disingenuous excuse for Romanticism here, but the comparison is what is important for the purposes of my essay, for Lurie's trajectory is from absorption in his own inner enculturated world towards an attenuation of that world via abrasion on the hard edges of the 'new' South Africa. In other words, intertexts and their use are tested within and by context. In many ways, Romanticism is found wanting in the new South Africa, even whilst its guiding revolutionary impulse is ratified in this context.

One of the major problems with Romanticism is its pastoral enclosure of femininity, which is seen not only in Lurie's relationship to women but also in the rape of Lucy. Her name is an allusion to St Lucy the Sicilian virgin martyr, patron saint of virgins, the blind, and writers, who has a silencing throat wound described in the novel thus: 'over the body of the woman silence is being drawn like a blanket. *Too ashamed*, they will say to each other, *too ashamed to tell*' (110). It is difficult not to infer that patriarchy is a rape which silences. This linkage between patriarchy and silence was developed in Donne's 'A Nocturnall upon S. Lucies day,/Being the shortest day' in which the speaker is an original nothingness and darkness, apparently due to mourning (perhaps for Donne's wife, daughter Lucy, or patroness Lucy Countess of Bedford).[13] St Lucy's Day falls on the thirteenth of December in the northern hemisphere, the winter solstice which emphasizes a long dark night of the soul and, of course, December is astrologically the time of Capricorn, the goat, with all its connotations of earthy lust. Ironically, it is Lurie who is reduced to silence by Lucy's experience. Her rape is all the harder for a father to bear because not only must it cause vicarious suffering via empathy, but it also emasculates him via his impotence and inability to imagine what was involved (97, 110, 158, 160), and this is compounded by Lucy's refusal to 'share' the experience in any way or to listen to any of his paternalistic advice. The reference to the rape of the Sabine women emphasizes Lurie's emasculation; a Roman myth, painted by Poussin and Picasso amongst others, in which the abducted Sabine women forced to marry Romans refuse to return to their Sabine men. Lucy's determination to get along with Petrus in the new South Africa, her determination not to leave the country, echoes this myth.

I think that it is worth noticing that Lurie is always at something of a distance from the pastoral despite his intellectual and academic championing of it. This is embodied in his strained relationship with Lucy and in his conflict with Pollux and Petrus, both representatives of indigenous naturalism. Hence he describes his re-entry to Lucy's world as an Orphean descent into the 'Stygian soup of souls' of Canto VII of Dante's Inferno[14] (Saute 1980: 209); as Graham Pechey points out, St Lucy is the patron saint of the mediatrix between Mary and Dante's Beatrice in the *Commedia*.[15] This descent into the natural and the visceral, an encounter with threatening otherness, forces him to feel otherness rather than just intellectually appreciating it: he realizes that Lucy is a different person to himself, not merely the offspring of his loins, when she confronts him thus:

David, I can't run my life according to whether or not you like what I do. Not any more. You behave as if everything I do is part of the story of your life. You are the main character, I am a minor character who doesn't make an appearance until halfway through. Well, contrary to what you think, people are not divided into major and minor. I am not minor. I have a life of my own, just as important to me as yours is to you, and in my life I am the one who makes the decisions (198).

It is not only the alterity of Lucy that becomes clearer through confrontation, it is also the weight of history that becomes apparent. Lurie had imagined that his daughter was indeed his, the delusion that all parents have that they control their offspring, but he comes to realize that it is perhaps history that has had the greater part in Lucy's evolution: 'Curious that he and her mother, cityfolk, intellectuals, should have produced this throwback, this sturdy young settler. But perhaps it was not they who produced her: perhaps history had the larger share' (61). However, history is not some settled fact but is constantly changing and hence constantly open to the potential of reinterpretation and agency: 'She talks easily about these matters. A frontier farmer of the new breed. In the old days, cattle and maize. Today, dogs and daffodils. The more things change the more they remain the same. History repeating itself, though in a more modest vein. Perhaps history has learned a lesson' (62). The lines 'History repeating itself, though in a more modest vein' having 'learned a lesson', could well be a summation of the novel as a whole which reinterprets history through culture. This not only shifts history, and perhaps politics, away from the epochal and towards the local, specific, and embodied, but also hollows out a tiny space of agency within its broad canvas, for it is the cultural that allows for some intervention into history.

This cultural agency can hardly be viewed as political in the usual sense, but that does not mean that it does not exist. If agency is about change, then the question is, has David Lurie changed? Specifically, has his attitude towards sex changed? Is Lurie able to view himself ironically in relation to Melanie Isaacs now, as a historically-situated subject? Coetzee does not provide us with a neat conclusion to these questions, not least because Lurie is his focalizer and hence it is difficult for the reader to fully trust his judgements. His attitude towards Bev Shaw, the manager of the animal clinic, is initially condescending in extremis and symptomatic not only of his sexism but of his 'looksism' or extreme aestheticism (72, 79), but he does come to some awareness of her alterity via Flaubert: 'His thoughts go to Emma Bovary strutting before the mirror after her first big afternoon. *I have a lover! I have a lover!* sings Emma to herself. Well, let poor Bev Shaw go home and do some singing too. And let him stop calling her poor Bev Shaw. If she is poor, he is bankrupt' (150). This is a reprisal of Lurie's self-regarding approval of his 'snake-like' cool sexuality at the beginning of the novel: 'He thinks of Emma Bovary, coming home sated, glazen-eyed, from an afternoon of reckless fucking. *So this is bliss!*, says Emma, marvelling at herself in the mirror. *So this is the bliss the poets speak of!* Well, if poor ghostly Emma were ever to find her way to Cape Town, he would bring her along one Thursday afternoon to show her what bliss can be: a moderate bliss. A moderated bliss' (6). The irony here is that it is Lurie who is being taught moderation.

It seems that Lurie is now not only aware of his own disgraced situation, but is also groping towards some sort of awareness of otherness, particularly female otherness, and he describes his relationships as having 'enriched' (192) him. So Lurie, having seen that he is now in no country for old men, reaches a monk-like kind of sexual purgatory in which he is no longer a Don Juan, has no lover, a place 'not cold but not hot' (195). This is ambiguated by his intercourse with a prostitute, which could be seen as a sign that he does not change, or as a valediction to his previous life. It seems that this intercourse is indeed a goodbye to his previous life, particularly if we consider this passage:

If the old men hog the young women, what will be the future of the species? That, at bottom, was the case for the prosecution. Half of literature is about it: young women struggling to escape from under the weight of old men, for the sake of the species.

He sighs. The young in one another's arms, heedless, engrossed in the sensual music. No country, this, for old men. He seems to be spending a lot of time sighing. Regret: a regrettable note on which to go out (190).

This echo of Yeats' 'Sailing to Byzantium'(1982)[16] (in the words 'The young in one another's arms …') emphasizes the low point of Lurie's roue career. He has to face the fact that he is no longer able to appeal to women as he used to, that he is in decline, that his kingdom has come and gone, that mortality is stalking him. As Mark Sanders points out, this is also embodied in language which is romantic for Lurie—he is always being etymological (102), and grammatical, often emphasizing the perfective tense (Sanders 2002: 21, 71).[17] The perfective suggests that Lurie is living the after-effects of an already completed event, that his life is now merely a comet's tail after the comet has already burnt out. Again, as in Donne, the speaker is immune to the renewal of life, it is over for him. Yet he has to continue to live, to somehow find a role and subjectivity within much diminished circumstances. So the 'perfection' that he finds in life is somewhat different from what he might have expected as Professor of English, yet the logic of his trajectory is 'perfect' in the sense that it is an inversion of his previous path and connotes a secular metaphysics of inevitability.

If some of Lurie's rather sedimented attitudes to sex do not fully change, his attitude towards animals slowly does. He attempts to look after Lucy, and when it is clear that his attempts are far too clumsy and that he is alienating her instead of helping her, he transfers care to the doomed sheep and then to the dogs; importantly he does not understand these bonds, they are intuitive or precognitive for him: 'A bond seems to have come into existence between himself and the two Persians, he does not know how. The bond is not one of affection. It is not even a bond with these two in particular, whom he could not pick out from a mob in a field. Nevertheless, suddenly and without reason, their lot has become important to him' (126). This intuitive bond is important, for whilst the novel may be seen as ameliorating Romanticism into something unrecognizable, what we have here is the mode or action of Romanticism, which is the accessing of extra-rational states of being as part of a wider connectivity. Of course this is Coetzee, so such access to the extra-rational is not romanticized; what we are presented with is a harsh vision of abjection and tiny gestures of compassion. Lurie's dog euthanasia is sacrificial and linked to Abraham and Isaac, echoed in Melanie Isaacs. So the point is that Romanticism within South Africa is redefined by Coetzee into an extremely humble yet proactive agency.

The savagery of this dog euthanasia is made clear in the use of the German word '*Lösung*' (142, 218) or solution, a word used by the Nazis to indicate the 'final solution', and echoing Elizabeth Costello's controversial equation of battery farming with the Nazi death camps in *The Lives of Animals* and *Elizabeth Costello*. It is also Kafkan in the quotation of Joseph K's stabbing in the final line of Kafka's *The Trial*: 'Like a dog! He said, it was as if he meant the shame of it to outlive him' (Heyns 2002: 205),[18] a phrase utilized by Lucy to describe her abject position in the new South Africa. Perhaps Kafka's stark modernism is just the antidote to Romanticism's excesses, and hence Coetzee's reference to it here. When Lurie decides to work in Bev Shaw's dog sanctuary he echoes Petrus in that he has now 'become a dog man: a dog undertaker, a dog psychopomp; a *harijan*' (146), a reference to Gandhi's attempt to dignify the untouchables with a new name.

So the novel critiques the excessive in suggesting that the first shall be last and vice versa, a suggestion visible in the metaphysical equation between the anagrams god and dog. Aphrodite and Eros have become Katy the three-legged male, nameless others. This is an attenuated middle-path, an anti-eschatological gradualism which would seem to be far from Romanticism. The novel itself suggests this through Lurie's desire to teach Emma Bovary 'a moderate bliss. A moderated bliss' (6), though it is Lurie who learns that 'his hopes must be more temperate' (214). A number of critics have noticed this amelioration, Elleke Boehmer saying that the novel is about 'enduring rather than transcending the degraded present ... reduced secular atonement',[19] Graham Pechey arguing that Lurie's creativity at the end of the novel is 'a small compensation in most ordinary contexts, huge in Coetzee's universe of parsimonious affirmation' (382). Michiel Heyns points out that this narrative trajectory of attenuation follows the pattern of tragedy, the primary intertext of which is *Oedipus*.[20] Lurie quotes the final chorus of the drama on page two of the novel, 'call no man happy until he is dead'. Heyns links this tragic inevitability to *King Lear* and to Hardy's *Jude the Obscure*.[21] It is also clear that this is something of a linguistic exercise, for Lurie now must embrace the imperfect partiality of life lived after the perfective tense.

Having said this, we should keep in mind that this secular metaphysics is hardly lacking in drama; indeed, as I suggested earlier, the narrative drama of shocking present-tense events is the means by which alterity or otherness is encountered and is Coetzee's method of defamiliarization in this novel. In other words, Coetzee seems to be rejecting the classic tenet of Lurie's liberal humanism which is that it is imagination that enables the perception of otherness. This is a critique of Shelley's 'The great secret of morals is love, or a going out of ourselves in identification of that which is different.'[22] Coetzee is suggesting, I think, that imaginative sympathy or empathy is not enough in itself, that otherness will often involve violent confrontation. The theorist who perhaps has most to say about this is Emmanuel Levinas, particularly in *Otherwise than Being*,[23] where he describes the irreducibility of the alterity of another person that interrupts the self, a divine moment of face-to-face transcendence. This might explain the pathos of the ending of the novel where the 'face of God' that confronts the Dionysian Lurie is a 'vast circulatory system to whose working pity and terror are irrelevant;' the karmic destiny of the Dionysian sensualist and egotist is to love dying dogs and become like Lucy 'rolled round in earth's diurnal course, with rocks and stones and trees'. So if Romanticism is the central intertext in the novel, it is an intertext that is stripped of Dionysianism and any rose-coloured gloss in order for it to be meaningful within South Africa's context.

Hence Lurie is able to find some kind of grace through looking after dead dogs, through being concerned with the marginalized, which is why in his new opera it is Teresa, the jilted lover of Byron, who comes to be the main character (182, 184). This movement of emphasis from the master to the marginal was anticipated in Henry James' *The Aspern Papers* which similarly focused on a former lover of Byron, Claire Claremont, though it often conflated her character with Teresa. Moreover, the descent from Gluck as his initial operatic ambition to the plink plonk of the chamber banjo-opera echoes in sonic form his trajectory from the baroque filigree of excessive romanticism to a stripped minimalism. Lurie claims that he loses Melanie Isaacs because he lacks the 'lyrical' (171), and his search for this lyrical takes him through the 'masters' (Boito: [4] 'Beethoven and Janacek' [176], Scarlatti's 'cat music' [15]); 'So much for the poets, so much for the dead masters. Who have not, he must say, guided him well. *Aliter*, to whom he has not listened well' (179). He rediscovers the lyrical, to the extent that he does, by learning from the masters, not by copying them, but rather by inserting their lessons into his context—hence the plink plonk Cape Coon banjo in the quasi-opera that 'consumes' Lurie. Whilst he was intent on copying the masters, his opera was on 'the monotonous track on which it has been running since the start. It has become the kind of work a sleepwalker might write' (214); it was as though he were drowning out the voice of local nature with grandiose Eurocentric melodies. His intent has been ambitious and even egotistical, 'it would have been nice to be returned triumphant to society as the author of an eccentric little chamber opera' (214), so he cannot create authentically; 'that is why he must listen to Teresa ... Teresa is past honour' (209).

Now he has created a soundtrack with which 'the dog is fascinated' (215) and nearly howls in tune to. So creativity consists in learning from the masters but applying their lessons humbly and authentically within his own local context, an argument against the sterilizing stasis of canonization. Whilst literary forebears are questioned by contrasting them with the local, the local is challenged by these masters; creativity lies in the lyrical straining to escape from the local:

> But he was wrong. It is not the erotic that is calling to him after all, nor the elegiac, but the comic. He is in the opera neither as Teresa nor as Byron nor even as some blending of the two: he is held in the music itself, in the flat, tinny slap of the banjo strings, the voice that strains to soar away from the ludicrous instrument but is continually reined back, like a fish on a line.
>
> So this is art, he thinks, and this is how it does its work! How strange! How fascinating (184–5)!

Through just such a creative utilization of intertextuality within the local *Disgrace* attempts to resist or evade being 'reined back'. Lurie is now something of a hierophant, a mediator between life and death, he conducts the reader to the isle of the dead past the dog Cerberus where they find their own role within history and are able to imagine a new role for themselves.

So I think that what we have in the novel is an affectionate deconstruction of Western culture, a deconstruction of the earlier Romantic effort to oppose the instrumental rationality of Modernity in the interests of an effort to resist similar instrumentalism in the latest instalment of globalizing capitalism within the postcolony. This helps to explain the resonances that the novel has had for those outside of South Africa. What we seem to be looking at in *Disgrace* is a complexly metafictional novel that suggests that not only is creativity a partial and humbling process, but that creativity cannot occur within a vacuum and so requires the careful selection and use of past texts in order to inform and vivify the present. However, many of the intertexts available for use in the creative process are partially inappropriate to contemporary contexts, not least South African, to the extent that they are imperial, sensationalist, apocalyptic and/ or eschatological, and will need to be carefully rewritten.

What is the value of this partial, temperate, and moderate narrative that includes a plenitude of intertexts and is continually modifying its trajectory? What is the valency of a postmodern postcolonialism? Is Coetzee merely constructing the reader as a highly educated sniffer-out of intertextual sophistications, expecting that the reader be highly enculturated? Or is Coetzee, in constructing this narrative chain of provocations, inviting a realist reading of *Disgrace*, and, if so, did he want to achieve the canonization of the text as the authoritative commentary on South Africa that has in fact occurred, or was he merely attempting to prompt debate about the issues of gender, sexuality, violence, restitution, justice within the postcolony? My feeling is that we could certainly accuse him of these motives, but such a reading could learn much from the diminutions of mastery that Lurie's humbling trajectory embodies. First, the anti-eschatological elements of the text are of value in an instrumentalist world/context for they tend to prevent extremism. Indeed, the instrumentalism of the reader is challenged in such a text. Coetzee has pointed out that empiricist mimesis is not only the cultural phenomenon accompanying Western imperialism, but is also inherently imperialist, as suggested by its links to desire.[24] Coetzee's fiction consists of the attempt to create a way to speak and write without the dynamic of rivalry and the mimetic violence of desire. Hence his fiction is of the West, but about Africa, preventing the establishment of a simplistic rivalry between the two and challenging the reader. Second, a highly intertextual text of this sort is all-embracing, non-exclusionary; if we do not grant a text its full scope, we are doing it a disservice. Third, Coetzee has no truck with false consolations, does not waste time with rationalizations. That Lurie is not able to sustain his Romantic ideals, partly because various realities violently haul him out of them, suggests that solipsistic idealisms cannot last and are inappropriate. This is an argument against canonization. It may also be an argument against putting one's faith in any single text, movement or ideal. Finally, Coetzee's intertextuality appears to be particularly historical and political, perhaps suggesting that post-colonial intertextuality is more *engagee* than its postmodern analogue, eschewing a self-reflexivity that becomes a *mise-en-abyme*. The question of what such a degree of metafictional intertextuality means in Africa is tackled by Coetzee in a chapter entitled 'The Novel in Africa' in *Elizabeth Costello* where the eponymous white Australian writer is at odds with the African writer Emmanuel Egudu, partly because they were once in bed together. Perhaps unsurprisingly, this debate is not only sexual, not only about power, but is also a debate about the valency of writing, between an essential/visceral understanding of African writing as oral and traditional and Costello's Derridean understanding of writing as play, a play of difference. This debate is not solved by Coetzee, for Egudu's emphasis upon physical authenticity has a point, as does Costello's argument that this authenticity is often merely the repackaging of Africa as a consumable primal exotic for Western audiences today. It seems that neither a Western audience wanting exoticism nor an African audience wanting authenticity desire a highly intertextual or postmodern African fiction. Nevertheless, this is what audiences receive in *Disgrace*, though it is a peculiarly postcolonial version of intertextuality that is on offer, a version that Michael Marais describes as having 'a well-defined metafictional dimension that articulates the text's intention to engage affectively with history'.[25] Marais, and I support him in this, is suggesting that postcolonial metafiction tends to be more politically engaged than many Western postmodernisms, but it also allows for more distance between the author and society than most nationalisms or realisms allow for, arguably even reinforcing a Modernist split between artist and audience. Nevertheless, there are historical/appropriateness limits to intertextuality; in relation to South Africa and South African literature Coetzee's focus on Romanticism in *Disgrace* is appropriate and canny given the political and pedagogical heritage of the country and Coetzee's ability to use a reformatted Romanticism to understand and redefine the present. Still, I do think that intertextuality often works in a chaotic way for writers; there are often happenstance and syncretic connections between hugely disparate times/places/things/ideas; 'If it works, make the links' is, I suspect, how most artists work in relation to intertextuality, and I think that critics have little right to be critical about this unless they have better (richer, more fruitful) connections to suggest.

Intertextuality, Kristeva's notion of textual interdependence, was an acknowledgment that texts do not merely allude to other texts but are profoundly dependent upon them; that the present or the self is a mosaic of the past and of others respectively.

Kristeva advances the notion that intertextuality 'involves an altering of the thetic *position*—the destruction of the old position and the formation of a new one'.[26] However, the problem with this notion is that it does not aesthetically or otherwise differentiate between uses of intertextuality that are merely new, in the sense that every production is new, and those that appear to provide a strikingly new vantage; an originality that provides defamiliarizing affect, or a new mode of thought, or analysis or seems to be seminal, or sum up something of the *zeitgeist*. In the less interesting forms of postmodernism, for instance, intertextuality results in pastiche or parody, without a new vantage point being attained. I think that Coetzee provides us with a powerful form of postmodern/postcolonial intertextuality within which carefully selected texts and contexts are subjected to such a sustained critique that they yield something new that redefines its constituent parts in a proactive fashion. Indeed, the postcolony can reinvigorate the world's texts, but likewise those texts can also provide some harsh lessons for the postcolony to learn, particularly in relationship to intransigent instrumentalist ideologies. In conclusion, I would add that it is the realization that kingdoms come and go that is the profoundest lesson at the heart of postcolonialism; Coetzee transmutates this realization into a new art by utilizing the art of lost empires in a new way. What is that way? That way is a new minimalist multiplicity—a plenitude of powerfully resonant intertexts is utilized towards the minimalist end of moving us away from singularity and towards ameliorated multiplicity. Is intertextuality a metaphor for hybrid cosmopolitanism? If so, Coetzee shows how a careful use of intertextuality produces a hybridity that is free of the blandishments all-too-often adhering to cosmopolitanism. Coetzee's intertextuality is a revisionist and discretionary one which is sanguine about the limitations of texts and of individual agency, but is nevertheless able to create. It seems, then, that the imagination and the nation are likely to be somewhat opposed, perhaps even in perpetuity.

## Notes

1. Cuddon, J.A. (Ed.). *The Penguin Dictionary of Literary Terms and Literary Theory*. London: Penguin, 1998, 415.
2. Coetzee, J.M. *Disgrace*. London: Vintage, 2000. All subsequent references are to this edition and will be cited in the text.
3. A number of reviewers have been indisposed towards *Disgrace*, in some cases virulently so: Blatchford, Matthew. 'A Good Book—Burn It', in *Mail and Guardian*, Johannesburg, 24 October 2003, 24. Christensen, Anna. 'Denial of Humanity', in *Financial Mail*, 17 December 1999, 59. Cornwell, Gareth. 'The Recovery of Grace', in *English Academy Review*, 16, 1999, 248–54. More substantial reviews which have read *Disgrace* sociologically, or have considered sociological critiques at length, include: Farred, Grant. 'The Mundanacity of Violence: Living in a State of Disgrace', in *Interventions*, 4, (3), 2002, 352–62. Peter D. McDonald. '*Disgrace* Effects', in *Interventions*, 4, (3) 2002, 321–30. Mary Eagleton. 'Ethical Reading: The Problem of Alice Walker's "Advancing Luna—and Ida B. Wells" and J.M. Coetzee's *Disgrace*', in *Feminist Theory*, 2, (2) August 2001, 189–203.
4. Williams, Michael. ' "—most of the men being already adulterated—" Byron and Coetzee', *AUETSA Conference*, 2004, 8, unpublished.
5. Coetzee, J.M. *Elizabeth Costello*, London: Secker and Warburg, 2003. All subsequent references are to this edition and will be cited in the text.
6. There is a substantial literature on how certain management ideologies have come to be globally pervasive in global capitalism. Volcker points out how pervasive management styles and ideas have become: 'the economic logic of living in a world of global capital markets is to have much more integration … The obvious counterpoint is a growing lack of autonomy in economic management, easily perceived as an affront to sovereignty' (2001, 82). The

pervasive macroeconomic policy of market laissez-faire is parallelled by 'deregulation' of the workplace, which 'amounts to a regime of indifference … the employee labours in a vacuum … [which] puts serious obstacles in the way of deriving an identity from work' (Sennett 2001:187). Sennett goes on to argue that 'There is a regime of power operating on the principle of indifference to those in its grip, a regime seeking to evade, in the workplace, being held accountable for its acts. The essence of the politics of globalization is finding ways to hold this regime of indifference to account. If we fail in this political effort, we will suffer a profound personal wound' (190). It seems to me that Coetzee's novel demonstrates this regime of indifference in the workplace that derives from globalization and that his novel seeks to hold this regime to account in a highly political manner.

Volcker. Paul A., 'The Sea of Global Finance', in *On the Edge: Living with Global Capitalism*. Eds Will Hutton and Anthony Giddens. London: Vintage, 2001, 75–85.

Sennett, Richard. 'Street and Office: Two Sources of Identity', in *On the Edge: Living with Global Capitalism*. Eds Will Hutton and Anthony Giddens. London: Vintage, 2001, 175–90.

7.  I use the term 'womanist' as opposed to 'feminist' here in order to signal Coetzee's suggestion that 'the new South Africa' has often tended to become somewhat politically-correct and essentialist in its determination to oppose exploitation.

8.  Foucault, Michel. *The History of Sexuality*. Trans. Robert Hurley. London: Penguin, 1978.

9.  Coetzee, J.M. *White Writing: On the Culture of Letters in South Africa*. New Haven: Yale University Press, 1988, 7. All subsequent references are to this edition and will be cited in the text.

10.  Goethe, Johann Wolfgang von. *Faust: Part 2*. Ed. H.G. Fiedler, Oxford: Blackwell, 1943.

11.  Wordsworth, William. 'A Slumber Did my Spirit Steal—Poems of the Imagination XI', *Poetical Works*. Ed. Thomas Hutchinson. London: Oxford University Press, 1969, 149.

12.  Coetzee, J.M. 'Noël Mostert and the Eastern Cape Frontier', in *Stranger Shores: Essays 1986–1999*. London: Secker and Warburg, 2001, 332–43.

13.  A. J. Smith's commentary on the poem is particularly enlightening, pointing out that Donne could have been writing to Lucy, Countess of Bedford.

Smith, A. J. *John Donne: The Complete English Poems*. London: Penguin, 1970, 390–3.

14. Alighieri, Dante. *Inferno*. Trans. Allen Mandelbaum. New York: Bantam, 1980.

15. Graham Pechey's comments on Coetzee's use of Dante are particularly illuminating. See Pechey, Graham 'Coetzee's Purgatorial Africa', in *Interventions*, 4, (3), 2002, 374–83. All subsequent references are to this edition and will be cited in the text.

16. Yeats, W.B. 'Sailing to Byzantium', in *Collected Poems*. London: Macmillan, 1982, 217.

17. Sanders, Mark. 'Disgrace', *Interventions*, 4 (3), 2002, 363–73.

18. Kafka, Franz. *The Trial*. Trans. Willa and Edwin Muir. Harmondsworth: Penguin, 1975.

19. Elleke, Boehmer. 'Not Saying Sorry, Not Speaking Pain: Gender Implications in *Disgrace*', in *Interventions*, 4, (3), 2002, 342–51, 343.

20. Heyns, Michiel. ' "Call No Man Happy": Perversity as Narrative Principle in *Disgrace*', in *English Studies in Africa*, 45, (1), 2002, 57–65.

21. Heyns points out that 'The dogs are brought to the clinic because they are unwanted: *because we are too menny*' (146) is a quote from *Jude the Obscure* highlighting the importance of the sympathetic imagination in Lurie's compassion for the abandoned dogs (Heyns 61).

22. Coetzee, J.M. *The Lives of Animals*. London: Profile, 2000, 48–9.

23. Levinas, Emmanuel. *Otherwise than Being, or Beyond Essence*. Trans. A. Lingis. Pittsburgh: Duquesne University Press, 1999, 185.

24. Coetzee, J.M. 'Erasmus: Madness and Rivalry', in *Giving Offense: Essays on Censorship*. Chicago: University of Chicago Press, 1996, 83–103. Coetzee derives his analysis from the Girardian schema of mimetic violence: 'desire is mimetic—that is to say, it seeks models for itself' (*Giving Offense* 92). Desire is insufficiency to itself, it is generated from a sense of lack or absence or incompletion, and seeks to eradicate that sense or feeling with fullness, fulfilment, which are primarily derived from acknowledgement. In a very basic sense, I only know myself to be present within the context of others, and I particularly feel myself present, sense my own being, when acknowledged by others in some way. The means by which desire slakes itself is by copying fullness, by copying that mode of being which others recognize and acknowledge, which explains the self-reproduction of society, socialization, and which is embodied in the commonplace phrase 'monkey

see, monkey do'. This mimesis within desire, this desire to ape, takes on a more sinister cast when we consider the implications of copying what it is that others see, desire, copy, acknowledge, for as soon as the desirable is mediated by an 'other', then a relationship of rivalry is established, an Oedipal economy that cannot but lead to conflict and violence. As Coetzee notes, 'desire does not involve only a desiring subject and a desired object: the object acquires its desirable value through the mediating glance of an Other whose desire serves as a model for the subject's imitation' (*Giving Offense* 91). This economy of rivalry within desire can be linked back to the socio-historical, in this case the rise of imperial modernity and capitalism, via another clichéd phrase: 'the law of the jungle', a law which depends upon an economy of scarcity, lack, and hence conflict. Desire leads to mimesis, which in turn leads to a mounting cycle of rivalrous violence, which in turn spirals into the erasure of difference, for it is the loss of difference that causes rivalry; it is always the similar, the twinned, who fight hardest: 'the appearance of doubles is a sign that the mimetic process has been carried to its ultimate reaches' (*Giving Offense* 92). Hence the peculiarly piquant irony of realism in Africa: in its desire to escape the hegemonic and obliterating gaze of the West and to establish a presence of difference, it imitates that rivalry and erases its difference. We have here a strange and monstrous twinning whereby Austen, Dickens, and Hardy are mirrored by Ngugi, Iyayi, and Achebe.

25. Marais, Michael. ' "Little Enough, Less than Little: Nothing": Ethics, Engagement, and Change in the Fiction of J.M. Coetzee', in *Modern Fiction Studies*, 46, (1), Spring 2000, 159–82, 177.
26. Kristeva, Julia. 'Revolution in Poetic Language', in *The Kristeva Reader*. Ed. Toril Moi. Oxford: Blackwell, 1986, 89–136.

# Shoring Up Britain
## David Dabydeen's Oceanic Sublime

JOHN CLEMENT BALL

The sea is a multivalent sign in West Indian literature and culture. In the work of Jean Rhys, Derek Walcott, George Lamming, V.S. Naipaul, and Caryl Phillips, among others, ocean-space may signify the salt-sweat of slavery and indenture, the blank surface of ancestral memory and buried history, the circumscribed possibilities of 'shipwrecked' lives, the restless fluidity of diasporic identity, a homesickness that can be as enervating as seasickness, and the complex relationality of what Paul Gilroy calls the 'Black Atlantic'. The cultural theorist Edouard Glissant, who defines 'the Caribbean' as 'a multiple series of relationships', also calls it a 'sea [that] exists within us'. This internalized space of outreach, this 'estuary of the Americas', as he calls it, makes the Caribbean islands not isolated and 'insular', as some would have it; on the contrary, Glissant writes, 'each island embodies openness. The dialectic between inside and outside is reflected in the relationship between land and sea' (139). The many oceans and seas that separate lands and peoples around the globe are paradoxically also a single space of continuity and connection; a naval historian observed this at the height of Britain's imperial dominance of the world's oceans. 'Though it has different

names in different parts', Spencer Wilkinson wrote, the sea 'is one
single uninterrupted surface', a fact that 'implies some kind of
community between all mankind' (qtd in Behrman 27). Glissant
would doubtless want to qualify that universalizing sentiment, but
his syncretistic view of Caribbean society and culture endeavours
to transcend the obvious oppositions engendered by a brutal,
violent history. His translator, J. Michael Dash, looks to the oceanic
shoreline as a place to ground the migrant individual when he
articulates one imperative at the heart of Glissant's relational poetics.
'The "unhoused" wanderer across cultures', Dash poetically writes,
'must be "rehoused" in the fissured history, the exposed sands, before
the surging sea' (xx).

One such transcultural wanderer is at the centre of David
Dabydeen's second novel, *Disappearance*. Its meditative narrative
loosely depicts the efforts of an engineer, from Guyana, to protect
some English cliffs against what he calls the 'rogue and monster
sea' that is eroding them and threatening a seaside village (20). Set
near Hastings—the same bit of coast where canonical English
history began in 1066 and where the protagonists of *The Satanic
Verses* would land over 900 years later—*Disappearance* turns the
ravaged English shoreline into an ambiguous symbol. Reviewers
typically describe the book as a 'condition of England' novel (e.g.
Jaggi; Rev. [*JCL*]); the disintegrating cliffs and the bucolic village
on top thereby represent a nation whose empire has collapsed,
shrinking its territory and its oceanic reach back to its original island
shores. Dabydeen, who wears his metaphors on his sleeve in this
novel, encourages such identifications. His unnamed narrator—a
'self-consciously post-colonial' voice, in one critic's view (McWatt
1997)—writes that 'the cliffs around Hastings were collapsing as
the Empire had crumbled' (121); 'the Empire had ended and what
was left was a palsied decay, like the state of the cliff' (133).

Post-war decolonization coincided with the arrival in England
of hundreds of thousands of West Indians—migrants who could
be discursively rendered as either building a newly constituted
nation or as eroding its foundations, depending on whether one
took an open or an insular view of national identity. Given that

context, what kind of England or Britain is implied by this novel's central image and event: a West Indian of African ancestry building a wall to protect the coast? If Dabydeen's protagonist is identified with the imperial and post-imperial sea—the slaves transported across the ocean as well as the waves of migrants washing up on England's shores and reshaping the nation's boundaries—can he, without self-contradiction, also be the one to, in his words, 'conquer' that sea: protecting the houses and gardens of elderly white Britons from disappearance? Is there a coherent vision of the nation—the land—swimming around in this overdetermined imagery of assault and defence? In a text driven more by association than narration—by ideas rather than incident—Dabydeen invites us to wring his symbolic spaces dry for every ounce of significance, however slippery his meaning may seem to be.

The narrator has it both ways. In one important paragraph he identifies himself with both the sea and the seawall. The sea appeals to him as something 'more restless than myself, belonging everywhere and nowhere'; its ability to 'dissolve' or erase the very history that was staged upon it liberates him, he says, from 'all disquieting thoughts about how I could belong or not belong'. 'I was seduced by its endless transformations, which promised me freedom from being fixed as an African, a West-Indian, a member of a particular nationality of a particular epoch' (132). But he immediately goes on to say that he longs for definition, 'to be a somebody, not any thing, and [I] resisted the sea's indiscriminateness' (132). And so he thinks of the wall as 'my identity, the obstacle I sought to put between shore and sea to assert my substantialness, my indissoluble presence, without reference to colour, culture, or age' (132–3). This oscillation between the countervailing attractions of fluidity and fixity, the ephemeral and the permanent, connection and division, evokes something of the ambivalence towards the sea that has marked English and European cultural history.

In Guyana, where reclaiming and protecting land from the sea has a long history, the narrator learned to admire the sea's eternal, patient, mindless power; he felt dwarfed by it even as he worked professionally to 'enslave it to my will'. 'What destruction could Europeans wreak on Africans or Africans on Asians compared to the sea's frenzy?' he wondered: 'How feeble were our strategies to colonise the land compared to the sea's ambition!' (17, 18). The English did colonize many lands and celebrated that taming of purportedly wild overseas places and peoples—the unruly in need of rule—as a domestication of the wild, restless ocean. Britannia, as the song went, 'rule[d] the waves'; as in Tennyson's characterization of Britain as 'the mightiest Ocean-power on earth, / ... the lord of every sea' (qtd in Behrman 28), the workings of metonymy extend those 'waves' to embrace the lands that Britannia crossed the waves to reach. It was a commonplace at the peak of the Empire and of British naval supremacy to call the sea the 'natural home of the Englishman', as James Anthony Froude did (qtd in Behrman 28). As Cynthia Behrman writes in *Victorian Myths of the Sea*, the English complacently claimed a sense of belonging to the sea, and a possession of it, greater than other nations'—a result of superior virtue and God's favour (22). This national feeling was part of the sense of entitlement to other lands that this substitution of sea for land and land for sea suggests. But as with all metonymic and metaphoric substitutions, the identification is imperfect, marked by difference as well as similarity. Foreign lands and peoples take enormous effort and power to rule, however incompletely; but no amount of effort or power can really enslave or control the sea, which will always be its own master.

This fact prompts Dabydeen to engage in some verbal punning with the word 'rule' that helps contextualize the narrator's own efforts to tame the sea. In Guyana, the acerbic labourer Swami mocks the engineers he works for, including the narrator, as 'straight-line folk' based on the way their 'bulldozer blade does slice a line in the land'. He says, 'all-you does live along ruler's edge. The white man who used to rule you left you with a plastic ruler to rule you. If you take the ruler away, what you will do? Without the edge, you'll wander off in the bush and get lost' (6). The cluster of intersecting binaries this passage implies recurs throughout the novel: the straight and narrow 'rule' of science—like that of imperialism—tames wild nature through the powers of civilization, culture, and technology. That which eludes or escapes such rule— that which is not straight or 'straightforward'—is 'the sinuous, the curved, the circular, the zigzagged, the unpredictable', the 'crooked' (75). The narrator's unconventional and anti-imperialist English landlady, Mrs Rutherford, recites that list as she encourages the narrator to transcend his engineer's habits of mind. But his work is premised on this very kind of hierarchical opposition: using science and technology to put a straight wall between the unruly sea and the crooked cliff, thus preventing the gardens and houses of civilization from being swallowed up and disappearing.

What they are threatened by is a sea that, as an implacable force in European history and global geography, comes saturated with symbolic and mythic associations that favour the side of crookedness and anarchy over the straight and ordered. As Alain Corbin shows in his masterful cultural history *The Lure of the Sea*, prior to the eighteenth century the Biblical creation and flood stories underpinned a dominant attitude of horror and repulsion towards the ocean. It was seen as a primordial remnant of chaos, the disorder that preceded civilization and still threatened it, so difficult was it to contain the sea's power or predict its behaviour. The Garden of Eden has no sea and, as Auden observes in *The Enchafèd Flood*, 'the first thing ... the author of the Book of Revelation notices in his vision of the new heaven and earth is that "*there was no more sea*" ' (6–7). Corbin writes, 'the ocean spoke to pious souls. Its roaring, its moaning, its sudden bursts of anger were perceived as so many reminders of the sins of the first humans, doomed to be engulfed by the waves; its sound alone was a permanent appeal to repent and an incitement to follow the straight and narrow path' (2–3). Add to that associations with sea monsters, the cruelty of the underwater food chain, the many natural and human dangers involved in sea travel, and the amorphous openness of a space that has no visible pathways, and the ocean accumulates a host of negative and threatening associations. It becomes a space of purgatory and exile, of drift and madness, and life itself becomes figured as a perilous journey through a world as unstable as the sea. In such a world, the straight and narrow was not an easy course to follow; it might even require divine support of the sort Moses received in finding a straight and narrow path across the Red Sea.

Over the eighteenth century, however,—a period of special interest to Dabydeen—ocean-space, along with the coastlines where it was imperfectly contained and accessed, was redeemed. The seaside became a place of renewal, refreshment, and pleasure; a place of meditative seclusion away from the madding crowd, but not entirely solitary; one could engage there in the pleasures of conversation with a select few individuals while being soothed by the rhythms of the waves. The narrator of *Disappearance*, with his solitary, meditative ways and his long conversations with just a few villagers, comes to the seaside with something of this agenda. The discursive taming of the sea in the eighteenth century led to a domestication and commodification of its benefits that continues in our own time: one went to the sea to be symbolically reborn or baptized by immersion in cold salt water that was now seen as physically and spiritually beneficial. Dabydeen's narrator doesn't bathe in the sea, but his perspective on it does draw on the sublime, a contemporaneous way of framing the sea (and other large phenomena such as cliffs) which combined that new sense of pleasure and personal uplift with the older view of the sea's primal mystery and danger. The sublime view emphasized the boundless vastness of the sea's surface and the profound mysteries of its depth, as well as its endless energy, mobility, and indifference to human activities or values. The very qualities that caused civilizing orders to construct the sea as a space of otherness now present what Edmund Burke would see as an 'agreeable amazement' that overwhelms the senses and emotions, even as the observer of this spectacle is reassured by his or her safe, if dizzying, position apart from it. Contemplation of primitive natural phenomena such as the sea, Corbin writes, 'invite[s] the observer to delight in any setting that demonstrates that Nature has sufficient force to resist the pressures of civilization. From this desire for a compensatory tempo the sublimeness of the ocean is born. Remember that human activities leave no trace upon the sea. As a barren landscape that mankind can neither arrange nor endow with moral significance, the immensity of the waters is the antithesis of the garden' (125).

The garden, like the city, is a time-honoured emblem of human civilization. In my book *Imagining London* I discuss Dabydeen's rendering of the city in *The Intended* (see 166–73), which also has some significant, if smaller and more contained, waterscapes. *Disappearance* makes fleeting references to London but picks the private garden as its chief representation of a settled world—as nature tamed by culture. Mrs Rutherford's obsessively tended garden runs 'down the edge of Dunsmere cliff and a sheer drop of ninety feet' (3). It and the house are therefore directly opposed to,—but also next to,—the sea. The garden strikes the narrator as 'the very picture of order'. 'Everything she planted', he says, 'was *engineered* to present a gentle spectacle of shapes and colours' (67; emphasis added). Moreover, that garden is essential to the narrator's acculturation since, in Mrs Rutherford's view, 'You only know a place when you can identify the flowers'; he duly learns their names and comes to see her plants as 'rooted in English history' (68). But as a fellow 'engineer' of a sort, Mrs Rutherford is no more clearly identified with the traditional order of history, Englishness, and civilization's rule (in both senses of that word) than the straight-and-narrow-wall-building narrator. It is she who urges him both to resist Englishness and to favour the unruly and crooked over the straight. She insists that her garden is actually a 'wilderness' (75) and is remarkably unconcerned about its possible collapse into the wild sea. As she blurs conceptual boundaries between her green and pleasant land and its supposed antithesis, she provides a model of Englishness that can help us better understand the narrator (whom she nurtures as avidly as her flowers) and his own contradictory affiliations with land and sea.

The sea-space in question here is, of course, the English Channel, the so-called 'streak of silver sea' that provided Britain with what the Victorians celebrated as their 'happy confinement' and 'splendid isolation' from continental Europe (Behrman 38, 43). With its rough weather the Channel was seen as a protective 'moat' or 'barrier' against foreigners (46). As a Victorian anthologist smugly observed, 'Thanks to the "silver streak" which is worth an entire European army, the English race, instead of exhausting its force ... in defending frontiers, has been enabled to give all its energies to strengthening its limbs at home and finding fresh fields in which to exercise them abroad' (qtd in Behrman 47). The Channel, in other words, facilitated imperialism and a national identity premised on it. Among the many ironic reversals invoked by Dabydeen's novel is the Channel's changing image: the waters that used to protect have become waters from which England must be protected. Now that Britannia no longer rules the waves, a former colonial from across the waves (and identified with them) is charged with providing protection from them.

Once he has done so and finished the wall, the narrator feels ambivalent about his achievement. He thinks it looks out of place, too visible and obviously man-made. 'Everything else was made by sea and wind', he says, but the wall interrupts the rhythms of nature and tide, settling, in his words, 'monumentally and unnaturally in the sand, refusing to budge' so that it looks 'monstrous and cruel, stubborn and brutishly arrogant, an awesome deformity. I regretted that I had made it and half wished that the sea would breach it, break it down to mere pebbles' (177). As another famous writer once opined, 'Something there is that doesn't love a wall' (Frost 94), and Dabydeen's ambivalent narrator seems to agree with that sentiment; however, as Robert Frost's poem makes clear, the walls that separate can also gather and connect, even if they have to be regularly broken down and built back up to do so.

Some recent books on Englishness and empire have shown how the prevailing sensibilities of the imperial nation have historically vacillated between an inclusive, borderless, global version of English identity and territory, and a more racially and territorially exclusive one. Ian Baucom's study of 'spaces of instability in the geography of Englishness' argues that nineteenth-century uprisings such as the Morant Bay Rebellion in Jamaica 'served to collapse any conception of England as a discrete, ocean-bounded space' (41). At its extreme, this global embrace leads to the 'vision' John Stuart

Mill and his contemporaries articulated of what Baucom calls an 'empire without interruptions, … without boundaries, or breaks, or, quite frankly, oceans' (167). Simon Gikandi, in 'calling attention to the unstable zones and contested boundaries that conjoin and divide metropolitan cultures and colonial spaces,' pursues some of the geographical and political implications of the fact that 'it has never been clear where the identity between the colonizer and the colonized ends and the difference between them begins' (2). As Homi Bhabha, Stuart Hall, and Paul Gilroy have also shown, the tensions between inclusive and exclusive versions of Britishness or Englishness remain divisive, and in post-imperial, multicultural Britain the redefinition of the nation's territory, culture, society, and identity remains an urgent, ongoing project.

In this context, it is fitting that Dabydeen chooses the seaside for the investigation of post-imperial Englishness. The writer who once referred to England as 'the third largest West Indian island' (Birbalsingh 174) makes the restless sea and shoreline the keys to a migrant, black British thematics. In doing so he chooses spaces that defy fixity, embodying fluidity and instability and transformation. While the sea is obviously a space, even the shoreline is most appropriately thought of as a space rather than a line. With its tides and shifting contours, its inclusion of land and sea—culture's houses and gardens and people as well as the forces of brute nature that threaten them—the shoreline is an in-between area, a liminal zone where differences collide but also overlap and vie for dominance. The nation, Dabydeen implies, is still a site of contestation, and locating 'the "unhoused" wanderer between cultures' at the seaside enables him and the novel to enact that contestation in a highly symbolic space: to shore up the nation so there will continue to be one and to break down any straight and narrow symbols of what its boundaries should be.

## Works Cited

Auden, W.H. *The Enchafèd Flood: or The Romantic Iconography of the Sea.* New York: Vintage, 1950; rpt.1967.

Ball, John Clement. *Imagining London: Postcolonial Fiction and the Transnational Metropolis*. Toronto: Toronto University Press, 2004.

Baucom, Ian. *Out of Place: Englishness, Empire, and the Locations of Identity*. Princeton: Princeton University Press, 1999.

Behrman, Cynthia Fausler. *Victorian Myths of the Sea*. Athens, OH: Ohio University Press, 1977.

Birbalsingh, Frank. 'David Dabydeen: Coolie Odyssey.' [interview]. in *Frontiers of Caribbean Literature in English*. Ed. Birbalsingh. New York: St Martin's, 1996, 167–82.

Corbin, Alain. *The Lure of the Sea: The Discovery of the Seaside 1760–1840*. Trans. Jocelyn Phelps. Harmondsworth: Penguin, 1994.

Dabydeen, David. *Disappearance*. 1993. London: Vintage, 1999.

Dash, J. Michael. Introduction. Glissant xi–xlv.

Frost, Robert. *Robert Frost's Poems*. Ed. Louis Untermeyer. New York: Washington Square, 1960.

Gikandi, Simon. *Maps of Englishness: Writing Identity in the Culture of Colonialism*. New York: Columbia University Press, 1996.

Gilroy, Paul. *The Black Atlantic: Modernity and Double Consciousness*. Cambridge: Harvard University Press, 1993.

Glissant, Edouard. *Caribbean Discourse: Selected Essays*. Trans. J. Michael Dash. Charlottesville: Virginia University Press, 1989.

Jaggi, Maya. Rev. of *Disappearance*, by David Dabydeen, in the *Times Literary Supplement*, 3 December. 1993: 20.

McWatt, Mark. ' "Self-Consciously Post-Colonial": The Fiction of David Dabydeen,' in *The Art of David Dabydeen*. Ed. Kevin Grant. Leeds: Peepal Tree, 1997.

Rev. of *Disappearance* by David Dabydeen, in *Journal of Commonwealth Literature* 29, (2) 1993: 122.

# PART THREE

## Nations and Empires

# Reading 1857

## The Government Report and
## Indigenous 'Narrative'

SUKESHI KAMRA

Legend has it that the last Mughal emperor, Bahadur Shah Zafar, exiled to Burma in 1858, composed a couplet by which today many Indians remember the 'mutiny'. It has emerged as a short hand for the brief moment of seemingly sweeping expression of the outrage of a subjugated people. It reads 'Kitna hai badnaseeb Zafar, dafn ke liye / Do gaz zameen bhi na mili koo-e-yar mein' (How unfortunate is Zafar that for his burial / He could not get even a couple of yards in the beloved land). A history of brutality and humiliation, made only too visible in 1857, had transformed itself into the more palatable language of nostalgia. The realpolitik, one could say, is domesticated in the trope of exile. In this very fact is proof of the unsayability of unbearable knowledge of defeat.

---

*I am grateful to the Social Sciences and Humanities Research Council of Canada and the Shastri Indo-Canadian Institute for funding the research on which this paper is based.

I am reminded of an extended email conversation that took place in December 2000 between Amitav Ghosh and Dipesh Chakrabarty in which the insurrection of 1857 emerges as one of the points of discussion. Ghosh, the more interested of the two in probing the possible significance of the insurrection, wonders about the impact of defeat on the people. The 'real' question 1857 raises for him, he states, is whether there is any option other than refusing to represent one's subordination to oneself in conditions of defeat.[1] This conversation, that ranges much further and wider than I have here suggested, pinpoints what are no doubt the more major obstacles facing any investigation of a historical moment that has left scant record of the opinion of the losing side.[2] These are: locating places where a resistant subordinated opinion and history registers and negotiating the Scylla and Charybdis of history writing—that Rosalind O'Hanlon has usefully described as the choice between declaring the alterity of the othered, subordinated, and victimized of history (and thus ensuring their continued erasure from the politics of presence that is history) on the one hand, and declaring the discoverability of a sovereign consciousness in the traces of subordinated opinion, wherever these may reside, on the other. O'Hanlon describes the uncomfortable interpretative place in which this leaves us: 'If we accept, as I assume we should, that no hegemony can be so penetrative and pervasive as to eliminate all ground for contestation or resistance, this leaves us with the question as to how we are to configure their presence, if it is not to be in terms of liberal humanist notions of subjectivity and agency' (74). And although the waters are proverbially more muddy than a racialized reading allows of the insurrection of 1857 (class interests, as Marx and Engels pointed out in their articles on the insurrection, for instance), in general subordinated opinion was indigenous. Thus associating 'Indian' with 'losing side' here is done advisedly and in the interest of covering subordinated opinion but acknowledges that a race-identified collective identity was not quite a reality.[3]

The reading Ghosh provides of 1857, as a rupture/juncture of overwhelming significance because it marks a shift in knowledge on the part of the colonized (proof of which lies in the refusal to represent their subordination to themselves), gives the kind of resistance that O'Hanlon prefers to find is practically structurally predicted short shrift.[4] Further, it is not borne out by the rather large, rather bald, and often emotional representations of abjection and despair that one encounters in regional language newspapers of the 1870s—a period and indigeneous public culture that writes from within the shadow of 1857. For instance, the Native Newspaper Report for Bengal for the week ending 18 March 1876 reports on an editorial article that appeared in the *Bharat Mihir* on 8 March 1876.

The same paper writes the following in its opening editorial, headed 'Then what has India to hope?':

Even a dangerously sick man speaks out his mind in a delirium, and in broken and indistinct language, if not in an intelligible and methodical way. But India has no life, no capacity of feeling. For if she had, we would not have become, for all time, the sport of others, an instrument of their will, to pander to their pleasure. […] The people of India are wanting in courage; they are weak, cowardly, ignorant and timid (p. 2 of report).

This does not mean that 1857 is better theorized as part of a continuous narrative of resistance (with us seeking for evidence of such resistance) instead of as a rupture. Instead, I would suggest, it is more profitably regarded as a particularly heightened moment of contest in which hegemony was as much defined and shaped by its own sense of a limited knowledge of actual and potential sites and forms of resistance, as resistance was by its own sense of uncertainty of the shift in relations so boldly and confidently announced in government proclamations and its applicability to the individual (native). I am by no means suggesting that the very real power imbalance should be ignored in discussions of forms of rule but that an assumption that abjection best describes the position in which the defeated find themselves is best interrogated. My choice of method owes much to the work done by anthropologists such as Marshall Sahlins, whose analysis of

colonialism for its forced encounter between radically different
societies led him to conclude that the moment of encounter is
marked by both reproduction (of attitudes and inherited ways of
making meaning) and transformation.[5] I am, of course, also heavily
indebted to O'Hanlon who suggests that a possible way out of the
binary she describes, while still keeping faith with the victims of
history, is to apply strategies associated with thinking of the subject
as a 'decentered' subject and thus to consider texts in which
government suborns native opinion, for instance, as texts that 'reveal'
not essence (whether governmental or native) but the production
of a momentarily solidified identity as opposing sides engaged one
another. This she describes as a 'Subaltern strategy' (87).[6] The
advantage of both approaches for me is that they focus attention
on the need to factor in conflict and its economy into any attempt
to read texts produced from within this economy. They require,
that is, paying attention to the government report as a place that
expresses what Sudipta Kaviraj has described as 'conceptual habits'
(309), produces strategies in its 'descriptions' of governmental
'response' to the insurrection, and stages the conflict in very
particular ways. And it is also the place which registers practised
ways of interacting with governmental representatives an indigenous
populace had developed in the form of native deposition.

The colonial text to which many interested in early colonial
India turn is of course government record. By 1857, record keeping
and archiving was a well established function of the Company
government (the Imperial Archives were formally constituted only
in 1891).[7] This genre of colonial text (government literature) is
described somewhat expansively by Ranajit Guha as inclusive of
official forms of correspondence such as 'the exordial letter,
telegram, dispatch and communiqué to the terminal summary,
report, judgement and proclamation' (4) and writings of the nonofficial sector 'symbiotically related to the Raj' (3). And, as Spivak
has pointed out in her piece on the Rani of Sirmur, amongst other
places, it is one of the places where native opinion is prominently
recorded. Instrumentalized as such opinion is, it is, she goes on to
prove, the place where colonial anxieties and desires are inscribed

or find expression.[8] Given that the government record is a text that originates solely within the province of one of the two constituent groups that make up government records—government and the 'public' it administers—with its very particular stakes vis-à-vis the 'mutiny', to undertake a reading of government's act of interpretation of native intent seems only fitting. However, even in so doing it is not as if that monolithic thing we refer to as government opinion can be assessed: the Civil Service was a complex arrangement of class and regional interests (as the body of literature on the Civil Service, in its discussions of internal politics suggests).[9] Thus acts of reading occur at every level: the junior official producing the report interprets indigenous culture for his senior, generally the district magistrate, who in turn forwards it to the office of the governor of the province, sometimes appending comments that interpret the junior official's intention and opinion, from where the report makes its way to the Government of India, based in Fort William in Calcutta, where its receipt is recorded, as is the acknowledgement sent to the government of the province, and note is made of the status of the report—whether it is simply filed as report, or as a report requiring follow up (in instances where action is recommended) and, of course, specifying the Governor-General-in-Council's orders.[10] What influences the readings—shared orientalist assumptions that appear to have formed part of the common sense of civil and government cultures for instance—and shifting patterns of influence (with reports filed by junior officials being legitimized by senior offices in some instances and not in others, so that they are at the basis of some governmental orthodoxy for instance) make administrative culture a rather amorphous collection of mixed registers, received knowledges, and regional interests and variations. This is of course in contradistinction to a training that emphasized regularized and invariant rule and ill-prepared officials to deal with the contingent.[11]

Consider the following entry, typical of reports whose main function was to detail insurrectionary activity and text and that grounds some of my observations. No. 137 in the report for the week of 7 August 1857 opens with a summary of the proclamation issued by Nana Saheb on 6 July 1857, goes on to reproduce the (translated) text of the proclamation, and concludes with a summary comment. The proclamation rehearses the most common of rationales for insurrectionary activity—conversion of 'Hindustanis' to Christianity.[12] The interpretative comment that follows reads: 'The style of the Proclamation is exceedingly simple and clear—evidently intended for the common people. It is very remarkable for the Mahomedan tone and language used, although issued, by the Nán4, a Hindu' (P 188/46: 154). What is remarkable about the official act of interpretation here is what it does not identify as a concern: the proclamation's playing on what were prominent debates within the Anglo Indian press—over the civilizing mission and its relationship to Christianity. In general, in the press, the category of native emerges as both proof of the need for the civilizing mission (with the debate being over whether civilizing could or could not be accomplished without Christianizing) and also as proof of the danger attending it (after all, the native was considered stubbornly attached to an inherited cultural logic).[13] For instance, the *Bombay Times* of 7 May 1857 reproduces an article that it claims appeared in the *Dacca Times* of 25 April 1857. In this piece, the paper comments on the absence of Christianity in 'state' policy and institutions and takes to task two Anglo Indian papers, the *Hurkaru* and the *Phoenix* (that argued against Christianizing on the grounds that it was endangering the empire in the East), for taking another Anglo Indian paper, the *Friend of India*, to task for what the piece describes as the *Friend's* 'noble' article on the subject. The *Dacca Times* states: 'We forbid the Bible in our colleges and schools. We are now about to forbid preaching; and yet the writers in the *Hurkaru* and *Phoenix* suppose that India will become Christian.'[14] Thus what is identified in one Anglo Indian paper as a potential cause of revolt is identified in the other as a reason to revolt. In other words, official comment (or this official's comment) shows little interest in interrogating native text for signs of intellection and strategic thinking. It reads, instead, by terms made available by the a priori of civilizational arrest—religion rationalizes everything native, including forms of language—and focuses attention on formal aspects of the text. In both of its conclusions (religion marks an absolute difference in communities and that the common folk speak a plain language), the reading is remarkably inaccurate.[15] The only hint there is of the discomfort produced in the official by the native text's refusal to fit the only coordinates he appears to possess—to rationalize indigenous reality—is his 'it is very remarkable'. Not enough, though, to make him question his reading.

In this somewhat bafflingly calm and lazy interpretative act (noticeable all the more for the panic in newspapers),[16] we find validation of Hannah Arendt's conclusion that bureaucracy in India was a 'substitute for government' (185), one that marks (European) imperial culture's discovery of 'bureaucracy as a principle of foreign domination' (185). Surprisingly enough, the same kind of acute comment was made by the *Daily News* and reproduced in the *Bombay Times* of 22 August 1857. Entitled 'The Indian Crisis', it says 'the fatal vices of our Indian system' is that there is 'a paper government' that rules 'not through its own institutions, by its own people, or by the ears and eyes of all earnest and efficient men of their own nation, but by reams on reams of written records of functionaries, stunted and dwarfed by the restrictions of bureaucracy'.[17] Thus I read government reports of November and December 1857, but that have entries that date back to July in some instances, for their particular forms of occupation of a space of indeterminacy.

If we turn our attention to 'the native', surely the knowledge that they, the indigenous population, were the subject of a heightened enquiry—required to prove their innocence (loyalty), bombarded with threatening governmental announcements and so on—informs the text of narratives by the class of testifier we find represented in government records. This is to say that I expect native narratives produced under conditions of threat to be always already strategic. As Ghosh remarks in the conversation with Chakrabarty, a writing always already informed by fear is expected of colonial culture.[18] His conclusion is supported by Bayly's finding that Indians adapted to censorship before and after the rebellion, 'wrapping up political information in everyday phrases', and in general pursuing a policy of careful expression (322). Of the class of informant, in particular, he observes that this class was 'aware of what their masters wanted to hear: "the citizens pray anxiously for the return of British power" was a constant refrain' (328).[19] The same observation, when turned around, would find utterance to be intentionally strategic and thus involved in maximizing the 'ambivalence' that Homi Bhabha has found to be definitive of colonial apparatuses. If we factor in the possibility of strategic expression, native deposition in whatever form it was required (narrative, diary, deposition, protestation of loyalty) is readable as a space of equivocation surrounded by strategies of reading that are themselves informed by anxiety of interpretation. In the government report, then, the performative has a significant presence, although the entire exercise of requiring deposition and its attestation by an Anglo Indian official, and recording of it in as factual a manner as possible suggests the entire act is presumed to fall under the category of constative (in this it shares with legal procedure, rhetoric, and apparatus in general)—where government interest is in nailing down 'the truth' and the interrogated's act is confessional (hence 'truthful'), a narrativizing of event in which all levels involved share in the process of arriving at 'the truth'. The production of truth in what was the discursive nerve centre of colonial government had of course very real effects, some of which I will describe in the conclusion.

The government department under whose jurisdiction surveying, recording, judging (what we would describe as 'managing'), and filing correspondence from the civilian population lay was 'Public', a sub-department of the Home Department.[20] Collected into weekly reports, with a 'Table of Contents' in which dates, originating point of report, subject, and status of report are noted, Public Consultations Records—as they were then called—have as routine entries from January to August 1857 requests and decisions on furloughs, resignations from the East India Company, complaints about the conduct of officials, submission of copies of the Classified lists of books, quarterly reports of the board of examiners for the Civil Service, and proceedings of legislative councils of the presidencies. In the July–August weekly reports, however, there are more entries related to the insurrection. Newly introduced punitive measures, such as laws and promulgations, conferring on various levels of government the legal power to prosecute Indian presses and newspapers, put suspects on trial and so on, circulars intended to inform the many levels of the Civil Service of the extent of their power in these extraordinary circumstances, appear routinely. And then there are extracts from articles considered seditious and from rebel proclamations, narratives and diaries of natives, and individual and collective letters professing loyalty to the Company government.

Any and all of the various forms of government activity recorded in correspondence speak of the centrality of the Civil Service in 'managing' the crisis, as much as the detailed recording speaks of the centrality of the administrative record to the writing of official history of the mutiny (it is the 'source book' so to speak). Needless to say, government record is also where the language with which the mutiny was to be represented (thus claiming the space of the legitimate) circulated in these early days of the insurrection, also the days in which government control was least secure. If one had to single out a text around which Civil Service activity, writing (reports), and internal dialogue was mobilized it would have to be the memorandum sent by the Governor-General- in-Council on 10 July 1857, announcing the government's decision to implement a system of reward and punishment and asking for the widest circulation of the same within indigenous circles.[21] The memorandum is thus as much interested, if not more, in ensuring that an indigenous civilian and military population is made aware of the terms separating loyal from disloyal intention and of the extensive surveillance activity of the Civil Service as it is in operationalizing a system of control. The order reads: 'The Governor General in Council hereby offers, and authorizes the payment of the under-mentioned rewards by British Civil or Military Authorities in every part of India' (182). Rewards are for apprehension of deserters or those guilty of seducing, for information leading to apprehension, and for delivering to government property plundered or carried off by force. Punishment is associated by the same logic with a refusal to do the above. Thus the concluding paragraph reads:

Every Pensioner of the Government who conceals or harbors any person whom he knows or has reason to believe to have been guilty of mutiny or desertion, or of waging war again˙˙ the Government, or of seducing or attempting to seduce any Officer or Soldier from his allegiance or duty, or who fails to do his utmost to secure the apprehension and conviction of such offender, or who neglects to give immediate notice to the Civil or Military Authorities of any mutinous or rebellious designs of which he may become cognizant, will, in addition to punishment to which he is liable by law, forfeit his pension (P88/46: 183).[22]

Government's dependence on the Civil Service at this critical time for the wide circulation and operationalizing of what Foucault has described as positive mechanisms of power (rewards in the form of money and land), to which negative mechanisms are attached in the workings of government power (forfeit of pension and land), is clear. Given that this was meant for circulation among the indigenous population, it is not surprising that what is absented is how precisely the 'truth' is to be discovered. As for the official reading of civil participation produced in this memorandum, it is already primed to find the civilian population's participation to be of a second order—guilty chiefly of harbouring or refusing to inform on the movement of fugitives from justice (government).

The other part of this key strategy of managing the crisis is Canning's Resolution of 31 July 1857. Saul David states that this resolution followed on the heels of Canning's hearing of 'the indiscriminate slaughter of Indians' (237) by officials and military.[23] It was meant, he adds, to act as 'a series of guidelines on how the civil authorities were to administer Act XIV' (237). This memo was meant for internal circulation but was leaked to the Anglo Indian press and we can only speculate about the extent of its circulation in and via the Indian owned press.[24] The text of the memorandum suggests a strategic concern with discovering a loyal population (and in fact the leaked memo drew furious responses from the Anglo Indian community and press for its suggested leniency to the indigenous population).[25] The category of indigenous public identified as the concern of the Resolution is the seemingly overwhelmingly large indeterminate one, whose loyalty could not be established definitively. This is the group that could not or did not, for instance, provide certificates 'in their favour from Officers of their regiments' (P 188/48; weekly report for 13 November 1857: 50) or were 'without any such ready means of clearing themselves from the presumptive evidence of their deep guilt' (P 188/48; weekly report for 13 November 1857: 50).

Behaviour and attitude of this indeterminate native figure that Canning suggests are readable as proof of loyalty include a provable absence from the scene of the crime, and the ability to prove a reluctant participation in scenes of revolt. Even the choice of returning to the village upon the disbanding of the regiment (instead of joining rebels) is, Canning states, proof of loyalty: 'there were men who appeared to have had no heart in the revolt, though they failed in their duty as soldiers, and who have evinced their peaceable disposition, and their want of sympathy with those who are now armed in open rebellion against the Government, by dispersing to their villages when the Regiment broke up, and mixing quietly with the rural population' (P 188/48; weekly report for 13 November 1857: 51). Probably the most powerful and least acknowledged of places for the discovery of innocence lies with the persistent framing of the insurrection as a law and order problem, not a political one. Thus the Resolution encourages a finding of loyalty even where guilt is established if the native proves to be 'normally' a law abiding citizen:

Where the number of men guilty of what it is impossible to pardon is so great, the Government will gladly seize every opportunity of reducing the work of retribution before it, by giving a free pardon to all who can show that they have a claim to mercy on this ground, provided that they have not been guilty of any heinous crime against person or property, or aided or abetted others in the commission of any such crime (P 188/48; weekly report for 13 November 1857: 50–1).

The strategic nature of this 'finding' of innocence is baldly asserted in the introductory clause ('Where the number of men guilty of what it is impossible to pardon'). Interrogation, encouraging the filing of narratives, diaries, public protestations of loyalty (of which there are more than a few in the Anglo Indian press) all form part of the strategy of discovering innocence in as many places as possible, one found so distasteful by an Anglo Indian community that read this as proof of government's betrayal of its (own) public.

It is possible to argue that in the very contortions to which this subject people were forced—including abjection and protestations of loyalty (of which government records for this time are full)—are signs of psychological violence, signs that belong on a continuum that has at one end of a spectrum the infamous image of men being blown from cannons (turned into spectacle at that) and at the other verbal utterances in which equivocation, servility, and other modalities typical of depositions made under conditions of threat appear and which, needless to say are in themselves destabilizing of the very requirement that these be truthful.

❖

In the rest of this paper I will offer a reading of two native texts. One is somewhat innocuously described in the 'Table of Contents' of the weekly report dated 6 November 1857 as 'an account of the occurrences' in Cawnpore (Kanpur) from 5 June to 2 July 1857 by 'a native gentleman residing at Cawnpore' (P 188/48; report for week of 6 November 1857). We know from other sources that Nunna Nawab was suspected of affiliation with insurrectionists. The other is described as the 'deposition of Keramut Ally, Native Doctor of Golaghat, taken on solemn affirmation by Capt. Holroyd, Assistant Commissioner' (P 188/48; report dated 18 December 1857).[26] Both texts are riddled with an anxiety to declare innocence even though the subject headings in the table of contents and genre indicators ('narrative', 'report') suggest quite another purpose for the inclusion of these texts—that they are not filed for 'orders' but for information/archiving purposes.

The two texts share a strategy of narration. They begin with factual observations, offering the kind of detailed description that was typical of diaries maintained by government officials at the time. The entry that reproduces Nunna Sahib's diary begins thus: 'On the morning of the 5th June last, say about 3 a.m., the 2nd Light Cavalry and the 1st Regiment of Native Infantry broke out in open rebellion, and proceeded towards Nawabgunge, burning every bungalow that fell in their way;' (P 188/48; weekly report for 6 November 1857: 27). But the safe difference between him and the rebel other that forms his subject breaks down as Nunna Sahib introduces himself into the narrative as its subject and where we first witness a concerted attempt to situate himself as victim, subject to the whims of insurrectionists:

When they reached near Mirza Hajee's bungalow, some six or eight troopers were dispatched to take me to the Nana, but I not answering their first call, again a party of about 100 troopers was sent, and effecting their entrance by forcing open the backdoor, made me their prisoner. I of course mounted my horse with a few of my followers, and went to the Nana, surrounded by mutineer troops who threatened to take my life if I should decline compliance with their wishes (P 188/48; weekly report for 6 November 1857: 23).

The reiteration of this threat of bodily harm occurs too often to note here, including references to being placed deliberately in the line of fire by rebels. That is, the narrative employs threat of bodily harm to rationalize activities that are described in government releases as evidence of disloyalty. The activity of joining rebels is one (more neutrally, being in their vicinity) and the other is a refusal to act as informant. This too informs the Nawab's statement of disclosure that reads:

I had heard previously to this, from a sepoy who came to the guard which was over me at about mid-day, and appeared to me by his manner and language to be disaffected with Nana, that they intended to beguile the Europeans out of their entrenchment, and then take them by surprise and kill them. I satisfied myself about the truth of the information and tried to apprise the same to the

Major General of impending danger, but I am sorry I could not do so on any account. I imagine I would have succeeded in sending a man to the entrenchment with the news of the intended treachery, but the sepoys besieged it on all sides to the extent of a mile, and would not allow any body to pass through them. Besides, the two troopers who stood guard over me watched my movements (P 188/48; weekly report for 6 November 1857: 34).

Statements such as these of course do not of themselves set up the government representative as interlocutor, except by way of emphasis that links threat with otherwise, seemingly, voluntary action—of having physically moved to the Nana's camp.

The 'deposition of Keramut Ally, Native Doctor of Golaghat' as reported is remarkably similar, even though it is provided in quite another part of the country (Assam). It too begins with a factual account of the breakout of disturbance and the expected naming of names and quite of its own accord turns into a narrative of justification.[27] The part of the narrative that represents Ally's movements also indicates his position was the untenable one of ambiguity (regarding intent). He states:

I should have reported these matters before, but Mr. Mahoney was sick, and I was afraid to write in Nagree, for they had all sworn to kill any one who said any thing about it. At first I could not tell Rughoonath's (Subadar) mind, but when I found he was loyal, I then told him what I knew; I have been in great dread of what the Sepoys would do to me, for they said, even if they were dismissed the Service, still they would have their revenge (P 188/48; report dated 18 December 1857: 76).

There are a couple of compelling features of Nunna Sahib's diary and Keramut Ally's deposition as we encounter them in government record that I would like to note. One is the possibility that we are witnessing the presence of the formulaic, one that derives from or is appropriate to narratives of fear. Thus narratives do not attempt to display uniqueness, rather, rein in all uniqueness via an emphasis on fear. The rebel other is as instrumentalized as is fear itself in this attempt at securing the space of 'innocence'. The other is what these narratives accomplish as the subject of government reports.[28] The turning of native opinion (perceptions of that always already untrustworthy other) into the material of factual report (the function of diaries, which officials were required to maintain) acts to 'discover' a loyal citizen of government—willing, after all, when able to act as native informant, proof of which is the diary of course—in place of a potential insurrectionist. As texts that are labelled 'narrative' and 'diary' these indeterminate texts are entered into the same space as the innumerable diaries and narratives filed by officials.

There is a remarkable consonance between the choices made in these two 'narratives'—of a kind of formulaic that derives its form from the politics of intimidation and that prominently identifies fear and threat as the reason for an apparent absence of proof of loyalty—and Canning's Resolution. What I am suggesting here is the possibility that native accounts such as the ones discussed here reproduce a logic that is established and legitimized in Canning's memo.

There is a continuity of logic between reports that include indigenous accounts written in their own defence, and reports filed by regional Civil Service officials—the very officials to whom Canning's memo is directed—in which the indigene is represented or spoken for. Officials as much as an indeterminate indigenous public describe a politics of fear, which in turn rationalizes the absence of a conspicuous display of loyalty. No. 121 in the weekly report for 13 November 1857 records the Commissioner of the division of Nudea's submission of a letter received by a landowner from rebels in the area. Entry 121 is the commissioner's own communication with the governor-general's office. The Commissioner, identified as A. Grotke, in effect offers his interpretation of the letter, the intent discoverable in the landowner's action of turning it in to the authorities, and, in general, instructs on the extent to which the entire incident (including the rebels, the most distant of objects in this chain of information and manifest only by this reported letter) is significant. I reproduce a paragraph from the report filed by Grotke.

I agree with Mr Eden in thinking, that the letter has been composed and dispatched with the object only of alarming the old man, but the effects of such attempts at annoyance is mischievous on a community which depends on gossip for their knowledge of what is going on out of the Lower Provinces (P 188/48; weekly report for 13 November 1857: 97).

This rather lighthearted and dismissive reading refuses to legitimize the landowner's concerns and the possibility of strategic thinking on the part of the natives (that the landowner was hedging his bets is at least as much a possibility—given the letter which is entry 122—as is the possibility that his action is motivated by a genuine loyalty). Further, the memo brings the larger native community— 'community which depends on gossip'—as subject of comment and inquiry and appears equally unconcerned with the position of a populace caught between the fervour, propaganda, and threats of rebel groups and the claims of government, claims that are assumed in Grotke's condescending and casual reference to (his certain knowledge of) the psychology of the people. Reducing the threat posed by the otherwise assumed indeterminacy of the native population and opinion in this time by describing insurrectionary discourse as 'mischief' and dismissing native intelligence in the reduction of their political interests to 'gossip' Grotke recuperates the landowner and community in general for the much threatened relationship imagined in the term 'loyalty' (a term and conceptual apparatus linked with the notion of self-respect, and honour in elite native culture).

If we believe that discursive forms manage and regulate relations, then loyalty and its use by both government and the native elite in an exchange suited to differing purposes (discovering in an otherwise suspect population signs of empire loyalism that, for natives, translated into survival and even social gain) is the discourse by which the realpolitik was misrecognized. Situating this generalization within the specific context of the landowner and his letter, in his action of turning in the letter, he enacts inherited patterns of relating—between subject and ruler. At the same time, this very inherited pattern—of visible expression of loyalty—ensures protection of government. That is, in both the zemindar's action and Grotke's naturalized assumption of his own access to native intent, the naturalized is the sedimented relationship and the kind of self-regulation associated with loyalty.

Not surprisingly, loyalty is trotted out as much by regional officials in what is an act of interpretation of native behaviour by the absolute of loyalty (where native action is denied the rationale of instrumentality and strategy) as it is by natives no doubt anxious about punitive measures. Records are replete with such instances, of which a report originating in the office of the judge of Tirhut, R. Forbes (dated 9 November 1857), and sent to Samuels, Commissioner of Revenue, Patna who then forwarded it to the governor-general's office, dated 12 November 1857, is a typical example. Forbes commends the Nujeeb Guard for their loyalty on the occasion of the mutiny of the Irregular Cavalry between 31 July and 1 August 1857. Samuels adds his own comment before forwarding it in which he emphasizes the sentiment of the original by stating that in his opinion, had the guards not proved faithful, 'what has taken place at every other Station where there has been a mutiny, would to a certainty have occurred here' (P 188/48; weekly report for 14 December 1857: 56). Interestingly enough, this is the same guard that E.A. Samuels singles out in correspondence (dated 8 October 1857) as proof that native monitoring of the Anglo Indian press for strategic purposes was routine.[29]

Thus the Civil Service finds as much relief in the discourse of loyalty that combined with Canning's Resolution and its indicating of places for finding loyalty/innocence made the task of discovering a loyal population somewhat easier. At the same time, there is much anxiety about accurately discerning/reading emotional and psychological attitudes; after all, attempting to figure out whether there is a 'want of sympathy' with the rebels and little 'heart' in joining the revolt is a daunting task. Anxiety about the terms of engagement required of them is often frankly the subject of correspondence. For instance, a report filed by Muir in Agra (dated 17, 18, 19, 20 October 1857) and sent to J.W. Sherer in Kanpur, who then forwarded it on the 17 October to C. Chester,

Commissioner of Allahabad, who in turn forwarded it to C. Beadon in the office of the governor-general, has Sherer represent the opinion of Hope Grant on the situation in Delhi. The relevant part reads:

I have been talking with Hope Grant about the exile of all the inhabitants from Delhi. I have not quite made out what is the state of the argument against the return of the well-disposed. Besides the difficulty of guarding the city, he speaks of the impossibility of distinguishing the guilty from the innocent, requiring that all should be involved in punishment until they have been proved (as I understand) their active loyalty in our behalf throughout the struggle (P 188/ 48; weekly report for 6 November 1857: 16).

Other forms of this anxiety are everywhere noted, particularly in the language of hesitation and over-compensation: 'to the complete satisfaction of his European superior', 'it was the obvious duty of such native officers to communicate with British authorities', and 'that he exerted himself to the utmost of his power to support his Government', are as common as are assertions about the reliability of evidence in phrases such as 'The zemindar did undoubtedly display a marked degree of loyalty', 'He took our side very openly from the commencement', and other phrases that indicate the relationship between officer and native is proof of the reliability of the native (as is the word of the officer of course).

✧

In the extraordinary conditions of 1857, loyalty works—evidenced in government literature, including native declarations of loyalty filed with the government and submitted to Anglo Indian newspapers—the way in which symbolic domination normally does. It particularly masks the interrogative practices and culture of intimidation by transforming them into the more benign modes of interaction typical of the feudal mode. In fact, on occasions, officials even express outrage at the kind of homogenizing and criminalizing of (their) communities that the Anglo Indian and English presses were indulging in so widely at the time. Paternalism that is exhibited in much Civil Service correspondence and in which we find described the much discussed civilizational imperative, is thus the place of transformation of relations. Not unexpectedly, it refuses the possibility of instrumentality on the part of the culture being subjected to a more than usually heightened 'reading'; there are some reports in which civil officials speak of 'hedging bets' and so on, but more often than not excused on the grounds that equivocation and its forms identify the presence of a politics of fear. It is of course necessary if the fiction of the transparency of the native was to be maintained at the very moment of its erosion.

The colonial government's mobilizing of the rhetoric of loyalty at a time when symbolic forms of control were more available than material forms is not unusual. John Illiffe, for instance, notes the ways in which colonialism in African countries availed of and destroyed honour cultures—honour is of course the ideology and practice in which the rhetoric of loyalty is embedded.[30] Conflating Illiffe and Bourdieu, who in *Practical Reason* locates honour as the defining feature of aristocratic or precapitalist societies (87), government and populace participate in a homologizing of opinion that is meant to discover a loyal population for government and to re-establish, for the indigenous population, the terms of political relationship by which it could be 'assured' of the continued existence of paternalistic rule.

Further uses of a symbolic mode of control that surely was most effectively and latterly discovered in 1857 (or assumed to be so) set in almost immediately. Ritual, deliberately choreographed to merge English royalty into an Indian scene, becomes the means by which authority was represented in Victorian India, or so Bernard Cohn has argued. In 'Representing Authority in Victorian India', he lists the number of royal visits and major durbars that took place over the last half of the nineteenth century: 1869 marks the Duke of Edinburgh's visit, 1875–6 that of the Prince of Wales, 1877 marks the extravagant Imperial Assemblage to proclaim Queen Victoria Empress of India with sixty-three ruling princes, 300 titular chiefs, and men of the professional and business classes in attendance.

At the same time, the strong possibility that loyalty and its rhetorical apparatus was manipulated by many Indians, quite differently from the way intended by government and no doubt by which it hoped to establish empire loyalism, meant that loyalty was as much available for circulation within indigenous circles—both to articulate a deep unease with what 1857 had required and to redefine the political economy in place. The Native Newspaper Reports for Bengal for 1875 and 1876, for instance, suggest some kind of crisis of consciousness—primarily socio-political—that circulates around the terms by which the political culture of 1857–8 was definitively marked. It appears to arise from a desire, on the one hand, to name political culture in inherited terms (loyalty to the ruler) and, on the other, to name it as a symbolic violence. Suspended somewhere between these two theorizings of colonial rule are the many articulations we find in the press at the time of native that describe 'Hindustan' as the name of an abject people. The rhetoric of lament thus finds at least two objects: lament for the loss of a particular notion of political loyalty, occasioned by government's placing of this relationship on trial in 1857, and for the loss of sovereignty (as such an illusion is maintained in a symbolic economy). At the same time, there are articles that use the same knowledge of loss to discover, make visible, for their readership the economy of calculation informing Company rule. While it is true that knowledge of colonialism's economic objective appears earlier in the century in the Indian-owned press, the resolving of 1857 in the Proclamation of 1858 guaranteeing the colony the same rights as all British subjects produced a systematic critique of a symbolic economy.

It is in the epistemological interest in the terms 'loyalty' and 'rights'—one belonging to the symbolic economy and the other to representative government—that we witness some of the implications of government's investment in 1857 in the rhetorical and affective dimensions of the discourse of loyalty. It is with the two that I would like to conclude. In a piece that describes the confusion of registers and emotions—that links loyalty, and consensual political relationship implied by it, with the subjection that is a result of the rule of force, at the same time as it expresses outrage at government's questioning of the integrity of its people and laments the loss of the relationship implied by the term 'loyalty'—definitive of this period, an editorial in the *Sadharani* of 15 August 1875 (as reported) states:

We are powerless, disarmed, and held in utter subjection by the rigors of the Penal and Criminal Procedure Codes. Our rulers forget that men, whose loyalty to the British rule remained unshaken during the days of the Mutiny, when any disaffection on their part might have caused not a little trouble to Government, are not likely to entertain any disloyal feelings now, when they have been enfeebled by the rigors of law (NNR, Bengal, week ending 21 August 1875).

The *Sahachar* (NNR Bengal, week ending 29 July 1876), reportedly published the following anti-governmental piece: 'If we have no rights, then what are we? Are we the slaves of the English? Now, if it be impressed on the minds of the people that they are held by the English Government as slaves, they will have no longer any feeling of loyalty or love towards it' (p. 10 of issue). The genuflection that follows, 'But it is a happy thing, and a matter of considerable honor to our Government, that it has never given expression to such an idea' (ibid.) is just that and does not take away from the fact that the language of rights, and the naming of Company rule as a history that speaks of a rule based on symbolic economy, is made part of the public culture.

One of the ways of approaching this simultaneous expression of political critique and protestations of loyalty is to consider them as constituting the necessary confusions of a transformational moment in which 1857 is named as a critical juncture. I have depended largely on Native Newspaper Reports (NNR) for Bengal, which means that choices made by government translators turn these reports into very particular narratives, and conclusions about native intent must remain speculative. By the same token, these reports offer a sense of the forms political writing took in the 1870s and some of its pervasive concerns. What is striking is the presence everywhere—if we take translated texts at face value— and the discomfort generated by what can only be described as uncomfortable knowledge(s). How best to rationalize defeat, for instance, is one place that mobilizes much opinion: is 1857 proof of abjection or of that honourable practice called loyalty? Another is how best to square emergent terms of resistance—that forces a replacing of existing terms such as loyalty with other terms such as abjection/slavery—with foundational discourses of identity that link the language of rights with disloyalty and that require a withdrawal of the consensual terms predicated by the economy of honour.

Either way, what the 1870s NNRs for Bengal suggest is that the discourse through which government and indigenous population 'spoke' in 1857, that of loyalty, is also the discourse by which rethinking 'belonging' in a colonial raj is conducted within indigenous public culture at the same time as it is the discourse whose perpetuation is attempted by government at the affective level anyway in the form of durbars and royal visits. Given the very different uses of the rhetoric of loyalty by government and indigenous public culture, the 1870s is fascinating for its staging of contest via this rhetoric where in 1857 it was used to manage resistance by the one (government) and survival by the other (indigene).

## Notes

1.   Ghosh is responding at this point in the conversation to Chakrabarty's suggestion in *Provincializing Europe* that Bengali cultural discourse of the post-mutiny period reflects 'very little anguish about the colonial situation' (161). Ghosh expresses agreement with the finding but questions Chakrabarty's reading, asking: 'how else is it possible to assimilate subordination except by refusing to represent it to oneself?' (161). He goes on to suggest that 1857 is best read as a rupture, marking the moment in which 'a great mass of Indians did indeed acknowledge that they were a "defeated people" […] that there was really, truly nothing they could do about it and that resistance, as they had once thought of it, was futile—the only grounds left for resistance were within the conqueror's own terms' (161). It is this sense of futility he believes that informs 'all their subsequent attempts to appropriate modernity' (161).

2. In *Empire and Information*, Bayly mentions that records of resisters were destroyed (330) and P.J.O. Taylor states that over 95 per cent of documentary evidence on the insurrection is British. Francesca Orsini, in her book on the formation of the Hindi public sphere, attests to the same difficulty of locating unmediated indigenous opinion (106).

3. The term by which a collective identity is indicated in indigenous texts is, more often than not, 'Hindustani'.

   One of the more interesting ways in which Marx indicates his disapproval of the landowning class and its collaborating with the colonial government is in the form of comments on individual days and events that he noted in the form of a chronological chart. Collected as 'Notes on Indian History', the entry for 25 May 1857 notes the spread of rebellion to '20 different places simultaneously' (193) and concludes with the following: '*Rajah of Patiala*—for shame!—sent large body of soldiers in aid of the English' (193).

4. Ghosh argues that proof of a different attitude before the 1857 insurrection is the revolt itself—that speaks of an active insurrectionary opinion—and the many mutinies, and one could add civil unrest, preceding this one. There were many revolts before 1857. See Sashi Bhushan Chaudhuri. *Civil Disturbances During the British Rule in India (1765–1857)*. Calcutta: The World Press, 1955, for a detailed account of civilian participation. Sugata Bose, Ayesha Jalal, and Judith Brown are among the many who have noted that the colonial period was rife with resistance and revolts (see 85–7 of Bose and Jalal and 86 of Brown). Finally, it is worth noting that revolts were not uncommon in Mughal India. See Gautum Bhadra, 'Two Frontier Uprisings in Mughal India'. However, 1857 is regarded by most as a moment that marks a rupture as much as it does a continuity. Bayly has suggested that this was the first revolt in which technology played a significant role. In *Empire and Information*, he states: 'In 1857 a struggle unfolded between British and the insurgents over the control of modern media of information, which belies the conventional assumption that the rebel leaders were blind traditionalists' (317).

5. In *Historical Metaphors and Mythical Realities*, Sahlins suggests systems are always already subject to continuity and to alteration, that one cannot occur without the other. That is, the two are not phenomenally distinct (67). Thus, for him 'situations of culture contact' (68) such as those typical of the colonial age are usefully approached for the ways in which attitudes were reproduced on all sides and forced transformation of both as well.

6.  O'Hanlon writes: 'A Subaltern strategy, reconstructed along the lines I have suggested, might be used to recover the presence of the subordinate without slipping into an essentialism, by revealing that presence to be one constructed and refracted through practice' (87).

7.  The colonial archive is the subject of much discussion, one that I am unable to engage here. However, I would like to point to a few recent works that usefully problematize the use of colonial archives. Antoinette Burton offers a good summary of the intervention intended by Gayatri Spivak, Homi Bhabha, and Edward Said in their reading of colonial archives (141) at the same time as she points out the function of the colonial archive. The archive is where the class of native that constituted a 'historical subject' (Burton's term, 141) was determined. Betty Joseph offers an equally useful summary of some of the major statements made regarding the uses and abuses of colonial archives, as well as emphasizing the importance of these archives for those working on early colonial India. (See 16–23 in particular.) It is interesting to note that government archives formed source books for a variety of European and American governmental and civilian interests, especially once the Imperial Records department was established.

8.  Spivak writes that the Rani appears in official records 'because of the commercial/territorial interests of the East India Company' (227). For her, records such as this one work, collectively, to construct the fiction on which colonial rule was based and justified. It produced, she writes, 'a whole collection of "effects of the real" and this misreading produced the proper name, "India"' (203).

9.  For discussions of the civil service in the nineteenth century India see Brown, Judith. *Modern India: The Origins of an Asian Democracy*. New York: Oxford University Press, 1994; Misra, B.B. *The Central Administration of the East India Company 1773–1834*. Manchester: Manchester University Press, 1959; Robb, P.G. *The Evolution of British Policy Towards Indian Politics*. Delhi: Manohar, 1992; and Dewey Clive, *Anglo-Indian Attitudes: The Mind of the Indian Civil Service*. London: Hambledon Press, 1993. For studies focused more on the social and cultural organization of the civil service, see of course Said, Edward. *Orientalism*. New York: Random House, 1979; Nair, Rukmini Bhaya. *Lying on the Postcolonial Couch: The Idea of Indifference*. Delhi: Oxford University Press, 2002; Singh, Jyotsna. *Colonial Narratives/Cultural Dialogue: 'Discoveries' of India in the Language of Colonialism*. London: Routledge, 1996.

10. The importance of these reports is pointed out by Richard Sumarez Smith in an article on the development of forms of administration in the Punjab and NWP in the nineteenth century. He states that records (reports) were the basis on which 'Reports'—that he describes as 'the authorized version of knowledge about Indian society' (154)—were generated. These Reports were circulated widely within governmental circles in India and England.

11. Eric Hobsbawm makes this point in 'Inventing Traditions': 'Insofar as they [social practices] function best when turned into habit, automatic procedure or even reflex action, they require invariance, which may get in the way of the other necessary requirements of practice, the capacity to deal with unforeseen or inhabitual contingencies. This is a well-known weakness of routinazation or bureaucratization, particularly at the subaltern levels where invariant performance is generally considered the most efficient' (3).

12. The proclamation, as reproduced in this entry, reads in part: 'A traveller just arrived at Cawnpore from Calcutta states, that before the cartridges were distributed, a Council was held for the purpose of taking away the religion and rites of the people of Hindustan. The Members of Council came to the conclusion that as the matter was one affecting religion, seven or eight thousand Europeans would be required and it would cost the lives of fifty thousand Hindustanies, but that at this cost all the Natives of Hindustan would become Christians. The matter was therefore represented in an "Urzee" to this effect to Queen Victoria, who gave her consent' (P 188/46: 153).

13. An article in the editorial page of the *Bombay Times* for 26 November 1856 entitled 'On the Limited Capability of the Hindoos as a Nation for Civilization' is all too representative. 'The capability for civilization, it must be confessed, is very different in different races [....] The Hindoos as a nation were civilized long before the Britons were, but their civilization was not of a progressive character; it soon reached its limit, and there it stopped, nor have the Hindoos for a thousand years advanced a step beyond [....] If the Anglo-Saxon has subjected this race to his dominion, it is owing to the fundamental differences of character, and to a constitutional superiority conferred upon him by his Maker.'

14. The opinion expressed by the *Hurkaru* and *Phoenix* is of course expressed in Indian insurrectionary opinion and the latter uses opinion such as the one expressed by the *Friend of India* and the *Dacca Times* as proof of the validity of its conclusions about colonial intent. Another form that the pro-Christianizing view takes is one that links the absence of significant

insurrectionary activity in the provinces of Bombay and Madras with (more successful) missionary activity and thus argues for an official policy supporting missionary activity in India and in general a less 'secular' educational policy. For instance, the *Bombay Times* of 8 September 1857 reproduces an article from the *Record* (an Anglo Indian publication), that reads in part: 'The people amongst whom the missionaries have laboured, have given no visible signs of disaffection. The Madras presidency, where alone whole districts have been Christianized, escapes hitherto scatheless, and the smell of fire has not passed upon it. [...] What can be more humiliating for a Christian Government than to have frowned down Christian missions, for nearly half-a-century through fear of irritating the prejudices of the Hindoos.'

15. We know for instance that complex, metaphorical modes of expression formed part of propaganda literature circulated by insurrectionists. The *Bombay Times* reproduces an article from the *Englishman* in its 25 June 1857 issue in which the latter claims to be reproducing a report sent to General Low. The report offers a summary of an insurrectionary pamphlet making its way through the troops. In part, the summary reads: 'It consists of a number of couplets in Persian, alleged to be composed by Niamutoollah, a fukeer in the Punjab, about 700 years ago, 38 of which couplets are in circulation among both Hindoos and Mahomedans in the N.W. Provinces, for both classes have equal faith in the predictions of the Mahomedan saints and goes on to summarize the couplets. The strategy of employing religious history, drawing on established poetical forms of expression, and the very notion of predictive history that even this summary makes apparent were part of the naturalized forms of political communication and are everywhere to be found in the literature of the insurrection.

16. Anglo Indian newspapers recycled and recirculated the same accounts, thus further exaggerating already sensational accounts of 'native savagery'. The following that is reported by the *Bombay Times* (25 June 1857) as an eye-witness report originating in the *Lahore Chronicle Extra* of 17 June 1857 is typical in its hysterical tone and sense of security in the moral infallibility of an Anglo Indian civilization—that makes brutality exercised by the latter of a qualitatively different order than native brutality—so much so that it reports on Anglo Indian brutality with some candour: 'Give full stretch to your imagination—think of everything that is cruel, inhuman, infernal, and you cannot conceive anything so diabolical as what these demons in

human form have perpetrated. On the 2<sup>nd</sup> we marched from Painput [sic] to Race—at this place some of the poor fugitives from Delhi met with the most barbarous treatment. We burnt four villages and hung seven Lambadars [....] We hung many other villains, and burnt the villages as we came along.'

17. This is a point that Homi Bhabha makes in 'Sly Civility'. He describes colonial 'governmental discourse' as a 'colonial substitute' for 'democratic public discussion' that, he adds, is considered by J.S. Mill to be the defining feature of representative government. Records, or in Bhabha's terms, 'recordation' is the very place of this substitution: this is where events are transformed into acts of government in 'another place' and 'another time' (95).

18. Ghosh states: '[...] could it not be said [...] all (native) discourse in imperial India were shaped to a greater or lesser degree by the ever-present fear of intervention?' (149)

19. I have not brought in the more general discussions of power and its workings in society that argue for the impossibility of encountering hegemony without resistance. The most classic formulation of power remains that provided by Michel Foucault. In 'Power and Strategies', he writes: 'there are no relations of power without resistances; the latter are all the more real and effective because they are formed right at the point where relations of power are exercised; resistance to power does not have to come from elsewhere to be real, nor is it inexorably frustrated through being the compatriot of power. It exists all the more by being in the same place as power' (142).

20. The Company government was established in 1764 with two distinct departments, Public and Secret. Until 1833, the government of Bengal and of the Government of India were continuous. The Charter Act of 1833 established the Government of India, to whom governments of the provinces of Bengal, Madras, and Bombay and of smaller territories were responsible. The Public or General Department of the Government of India was constituted in 1843 as a branch of the new Home Department. This branch was responsible for general constitutional, administrative, and political matters within British India, including political movements and disturbances. In 1907, a separate Home (Political) Department was established.

21. No. 94 in the weekly report dated 10 July 1857 states the Government of India requests 'that the widest publicity may be given to this Proclamation in the native languages [and that at the same time the Zemindars may be reminded of the obligation imposed on them by Section VI. Act No. XVII

of 1857]' (P 188/46:183). The same entry also states that the proclamation was published in the *Calcutta Gazette*.

22. The first proclamation appeared in the 15 May 1857 *Mofussilite*. It speaks more of property—threatening insurrectionists with a forfeiture of property and offering reward to the loyal in the form of property. It reads: 'Whereas it has been ascertained that in the Districts of Meerut and in, and immediately around Delhi, some short sighted Rebels have dared to raise resistance to the British Government, it is hereby declared that every Talookdar, Zemindar, or other owner of land, who may join in such resistance, will forfeit all rights of property, which will be confiscated and transferred in perpetuity to the faithful Talookdars and Zemindars of the same quarters, who may shew by their acts of obedience to the Government, and exertions for the maintenance of tranquility that they deserve reward and favour from the State. The powerful British Government will in a marked manner recompense its friends, and punish its enemies' (qtd Taylor 274).

23. David is one of many historians to have pointed out that many trials were a travesty of justice, more noted for their breach of (even) the minimal requirement of court ported than for its observance. He writes: 'Trials were little more than drumhead courts martial with officers and men vowing to kill prisoners whether they were found guilty or not' (153–4). Of trials of the civilian population, he writes: 'Sometimes trials were dispensed with entirely. Tales of atrocities against women and children, many of them exaggerated, had infuriated the British soldiers and almost any Indian male was considered fair game' (154).

24. Bayly describes the flows of information back and forth between government and insurrectionists in *Empire and Information* and suggests that E.A. Reade, the Acting Lieutenant Governor stationed in Agra for much of 1857, read some rebel papers routinely. (See 325–6). Some reports filed in 1857 are by officials alarmed by what they consider the government's lackadaisical response to the flow of information. For instance, Appendix E to numbers 35–6 (the first dated 10 November) in the weekly report of 13 November 1857 (a letter from E.A. Samuels, Commissioner of Revenue for the Division of Patna to A. R. Young, Secretary to Government of Bengal dated 6 October 1857) observes: 'Many people endeavour to persuade themselves that the natives are not aware of the contents of the English papers, and that so far as they are concerned, it is immaterial what appears in those publications, but this is a very great mistake. The English papers

have for many years past formed the source to which the native news writers and the native papers looked for their intelligence of our movements and intentions. Since this revolt commenced the greatest anxiety has been manifested to learn what the English papers say, and every one fortunate enough to get hold of an English paper is called upon to translate it for the edification of large circles of listeners, who again retail the news and comments of the journals in their villages' (P 188/48: 54). The Home Miscellaneous Series, Manuscript 726, pp. 1109–57 details a post-rebellion trial in which in answer to the question: 'Do you think the newspapers assisted in the revolt in any way?' the native on trial answers in the affirmative. I reproduce part of his reply to this question: '[they] have been looked to by our people as their best source of information. Everything is published in the newspapers and not only your strong points but your weak ones, are made known through their medium' (1139).

25. David writes: 'The Resolution was never intended for public consumption. But inevitably a copy found its way into the Calcutta and English newspapers. It was savaged in both countries. The editor of one English-language Indian paper wrote: "Lenity towards any portion of the conspirators is misplaced, impolitic and iniquitous, and is calculated to excite contempt and invite attack on every side, by showing to the world the Government of India ... allows the blood of English and Christian subjects of Her Majesty to flow in torrents, and their wives, sisters and daughters to be outraged and dishonoured without adequate retribution" ' (237–8). David also quotes Canning as having remarked in essence on the strategic need that dictated his decision in addition to situating his action in an ethical requirement as well. As quoted, Canning told Lord Granville, 'As long as I have breath in my body, I will pursue no other policy than that which I have been following—not only for the reason of expediency ... but because it is just. I will not govern in anger' (David 238).

26. The significant gap between the time of events described in the diary and deposition on the one hand and the recording of the same in Government of India records leads one to wonder about the reasons for its recording. On the one hand, it leads to the conclusion that the bureaucratic system in place was being dutifully followed in spite of the crisis and, on the other to the conclusion that records were being maintained with an eye to the kind of control over collective memory Derrida has argued in *Archive Fever* is at the basis of archives.

David states that Nunne Nawab (as his name is spelt in David's book) was the leading Muslim noble of Kanpur. According to David, after his initial arrest by Nana Saheb, the nawab 'had embraced the rebellion enthusiastically and was in command of over a thousand Muslim soldiers and the rebel battery situated near to St. John's Church' (197).

27. The opening paragraph reads: 'The Sepoys at Golaghat used to hear the news of the Mutineers from the Amlah at Golaghat; the Amlah received the Samachar Chundrica, and these used to be read out and matters talked over. Narayon Naxzir and Gunuck Ram, Sudder Ameen's Mohurir, used to come to the lines to Ramtohul Havildar's house, where the Sepoys assembled and heard the news; the golmal in this way commenced, daily the news was disseminated of the king being on the throne of Delhi, the massacre at Cawnpore and other places, and of the whole of Hindoostan with the exception of Calcutta and Bengal, having been taken possession of by the Sepoys on part of the King' (P 188/48: 73). Of course whether this deposition is edited, or how much of it changes in translation is difficult to assess.

28. N. Krishnaswamy and Archana Burde write that writings by Indians, in English, indicate the extent to which a particular type of formulaic was observed by Indians in their correspondence with government (96). Of course these narratives are translated into English, but it is more than likely that the formulaic was one of the regulative features of indigenous exchange with the colonial overlord.

29. The relevant part reads: 'It came to my notice accidentally the other day that the Nujeebs at Mozufferpore were in the habit of having the English papers translated to them, and there can be no doubt that whatever appears in the English papers which can in any way serve the purposes of the disaffected is speedily made known to them by their agents in Calcutta or elsewhere' (Appendix E to Nos. 35–6, weekly report for 13 November 1857; P 188/48: 54).

   In *What Really Happened*, the incipient revolt referred to here is mentioned under '31 July'. A detachment of Holmes' Irregulars rebelled but the Nujeeb Guards, and the public, prevented them from looting the treasury (109).

30. Illiffe writes: 'African notions of honour survived vigorously until the colonial period and then fragmented, partly surviving, partly disappearing, but chiefly being transmuted and absorbed into other ethics, which themselves were most effective when drawing on traditions of honour' (227).

# Works Cited

*Government Records*
Government of India, Home Office Records. P 188/46.
Government of India, Home Office Records. P 188/48.
India Office Records, Home Miscellaneous Series. Manuscripts 726.
Native Newspaper Reports. (Bengal). 1875, 1876, 1877.

*Newspapers*
*Bombay Times*. 1856, 1857.

*Secondary Sources*
Arendt, Hannah. *The Origins of Totalitarianism*. Revised Edn. London: George
    Allen and Unwin, 1967.
Bayly, C.A. *Empire and Information*. Cambridge: Cambridge University Press, 1996.
Bhabha, Homi. *Locations of Culture*. London: Routledge, 1994.
Bhadra, Gautum. 'Two Frontier Uprisings in Mughal India', in *Subaltern
    Studies*, Vol. II. Ed. Ranajit Guha. Delhi: Oxford University Press,
    1983, 43–9.
Brown, Judith. *Modern India: The Origins of an Asian Democracy*. New York:
    Oxford University Press, 1994.
Bourdieu, Pierre. *Practical Reason: On the Theory of Action*. Stanford: Stanford
    University Press, 1998.
Bose, Sugata and Ayesha Jalal. *Modern South Asia: History, Culture, Political
    Economy*. Delhi: Oxford University Press, 1998.
Cohn, Bernard. 'Representing Authority in Victorian India', in *The Invention
    of Tradition*. Eds Eric Hobsbawm and Terence Ranger. Cambridge: Cambridge
    University Press, 1983, 165–210.
David, Saul. *The Indian Mutiny*. London: Penguin, 2003.
Derrida, Jacques. *Archive Fever: a Freudian impression*. Trans. Eric Prenowitz.
    Chicago: University of Chicago Press, 1996.
Foucault, Michel. *Power/Knowledge: Selected Interviews and Other Writings
    1972–1977*. Ed. Colin Gordon. New York: Pantheon, 1980.
Ghosh, Amitav and Dipesh Chakrabarty. 'A Corrspondence on Provincializing
    Europe', in *Radical History Review*, Vol. 82, 2002, 146–72.
Guha, Ranajit. 'The Prose of Counter-Insurgency', in *Subaltern Studies*,
    Vol. II. Ed. Guha. Delhi: Oxford University Press, 1983, 1–42.

Hobsbawm, Eric. 'Introduction: Inventing Traditions', in *The Invention of Traditions*. Eds Hobsbawm and Terence Ranger. Cambridge: Cambridge University Press, 1982, 1–14.

Illiffe, John. *Honour in African History*. Cambridge: Cambridge University Press, 2005.

Joseph, Betty. *Reading the East India Company, 1720–1840*. Chicago: University of Chicago Press, 2004.

Kaviraj, Sudipta. 'In search of civil society', in *Civil Society: History and Possibilities*. Eds Sudipta Kaviraj and Sunil Khilnani. Delhi: Cambridge University Press, 2002 (South Asian edn), 287–323.

Krishnaswamy, N. and Archana S. Burde. *Linguistic Colonialism and the Expanding English Empire: The Politics of Indians' English*. Delhi: Oxford University Press, 1998.

Marx, Karl and F. Engels. *The First War of Independence 1857–1859*. Moscow: Foreign Languages Publishing House, 1959.

O'Hanlon, Rosalind. 'Recovering the Subject: *Subaltern Studies* and Histories of Resistance in Colonial South Asia', in *Mapping Subaltern Studies and the Postcolonial*. Ed. Vinayak Chaturvedi. London: Verso, 2000, 72–115.

Orsini, Francesca. *The Hindi Public Sphere 1920–1940: Language and Literature in the Age of Nationalism*. Delhi: Oxford University Press, 2002.

Sahlins, Marshall. *Historical Metaphors and Mythical Realities: Structure in the Early History of the Sandwich Islands Kingdom*. Ann Arbor: University of Michigan Press, 1981.

Smith, Richard Saumarez. 'Rule-by-records and rule-by-reports: complementary aspects of the British Imperial rule of law', in *The Word and the World: Fantasy, Symbol and Record*. Ed. Veena Das. New Delhi: Sage Publications, 1986, 153–76.

Spivak, Gayatri. *A Critique of Postcolonial Reason: Toward a History of the Vanishing Present*. Cambridge: Harvard University Press, 1999.

Taylor, P.J.O. (Ed.) *A Companion to the 'Indian Mutiny' of 1857*. Delhi: Oxford University Press, 1996.

———. *What Really Happened During the Mutiny*. Delhi: Oxford University Press, 1997.

# Decolonization and the Progressive Writers Association in India

## PRIYAMVADA GOPAL

On 14 August 1947, a few hours before India attained formal independence from British rule at midnight, Jawaharlal Nehru addressed the Constituent Assembly of India in a now iconic speech:

> Long years ago we made a tryst with destiny, and now the time comes when we shall redeem our pledge, not wholly or in full measure, but very substantially. At the stroke of the midnight hour, when the world sleeps, India will awake to life and freedom. A moment comes, which comes but rarely in history, when we step out from the old to the new, when an age ends, and when the soul of a nation, long suppressed, finds utterance. It is fitting that at this solemn moment we take the pledge of dedication to the service of India and her people and to the still larger cause of humanity (1965: 336).

To present-day readers, after many such midnight ceremonies, inaugural trysts and speeches across decolonizing regions of Asia and Africa, the metaphors and gestures of Nehru's speech are familiar ones: an awakening from slumber, the dawn of a new era, the assertive, unitary vox populi, and the rebirth of a nation. Several such scenes where the motif of national emergence onto the world stage would recur were also played across Africa from 1957 onwards: 'With the passing of the world-historical era of colonialism a new world-historical era would dawn. In this new era, the slumbering giant of Africa would awaken and leave the imprint of its decisive action upon the world' (Lazarus 1990: 2–3). As Neil Lazarus has pointed out, these ceremonies were all imbued with a 'special aura of timelessness' testifying to 'the headiness of initial expectations of independence' (3).

Some ten years before Nehru gave his fabled speech, a group of young Indian writers issued a manifesto that also spoke of transition:

Radical changes are taking place in Indian society. ... We believe that the new literature of India must deal with the basic problems of our existence to-day [sic]—the problems of hunger and poverty, social backwardness, and political subjection. All that drags us down to passivity, inaction and un-reason we reject as re-actionary [sic]. All that arouses in us the critical spirit, which examines institutions and customs in the light of reason, which helps us to act, to organize ourselves, to transform, we accept as progressive (Anand 1979: 20–1).

The differences between the two calls to national action are marked even as both draw on an epochal sense of transition and on similar vocabularies of transformation. If Nehru is cautious about the extent to which India's 'pledge' can be redeemed as her ineluctable destiny unfolds, his words nevertheless speak to an inevitable renaissance, a national self-actualization that is now unstoppable. The 1936 manifesto drafted by Mulk Raj Anand and others to commemorate the inauguration of the All-India Progressive Writers Association (PWA) is also optimistic in its epochal vision but emphatic about the self-critique and work that postcolonial re*construction* (as opposed to re*birth*) will take. Despite its own schematic and teleological undertones, this document conveys a sense of the challenges involved in such a project.[1] The new, if it is to be brought into being, requires the development of a critical awareness of all that needs to be changed or reworked and of the labours that such transformations will require. The new is not the opposite of the old; instead, the latter is to be examined 'in the light of reason' and reworked into the future. Where Nehru's speech is replete with references to a singular national History to which national self-'discovery' is integral, the PWA manifesto speaks of a dynamic process of recognizing problems and working through them. The structure of the former is teleological; the latter is driven by utopian impulse but not a sense of manifest destiny.

The distinction between these two inaugural gestures is not unlike one that Lazarus, drawing on Anouar Abdel-Malek, maps between 'nationalists' and 'nationalitarians' in anti-colonial struggles in Africa. Nationalitarians (Frantz Fanon is one example) criticize 'nationalists for conflating independence with freedom' and for not undertaking the radical social and economic restructuring that would mean real freedom (Lazarus 1990: 11). Nationalitarians, like the founders of the PWA, do see the moment of independence as one with revolutionary potential; the postcolonial era must bring with it 'a wholesale reconstruction of society' (5). If Nehru's words have come to represent a certain kind of nationalism emblematic of the new-born Indian state itself, for the writers who came together to found the PWA, the nascent nation-state in 1936 was 'a terrain of struggle' (Ahmad 1993: 48). Rather than take the 'long-suppressed soul' of the nation for granted, a fundamental and urgent question here is how to democratically *build* an all-India character. If for Nehru, despite cautionary disclaimers, 'the past is over and it is the future that beckons us now,' the PWA manifesto eyes the future with a radical sense of the present and its challenges. Certainly both sides share the urgent sense that the day must be seized in the interests of bringing utopian visions to fruition.

For Nehru, this vision is troped as a quest, the discovery of an idyll that is always already part of India's historical being. Change has already occurred ('we have endured all the pains of labour and our hearts are heavy with the memory of this sorrow') and what follows in its wake are the labours of ensuring its fruits: 'The future is not one of ease or resting but of incessant striving ... the ending of poverty, and ignorance and disease and inequality of opportunity' (1965: 336). The PWA manifesto, in contrast, interprets the moment as one which demands active intervention in the interests of broadening the meanings and scope of 'freedom'. Even as it highlights oppression, the manifesto is a call to agency. The task of the radical writer is not the benevolent one of 'wiping tears from eyes' but one of active self-transformation (Nehru 1965: 336). Where Nehru uses the relatively benign phrase with a missing agent of action—'inequality of opportunity'—to indicate the challenges at hand, the manifesto speaks more forcefully of 'political subjection' as a problem. In the final instance, its polemical target is not all that 'we've endured' but all that enables 'us' to be passive, reactionary, and inactive.

Without over-emphasizing the distinctions between these progressive writers and mainstream nationalists (for there were also significant overlaps between the two groups), it is clear that the motley crowd who came to constitute the PWA were concerned with a diversity of issues beyond nationalism that they saw as integral to the transitional period of decolonization. Though deeply invested in anti-colonial activity, they spoke of an 'institutional change' that was to take place at several different levels. The writer's primary task in this context of the 'radical changes' already underway was to counter backlash, or 'reactionary and revivalist tendencies on questions like family, religion, sex, war and society' (Anand 1979: 20). The 'struggle' itself was framed as not a dyadic one of colonizer against colonized, but as a war to be waged against a range of social and political forces. Much of the output in this newly radicalized literary climate mandated that 'a critique of others (anti-colonialism) be conducted in the perspective of an even more comprehensive, multifaceted critique of ourselves: our class structures, our familial ideologies, our management of our bodies and sexualities, our idealisms, our silences' (Ahmad 1992: 118). In contrast to the axioms underlying Nehru's discourse of freedom at midnight, the initial work of many writers associated with the PWA does militate against any kind of 'sustained, powerful myth of a primal innocence, when it comes to the colonial encounter' (118).

The formation of the All-India Progressive Writers Association in 1936 points to a crystallization of radicalizing trends begun in the years before.[2] Many critics and writers, including founder members of the PWA, trace the literary radicalism of this period back to the publication in 1932 of a controversial anthology of short stories, *Angarey* [Live Coals]. This anthology contained some ten short stories contributed by four authors who would then go on to be involved with the PWA: Sajjad Zaheer, who edited it, Ahmed Ali, Mahmuduzzafar, and Rashid Jahan, the lone woman in this group. Both its many detractors and its enthusiastic supporters saw *Angarey* as the result of cultural and intellectual contact with Europe: 'It would be hard to say,' writes critic and translator, Shakeel Siddiqui, 'whether the vision for *Angarey* or an anthology like *Angarey* was conceived in Lucknow or London' (1990: 12). Siddiqui observes that both Zaheer and Ahmad Ali had been studying in England at the time; both were drawn to the radical and avant-garde literary movements that were gaining momentum in the Europe of the 1930s.[3] All four contributors were, however, members of the upper strata of the Muslim community in Lucknow. The publication of the stories, all of which thematize the morals and mores of this community, drew upon the authors the charge that they were 'intoxicated' by English education and brainwashed into attacking Islam and its tenets. Some religious leaders denounced the collection and even an official 'anti-*Angarey*' campaign was inaugurated; Ahmed Ali writes that he and his fellow authors 'were lampooned and satirised, censured editorially and in pamphlets and, were even threatened with death' (1974: 35). This campaign was ultimately successful in getting the British government to ban the collection and confiscate remaining copies almost six months after its publication.

The question of location is an important one with regard to this collection and the radical literary production that followed in the next two decades. Given the status of North Indian Muslims as a minority community and the overdetermined nature of any emancipatory project in colonial polities—where it inevitably overlaps with civilizing missions—the charges against the collection bear some reflection. What are the valences of self-criticism within minority communities in such a context? The answer that the

authors gave through Mahmuduzzafar's letter to the editor in the
*Leader*, dated 5 April 1933 was simple:

> The authors of this book do not wish to make any apology for it. They leave it
> to float or sink of itself.... They have chosen the particular field of Islam not
> because they bear it any 'special' malice, but because being born into that particular
> society, they felt themselves better qualified to speak for that alone. They were
> more sure of their ground there (Alvi 1995).

This idea that a self-critical literature, or more precisely, writing
that critically identified an 'us' and an 'our' in the interests of
reconstruction, needed to be developed was one of the defining
features of this emergent radical tradition. If the *Angarey* writers
had chosen their natal religious community and class as the target
of critique, in the radical literature that was to follow, such acts
of identification and self-criticism would take place along other
axes, including gender and caste. Critical identification, a radical
reappropriation of the communal 'we' and 'us', was a particularly
difficult and yet especially necessary task in contexts where
homogenized 'selves' defined themselves against equally
homogeneous 'others'—colonizer and colonized, Hindus and
Muslims, minority and majority. *Angarey* was to inspire a body
of literature that, by interrogating the 'we' of both communal and
national collective identities, attempted to break away from dyadic
models of conflict and oppression. As Aijaz Ahmad has suggested,
this literature—especially in the bloody wake of Partition—did
not 'construct fixed boundaries between the criminalities of
the colonialist and the brutalities of all those indigenous people
who have had power in our own society.... No quarter was given
to the colonialist; but there was none for ourselves either'
(1992: 118).

Some four years after the publication of the *Angarey* collection,
the All-India Progressive Writers Association was formally
inaugurated in April 1936 at a large conference in Lucknow. The
primary goal was to consolidate the gains of the last few years—to
open up institutional spaces where diverse issues pertinent to

regenerating nation and national culture could be discussed; and to create support networks for writers concerned with social and cultural change. While it is certainly true that the PWA had links to the Communist Party of India (CPI) (influential founder-members like Zaheer), it is incorrect to reduce the organization's mandate, as Aijaz Ahmad does, to that of a cultural front *for* or *of* the CPI. Many leading figures at that first conference, even those deeply sympathetic to communism, were not affiliated to the party and certainly did not see the organization as a front for the party. In fact, founder members like Mulk Raj Anand often went great lengths to point out the respect for political heterogeneity that the organization would maintain.

[T]he title of 'Progressive Writers' Association' has led to some confusion by suggesting some kind of regimentation of writers or at least by giving the appearance of a clique ... actually we were a collection of readers and writers groping together, in spite of our different individualities, towards the realisation of certain facts (Anand 1979: 2).

Anand also pointed out that, unfortunately, 'the naiveté of our catch penny formalists' and 'vulgar sociologists' allowed reactionary forces to dismiss Progressive and Marxian thought; he urged Progressive writers to 'be strongly on our guard against cheap simplifications and sensationalism' (8–9). Meanwhile, writers like Chughtai and Manto had deeply contentious relationships to the party and often distanced themselves from it, even as they retained a commitment to radical politics. In a famous essay entitled 'Progressives Don't Think', Manto wrote bitterly about the dismissive treatment he had received from more orthodox socialist and communist writers (1996). Ismat Chughtai—who unhesitatingly described lifelong Party member, Rashid Jahan, as her mentor—was also emphatic about her own independence: 'no association could dictate to me what I could or could not write' (Tharu and Lalita 1993: 128).

In ascribing the development of what he terms 'Critical Realism' primarily to the Party's influence, Ahmad weakens his own salutary insights about the importance of leftist and Progressive writing during this period in two ways. His claim that 'Critical Realism' became a 'fundamental form of narrativity' in response to the CPI's 'United Front' strategy seems suspiciously close to an endorsement of party-line aesthetics (Ahmad 1992: 118). This delineation also militates against the attempts of many in the PWA not to be regimented in this way, either aesthetically or ideologically. Although Ahmad's claim honours the role of organized communism and the CPI in forging cultural resistances and alliances (a necessary gesture in a contemporary critical climate which is marked by a sweeping and undifferentiated hostility towards communism), so schematic a causal linkage fails to provide us with a historicized account of why such a diversity of writers and intellectuals were prompted to come together at this particular historical conjuncture. Michael Denning has pointed to a similar blindness in readings of Popular Front public culture in the US; he argues that the politics of anti-fascist solidarity with Soviet socialism has erroneously 'led many historians to see the Popular Front, not as a social movement, but simply as a strategy of the Communist Party, a political line dictated by the Moscow-controlled Communist International' (1997: 11). While the PWA and its more mass-based sister organization, the Indian People's Theatre Association (IPTA, established in 1942), were not social movements in the strict sense of the term, they certainly had broader roots and a more heterogeneous membership in their heyday than a singular emphasis on the CPI's role would indicate. As David Roediger has noted, again in the context of the Popular Front in the US, a cultural moment with striking affinities to the moment of the PWA and IPTA: 'A fixation on the Party ... has left enormous gaps in our knowledge of the radical past' (cited in Denning 1997: 5). The task of the radical critic and historian is to reconstruct this past without either undermining the role of organized party politics or the enormous efforts of those who were not affiliated to the party or who worked in a kind of contentious solidarity with it.

## 'Radical Changes are Taking Place': The Historical Conjuncture of Transition

While it is beyond the scope of this essay to reconstruct in full the historical conjuncture that gave rise to the cultural radicalism of the PWA and IPTA, I will try to show here how it was that this conjuncture came to be seen as a transitional one that needed to be seized in the interests of social transformation. The 'terrain of the conjunctural', as Gramsci defines it, is one where

incurable structural contradictions have revealed themselves (reached maturity), and that, despite this, the political forces which are struggling to conserve and defend the existing structure itself are making every effort to cure them, within certain limits, and to overcome them (1971: 178).

This is 'the terrain [upon which] the forces of opposition organize' (178). In the context of India's transition from colony to nations, the Gramscian dyad of 'existing' versus 'oppositional' forces was marked by a certain fluidity of position. If, for instance, Gandhian nationalism functioned as an oppositional force in relation to the colonial government, it is also true that the same force could and did take a reactionary role with regard to, for instance, peasant militancy. Despite this fluidity—or perhaps as a consequence of it—the decades just prior to formal independence were marked by a proliferation of oppositional forces and social movements. Additionally, in 1935, the India Act gave a certain limited autonomy to provincial governments run by Indians and increased the electoral franchise from 6.5 to 30 million. The new constitutional structure, historian Sumit Sarkar has suggested, provided a frame around which a major confrontation between Left and Right within the national movement could play itself out (1983: 336). The India Act consolidated the terrain of 'nation' within which various struggles would now be enacted.

In his influential work on the discursive contours of Indian nationalism, Partha Chatterjee has argued that the Gramscian concept of 'passive revolution' best describes the general form of the transition from colonial to postcolonial states in the twentieth century (1986: 50). Because of its inherently contradictory nature—drawing on a modular Western form while attempting to assert a unique, oppositional cultural essence—non-Western nationalism adopts passive revolution as 'the historical path by which a "national" development of capital can occur without resolving or surmounting those contradictions' (Chatterjee 1986: 43). Accordingly, dominant nationalism (in this instance, Gandhism) attempts

a 'molecular transformation' of the state, neutralising opponents, converting sections of the former ruling classes into allies in a partially reorganized system of government, undertaking economic reforms on a limited scale so as to appropriate the support of the popular masses but keeping them out of any form of direct participation in the processes of governance (45).

Unlike a more frontal attack on the state, this process of manoeuvring in a 'war of position' prevents contradictions from coming to a head.[4] Though the general arc of his argument seems convincing, Chatterjee's analysis of the trajectory of nationalism and the transition to postcolonial statehood in India fails to give sufficient importance to the complexities of each historical conjuncture ('moment') that he analyses. Attempting to delineate a seamless trajectory from the moment of 'departure' to the moments of 'manoeuvre' and 'arrival' in Indian nationalism, Chatterjee alludes to, but does not sufficiently elaborate, the contestatory nature of the struggle for nationhood. For while the story of the establishment of the nation-state is certainly one of manoeuvre, cooptation and eventual domination by an alliance of the rural and urban bourgeoisie, it is also the history of opposition, counter-manoeuvres, appropriation from below, and alternative 'imaginings' of community. If it is true that 'the unique achievement of Gandhism' was to open up the possibility for 'the political appropriation of the subaltern classes by a bourgeoisie aspiring for hegemony in the new nation-state', it is also the case that the subaltern classes often undertook appropriations of their own (Chatterjee 1986: 100). In his brilliant case study of the ways in which Gandhi 'registered in peasant consciousness', for instance, Shahid Amin has shown how peasants often contravened orders from above to take militant action in their own interests, but in the name of the Mahatma (1988: 289). 'While such action sought to justify itself by reference to the Mahatma, the Gandhi of its rustic protagonists was not as he really was, but as they thought him up. Though deriving legitimacy from the supposed orders of Gandhi, peasant actions in such cases were framed in terms of what was popularly regarded to be just, fair and possible' (305).

The conjunctural terrain of Indian nation-formation in the decades just prior to Independence in 1947 is marked by the gathering of various forces of opposition. Their activities ranged from trade union activism to peasant agitation, and from the secularization of state institutions to the proliferation of diverse women's organizations. Though inflected by the struggle between British imperialism and Indian nationalism, the activities undertaken by these various forces suggest that a multiplicity of projects were to be undertaken as the transition from colony to nation took place. Gramsci's contention that oppositional forces on the terrain of the conjunctural 'seek to demonstrate that the necessary and sufficient conditions already exist to make possible, and hence imperative, the accomplishment of certain historical tasks' is borne out at this historical conjuncture (1971: 178). Even as the tide of Indian accumulation swelled and the Indian bourgeoisie were on their way to becoming captains of industry, labour activism was on the rise after a long quiescence. Sumit Sarkar points out that in 1934, the number of strikes began rising as 'British and Indian cotton mill-owners alike tried to pass through the burden of Depression on to the workers through retrenchment, rationalization and wage cuts' (1983: 335). As pressures applied by big business resulted in the formation of a nationalist right-wing in the Congress party and Gandhism manouevred itself into a position of ideological dominance, the Indian Left was also consolidating itself. With the disappointing Gandhian retrenchment of Civil Disobedience, the world crisis of over-production which stimulated the growth of fascism, and an as yet untarnished Soviet experiment with socialism, Sarkar suggests, many within the nationalist movement were drawn to communism, socialism, and Marxian thought (1983: 331). Importantly, this Left itself was a diversified one, ranging from radical nationalists to Marxian scientific socialists and communists.

In the face of superficial and minimal agrarian reforms, the period witnessed the growth of agrarian radicalism in the form of the emerging Kisan Sabha movement which made radical and un-Gandhian demands such as the abolition of Landlordism (zamindari). Sarkar points out that the umbrella Left organization, the Congress Socialist Party (CSP), was instrumental in 'stimulating thinking ... on questions like radical agrarian reform, problems of industrial labour, and non-Gandhian methods of mass mobilization and struggle' (Sarkar 1983: 333). Along with labour activism, peasant militancy rose in the years, 1933–4. Though the Communist Party was officially banned in 1934, the paradoxical result was a strengthening of the Left through a United Front strategy, 'with communists progressively developing contacts with Left-nationalist elements by work within the CSP and the Congress' (335).[5] While these elements pressed for more radical changes in property laws, land ownership, and labour regulations, the Congress itself officially maintained a Gandhian policy of 'helplessness' and 'non-interference', choosing simply to express the hope that princes, landlords, and capitalists could act as 'trustees' for property and wealth which theoretically belonged to all (341). Eventually, communists led peasant militancy in the case of landless labourers and sharecroppers who were effectively excluded even from the more radical Kisan Sabha. With the Quit India movement launched by Gandhi in 1942, nationalism became an increasingly polysemic concept with a proliferation of the meanings of 'swaraj' or self-rule. One rumour that spread is symptomatic of the radical potential with which Independence was invested: 'under a Swaraj Government no taxes would be paid and the paddy of the rich would be available to the poor' (401).

By the 1930s, women (largely from the middle- and upper-classes) too had entered the political and public sphere in unprecedented numbers; their presence was noticeable not just within nationalist organizations but also in trade unions and educational institutions.[6] Issues around women's rights and gender relations became linked to ideological diversity within the emergent national public sphere and to women's own increasingly varied political allegiances and activities. As Hajrah Begum's account of her years with the All-India Women's Congress (AIWC) suggests and as scholar Geraldine Forbes has shown more recently, '[by] the mid-1940s, the all-India women's organizations had lost their hegemony'; their claim to speak for all Indian women had been openly undermined (1987: 189). Not only was their mandate considered too Hindu and too urban middle-class, but even members of their existing constituency had become active in a variety of social and political movements. Many women were questioning Gandhian ideologies of women's nature and place even as they credited him with the entry of women into public life. Some, such as Hajrah Begum, Razia Sajjad Zaheer, and Rashid Jahan, joined Marxist, communist and socialist groups, and still others (like Preetilata Wadedar and Kalpana Datta) become involved with violent revolutionary organizations (Forbes 1987: 190; Kumar 1993: 74–95). Some Muslim women, led by Begum Shah Nawaz, reacted against Hindu dominance in the AIWC by organizing the All-India Moslem Women's League (Forbes 1987: 197). Both 'domestic and world-wide events demanded a new idealism and pragmatism from politically active women' (191). This involvement in a range of activities 'helped shatter the essentialist construction of the "Indian woman" that helped some women but hindered others in their quest for equality' (191).

My point here is that the history of nationalism and nation constitution in colonial India was one of contestation and mutually-shaping pressures between different political and social forces. Even as a certain kind of bourgeois nationalism was eventually to triumph in its manoeuvres, the birth of the Indian and Pakistani nation-states was a far more contestatory process than accounts like Chatterjee's would indicate. I am not just making the obvious point that all hegemonies are consolidated through a process of construction and articulation. The argument is, rather, that the historical conjuncture from the early 1930s to the years immediately after Independence made possible a range of historical tasks or, at the very least, a *perception* that it would be possible—and necessary—to undertake certain kinds of radical endeavours. It is these tasks—and the project of raising awareness about them—that the cultural front constituted by the PWA and IPTA placed at the centre of their agenda. As Gramsci has suggested, the demonstration that conditions for accomplishing such tasks exist, is developed in the immediate 'in a series of ideological, religious, philosophical, political, and juridical polemics, whose concreteness can be estimated by the extent to which they are convincing, and shift the previously existing disposition of social forces' (1971: 178). The PWA/IPTA combine can be seen as polemics that attempted to take seriously the role of culture in shifting these previously existing dispositions.

In his analysis of intellectuals and writers in working in Africa in a similar position of contentious solidarity with the national project in their respective countries, Neil Lazarus has suggested that even those who were critical of the conflation of independence and liberation, were susceptible to 'a preliminary overestimation of the emancipatory potential of independence' (1990: 23). This is because radical intellectuals, with few exceptions, themselves belonged to the bourgeoisie, the class that had most reason to believe in the good things that Independence would bring.

To the extent that they identified with the aspiration of the peasant and working classes as articulated in the rhetoric of anticolonialism, they may *theoretically* have appreciated that the mere acquisition of political independence was not to be confused with national liberation. But in practice they also experienced their class's sensation of being set free (1990: 11, original emphasis).

These intellectuals are 'guilty of an unwarranted conflation ... of independence with *revolution*' (11–12, original emphasis). Lazarus' observations about the classed nature of the nationalitarian position are pertinent to discussions of radical writing in contexts such as

India where literacy itself marked a relatively high class position. Most writers associated with the PWA were from middle-class, upper-class, and/or upper-caste backgrounds.[7] Ralph Russell has rightly observed that many Indian communists and fellow-travellers 'were able to take advantage … of the remarkable class solidarity of the Indian privileged classes to which most of them belonged', though his delineation of their literary activities as the 'gentlemanly practice' of revolutionary beliefs verges on caricature (Russell 1999: 73). Sajjad Zaheer was even to comment, with disarming frankness, that the PWA came into being as a collection of folks who did not know what to do other than write: 'We were incapable of manual labour. We had not learnt any craft and our minds revolted against serving the imperialist government. What other field was left …?' (1979a: 36–7) Both Russell and Lazarus are right to caution against any overestimation of the radical scope of nationalitarian or Progressive endeavours in the context of the transition to independence. It would seem necessary, however, to make a distinction between transformative *projects* undertaken as independence approached and the actual events that took place during the transition and after. Lazarus asks whether 'if the kind of revolutionary consciousness to which Fanon alludes had actually existed in the era of decolonization, [it could] have been so rapidly or so easily unraveled in the first years of independence' (1990: 15). In the case of the India, it is possible to argue that there were a range of radical *possibilities* that were thrown up by the very nature of the anti-colonial struggle and the process of decolonization; what happens after independence does not negate these possibilities even as it may eliminate, co-opt or reshape them.

## Culture, Community, and Nation

But why *organize* in the interests of culture? Beyond the *Angarey* phenomenon, the genesis of the PWA can be traced back to two curiously disparate influences outside India as well—the Bloomsbury circle, with whom both Zaheer and Mulk Raj Anand had developed a personal acquaintance, and the European group, 'International Writers for the Defense of Culture', whose 1935 Congress in Paris they attended. In his memoirs, *Conversations in Bloomsbury*, which consists of vignettes of meetings with luminaries ranging from the Woolfs, to E.M. Forster, T.S. Eliot, Clive Bell, and Lytton Strachey, Anand writes of being attracted to the stimulating intellectual atmosphere of Bloomsbury (while working part-time as a proof corrector at the Hogarth Press) but feeling 'nervous and on edge about the undeclared ban on political talk' (1995: ix). Though drawn to the literary brilliance of the European modernists whom he meets and eager to share his work with them, Anand also found himself dismayed by what he saw as a general acceptance, even endorsement, of British imperialism in India; these vignettes are replete with painful and illuminating glimpses of genteel ethnocentrism and racism. He writes of wanting to learn from the writers and critics he meets, but also 'out of my own disillusionment with Europe, to show the concave mirror to Western intellectuals, however eminent they may be' (1995: 169). Out of these encounters grew a desire to create a stimulating literary circle that would reproduce the excitement of Bloomsbury but one that would also be political and definitively anti-imperialist in its provenance. There was a sense that as subjects of a colonial regime, Indian writers necessarily had a political and activist role to play for they had seen 'the ugly face of Fascism in our country earlier than the writers of the European country' (Anand 1979: 17). For these writers, situated at the intersection of an encroaching fascism and an entrenched colonialism, each of these political ideologies cast light upon the workings of the other, and made culture visible as a zone of conflict and subjugation; as such, it was also a zone of intervention. It would not be enough, however, to simply posit an originary national culture in response to fascism and colonialism, for on these native grounds, 'narrow nationalists' and 'revivalists' waged their own war against the people at large (18). The most meaningful strategy in this minefield of contradictions and ambiguities would be to create spaces and institutions that would enable writers to 'popularize' culture.

The idea of 'popularizing culture' through organizing was, of course, one that had gained currency in the France of the Popular Front in the 1930s; influential cultural fronts—including one for African-Americans— were also being formed in the US in the post-Depression era of the Works Progress Administration.[8] The term, 'cultural front' was increasingly used by those on the left to 'connote their insistence on culture as one arm, or front, of a widening campaign for social, political, and racial inequality' (Mullen 1999: 2).[9] In France, the Communist Party played a pivotal role in this process, sponsoring the formation of the Association of Revolutionary Artists and Writers (AEAR) in 1932 'with the aim of gathering together, under the vague aegis of the party, all intellectuals opposed to fascism' (Jackson 1988: 119). Like the manifesto Zaheer and Anand would circulate to Indian writers in 1936, the AEAR's 1933 manifesto against German fascism was signed by a range of well-known non-party writers including the two Andres, Gide and Malraux, Romain Rolland, and Louis Aragon whom Zaheer consulted about the formation of the PWA. In keeping with the shift from valorizing proletarian literature to forging broad cultural coalitions, the 1935 Congress of 'The International Writers for the Defense of Culture' laid out relatively pragmatic goals: 'The guarding of our civil liberties, the organization of writers to safeguard their own economic interests and to render help to the writers exiled by fascism' (Anand 1979: 13). A range of European literary luminaries attended this Congress, including E.M. Forster, Julien Benda, Aldous Huxley, Heinrich Mann, Elya Ehrenburg, Isaac Babel, Boris Pasternak, Christina Stead, and Michael Gold (Coppola 1974: 14). Mulk Raj Anand writes that there was also a general sense at the 1935 Congress that it was important to gain 'the support of the labouring classes' and to join the United Front against fascism (1979: 13). This broad conception of a progressive cultural front resonated with the prevalent coalitional thinking among these London-based Indian intellectuals whose political views ranged from 'the radical socialist nationalism of which Nehru was the most representative, to the communism of Sajjad Zahir [sic]' and the Gandhian utopianism to which Anand was attracted (Russell 1999: 70). Indian communists like Zaheer had already accepted that the Indian National Congress and Gandhi, in particular, dominated the anti-imperialist struggle and 'that the radicals, the revolutionaries also should, therefore, work through this movement, radicalise it if they liked' (Zaheer 1979a: 43).

And so, as the Indian expatriates 'emerged from the slough of despond of the cafes and garrets of Bloomsbury and formed the nucleus of the London-based Indian Progressive Writer's Association' which met to read and discuss members' work, they confronted the question of their own location (Anand 1979: 1). Though aware of 'the advantages of forming the association in London,' they felt that a 'few exiled Indians could do little more than draw up plans among themselves and produce an orphanlike [sic] literature under the influence of European culture' (Zaheer 1979a: 39). At best, they could 'represent Indian literature in the West and ... interpret for India, the thoughts of Western writers and the social problems which were profoundly influencing Western literature' (40). The more urgent task at hand was to reinterpret India for Indians themselves. The past, writes Mulk Raj Anand, has to be rescued 'from the maligning of Imperialist archaeology on the one side and from its misuse by reactionary elements in our society, whether they be the narrow nationalist revivalists, the priestcraft, or orthodoxy' (1979: 18). As with the Popular Front in France, there was an attempt here not merely to inspire avant-gardism but to reclaim Indian culture tout court; the PWA nominated themselves 'to be the inheritors of the best traditions of Indian civilization' (Anand 1979: 21).

For the intellectuals who met in 1935 at the Nanking Restaurant in London to set up what was initially called the Progressive Writers Group, the question of location was, obviously, not one of authenticity, but that of the most effective site for cultural work and intervention. Invested as they were in anti-imperialism, it was the emergent Indian nation that would provide this site. This necessitated physical proximity; exile was not perceived as the most useful vantage point. At this early point, the primary aim does seem to have been to create a climate for discussion and debate: 'We knew, of course, that good literature could not be produced to "order". But we aimed at creating those conditions for our writers which would help them in their work ... [through] mutual criticism and just appreciation' (Zaheer 1979b: 49). These conditions would be fostered in institutional contexts in the form of cultural institutes, workshops, translation projects, advocacy groups for freedom of expression, seminars, conferences, and sponsored publications such as periodicals, books, and pamphlets. The idea, eventually put into practice, was to proliferate a number of local PWAs to correspond to various linguistic regions and to make Hindustani a common language written in the Roman script (which did not happen, of course). English came to be the predominant language of business and general critical discussion while it was in the Urdu and Hindi-speaking regions that the PWA became enormously influential among writers (Russell 1999: 79).[10] Other PWA goals included bringing literature into close contact with the people; this took place to a certain limited extent in the form of poetry and story recitals which included the participation of peasant and worker poets in some regions (82). Written texts necessarily had a limited and class circumscribed readership in a context where illiteracy was high. As Ralph Russell has pointed out, there was, in fact, fairly widespread support for the inauguration of the PWA from across the intelligentsia and literati. The support of literary luminaries such as Munshi Premchand and Rabindranath Tagore added enormously to the nationwide cache of the organization. The relatively free and supportive atmosphere in which many PWA associates worked was, however, to change with Independence and the emergence of anti-communism in Nehruvian circles, on the one hand, and the hardening of Communist Party control of the organization, on the other.

The early manifestos and essays do indicate some tension between the more programmatically-inclined members of the group, such as Zaheer, and those like Anand who were anxious to retain heterogeneity.[11] Even Zaheer, however, would concede that it was a 'consciousness, in many cases vague and undefined' of the need for change that led to the formation of the PWA (1979a: 48, my emphasis). Mahmuduzzafar argued that it was 'futile to search for all-embracing definitions' while Ahmad Ali understood the word 'progressive' not to mean 'revolutionary', but 'the consciousness of what we are, what we were, what we should or can be. It is dynamic in essence' (Mahmuduzzafar 1979a: 87; Ali 1979: 78–9). As such, 'Progressive writing' (or 'Progressivism' as some termed it), itself became the subject of productive discussion and debate. I map the ways in which some of the most interesting writers who worked in this radicalized environment evolved their own perspectives on what constituted the 'progressive'—and how they conceptualized the role of the writer in relation to projects of social transformation. As a broad imperative (perhaps because the organization was always already heterogeneous—filling its ranks with both established writers and newer ones), the 'progressive' emerged not so much prefabricated content, as a general critical spirit. Even Zaheer insisted that the definition of 'progressive' would be 'neither narrow nor sectarian' (1979b: 51). Instead, its meaning itself would emerge from discussions and debates that happened within broad parameters such as combating 'literary trends reflecting communalism, racial antagonism, and exploitation of man by man' (51). Nevertheless, essay after essay returns to one common 'purpose', that is, to make literature a revitalizing force of 'social regeneration' both at the level of the individual psyche and that of society at large (Russell 1999: 72). In his famous inaugural address at the 1936 Conference, for instance, literary *éminence grise,* Premchand, 'invoked the need for literature to "arouse in us a critical spirit", and to be "force-giving" and dynamic' (1979: 53). Literature's function would be to awaken a certain moral capacity in its constituency; not through 'fear and cajolery, reward and retribution' like religious morality, but by arousing our 'sense of beauty' (53).

Premchand's address invokes the two concepts whose pairing best describes the 'critical realism' of the PWA that Aijaz Ahmad alludes to without defining. (The term does not, however, appear in the literature itself.)[12] For Premchand, if, on the one hand, literature must engage our 'inherent sense of beauty', on the other, it must 'make us face the grim realities of life in a spirit of determination' (1979: 53). Realism, within this framework, is less a specific aesthetic technique than a philosophy that brings together an affective sense of justice, fairness, and harmony with an understanding of all that violates that sense. Beauty—our sense of the aesthetic and the affective—has to be recuperated from orthodoxy, and redefined. The literary perspectives developed by writers as diverse as Rashid Jahan and Saadat Hasan Manto attempt to combine the *cognitive*, or what Roy Bhaskar calls 'explanatory critiques' of existing conditions and the *affective*—discourses 'of place, body, inheritance, sensuous need' (Bhaskar 1993: 2; Eagleton 1990: 34). In an insightful essay where he discusses what he sees as the Western left's 'fatal surrender' of aesthetics to the right, Terry Eagleton points to the dilemmas of the left vis-a-vis discourses of the particular such as nationalism: 'The political left is then doubly disabled: if it seeks to evolve its own discourse of place, body, inheritance, sensuous need, it will find itself *miming the cultural forms of its opponents*; if it does not do so it will appear bereft of a body, marooned with a purely rationalist politics that has cut loose from the intimate affective depths of the poetic' (1990: 34, my emphasis). In some ways, it is this challenging project of bringing together the rational (systemic analysis of self and society, universal values) and the affective (cultural identity, particularity, and desire), in a context where the nationalist centre and religious-communal right had appropriated the latter, that marked the attempts—not always successful—of different writers in this radicalized climate to develop a literature that would think through questions of individual and social transformation.[13]

Any oppressed group, Eagleton suggests, also needs 'to generate a positive particular culture without which political emancipation is probably impossible. Nobody can live in perpetual deferment of their sense of selfhood, or free themselves from bondage without a strongly affirmative sense of who they are' (1990: 37). It is this recognition that alienation's true triumph 'would be not to know that one was alienated at all' that marks the importance accorded to the anti-colonial national within the Progressive movement: 'They attack the national character of our literature by preaching that all culture is cosmopolitan, that it has no national characteristic and form' (Eagleton 1990: 37; Sharma 1979: 135). This nation, unlike Nehru's, was defined not as much our expressive content as an enabling structure, a space where freedom must be defended so that 'we can discuss, criticise, and remould our varying ideals and develop our national culture' (Anand 1979: 12). This attitude to the national was also marked by an awareness of all that was problematic about nationalism as it was being articulated in the present, combined with a sense of its liberationist and revolutionary potential. Imperialism, capitalism, feudalism, fascism, and communalism came to be seen within this analytic as interconnected phenomena that needed to be part of the same sustained critique.

Ultimately, the question of what constituted the progressive was, for these important and influential writers, less an issue of 'external directives' or 'internal conscience' than the focus of literary and critical enquiry. As such, this literature merits as much consideration in terms of the *projects* it undertook as with regard to its actual *achievements*—or lack thereof—as some critics might have it (to borrow Neil Lazarus' useful distinction [1990: 222]). To understand the historical imperatives that engendered the radicalism of the transitional period is to open up space for more grounded investigations of our own narratives of progress and transformation. Rather than pit 'postmodern' ideas against somewhat reductive understandings of an 'old ideal of purely political commitment', as do the questions posed by *Indian Literature*'s editors in an evaluation of the legacy of Progressive writing, it may be more productive to examine the ways in which the PWA itself engendered a diverse body of texts deriving from shared literary and political concerns (1992: 152). If these texts found themselves defining transformation and moral vision with regard to the exigencies of their times, what do our times call upon us to do as critics, writers, and intellectuals? How do we understand our own historical moment and what are the ways in which that understanding should shape our commitments? It is my contention exploring the literary production of the period—in the case of Urdu and English, that of authors like Rashid Jahan, Ismat Chughtai, Sajjad Zaheer, Ahmad Ali, Krishan Chander, Rajinder Singh Bedi, Razia Sajjad Zaheer, Siddiqa Begum Seharvi, K.A. Abbas, and Mulk Raj Anand—will yield an even greater understanding of the richness of diverse endeavours to define and formulate progressive and socially transformative projects, endeavours that were simultaneously flawed and visionary.

## Notes

1. At least two published versions of this manifesto exist: the first was published in *Left Review* (1935); later, an amended version translated into Hindi was published in the literary journal *Hans*. For an interesting comparison of the two versions, see Coppola 1974.

2. Khizar Humayun Ansari suggests that there were other precursors to such literary organizations, such as the Tahzib al-Akhlaq and the Anjuman-I-Panjab. The latter 'aimed to advance 'popular knowledge' through the vernaculars and through discussions of social, literary, scientific and political interest' and expand the purview of poetry and poetry recitals to include new subjects and styles. The Anjuman-I-Taraqqi Urdu was founded in 1903, inspired by English liberalism, and was instrumental in encouraging Marxist approaches to literature and literary criticism (1990: 157).

3. Ansari points out that by the end of the 1920s, several Urdu-speaking Indian Muslim students including Sajjad Zaheer and Hajrah Begum were involved with the Oxford and Cambridge Majlises and were instrumental in taking those organizations leftwards; topics of debate they introduced included 'Imperialism', 'Communalism', and 'The Language Problem'. Some of them gathered into a Marxist study circle in London.

4. As mathematician and occasional historian, D.D. Kosambi observed in the mid-1950s. The big Indian bourgeoisie owes its present position to two war periods of heavy profit-making. The First World War gave Indian capital its first great impetus and initiated the process of Indianizing the bureaucracy. The Second World War vastly expanded the army and Indianized the officer corps; further it swelled the tide of Indian accumulation

and enabled the capitalists, by rallying the masses behind the Congress Party, to complete the process of pushing the British out of the country (1957: 25).

5.  Khizar Ansari points out, correctly, that the collaboration with the Congress while it had gone underground, allowed communist members of the PWA such as Sajjad Zaheer to develop closer relationships with their fellows in mainstream nationalist politics. This 'assured the Progressive Movement of a warm reception in larger sections of the Indian intellectual community' (1990: 167). As Ralph Russell has also pointed out, the PWA's closeness to Nehru and other nationalist figures did allow the organization a degree of mainstream acceptance.

6.  See Kumar 1993, esp. chapters 4 and 5 for an extensive account of women's 'doings' in political sphere during this period.

7.  See Ansari 1990, esp. Chapter IV, 'The social background of Muslim socialists of the 1930s and 40s'. Ansari makes a useful observation about the 'qasbah' background of many leading PWA figures, with its emphasis on Islamic culture and learning.

8.  For detailed accounts of Popular Front culture in the US, see Denning (1997) and Mullen (1999); and in France, Jackson (1988).

9.  Mullen argues that 'the 1936 opening of Chicago's black "cultural front" represented both a culmination and new beginning for African-American engagement of and revision within the U.S. Left' (6).

10. For a succinct account of debates among Hindi writers affiliated to the PWA, see Rai (2000).

11. Though there were to be common interests among its constituent members, at no point in the first constitution adopted at the 1936 PWA Conference or in any early manifestos do we see anything even as programmatic as the committed guidelines suggested for the John Reed Clubs in the US that had been established some years before. Where the latter had some interest in making 'industrial correspondents' of its affiliated writers, the manifesto adopted at the PWA Conference simply states that it is the object of the Association.

12. Ahmad does not appear to be using Lukacs' definition of critical realism either. Lukacs saw critical realism as a mainly bourgeois aesthetic which had a progressive stance in contrast to bourgeois modernism. Its subject matter was the 'social and ideological crisis of bourgeois society' (1962: 60). In contrast to modernism, which exalts 'life's very baseness and emptiness', critical realism 'transforms the positive and negative elements of bourgeois

life into "typical" situations' (68). While critical realism was not hostile to socialism, it did not include a socialist perspective which was fundamental to the more radical 'socialist realism'. My own use of the term with regard to the PWA is closer to Roy Bhaskar's 'dialectical critical realism' which combines anti-positivist 'explanatory critique' and emancipatory/transformative axiology (1993: 2).

13. In the context of the Indian Left, this argument has particular resonance. The Left has, indeed, been conventionally associated, as even the PWA manifesto seems to suggest, with 'a rational and scientific basis for social change' (Panikkar 1990: 9), while the communal Right has been more successful in deploying the rhetoric of sensuous particularity and cultural identity. Recent debates within the broad spectrum of the Indian Left has returned repeatedly to the idea that the Left needs to recuperate the ground of the aesthetic, the cultural and even the religious-ecumenical. While Panikkar problematizes the recuperation of religion within secular traditions, Aijaz Ahmad has suggested that an 'ideological struggle against Hindutva fascism must recoup, as a significant element, those traditions of humanism, ecumenism, agnosticism, and anti-casteist worldview which we have inherited from our medieval anti-Brahmininical movements' (1993: 65). These were debates that were familiar to those associated with the PWA and IPTA.

## Works Cited

Ahmad, Aijaz. *In Theory: Classes, Nations, Literatures.* London: Verso, 1992.

————. 'Fascism and National Culture: Reading Gramsci in the Days of Hindutva', in *Social Scientist* 21 (3–4), 1993. 32–67.

Ali, Ahmad. 'Progressive View of Art', in *Marxist Cultural Movement in India*, Vol. 1. Ed. Sudhi Pradhan. Calcutta: National Book Agency, 1979.

————. 'The Progressive Writers Movement and Creative Writers in Urdu' in *Marxist Influences and South Asian Literature.* Ed. Carlo Coppola in South Asia series occasional paper, No. 23. East Lansing, MI: Michigan State University, 1940.

Alvi, Khalid. (Ed.) *Angare.* Delhi: Educational Publishing House, 1995.

Amin, Shahid. 'Gandhi as Mahatma', in *Selected Subaltern Studies.* Eds Ranajit Guha and Gayatri Spivak. New York: Oxford University Press, 1988.

Anand, Mulk Raj. 'On the Progressive Writers Movement', in *Marxist Cultural*

*Movement in India*, Vol. 1. Ed. Sudhi Pradhan in Calcutta: National Book Agency, 1979.

————.'Mulk Raj Anand remembers', in *Indian Literature*. New Delhi: Sahitya Akademi Publications, 1993.

————.*Conversations in Bloomsbury*. New Delhi: Oxford University Press, 1995.

Ansari, Khizar Humayun. *The Emergence of Socialist Thought among North Indian Muslims (1917–1947)*. Lahore: Book Traders, 1990.

Bhaskar, Roy. *Dialectic: The Pulse of Freedom*. London: Verso, 1993.

Chatterjee, Partha. *Nationalist Thought and the Colonial World: A Derivative Discourse?* Minneapolis: Minnesota University Press, 1986.

————.*The Nation and its Fragments*. Princeton NJ: Princeton University Press, 1993.

Coppola, Carlo. 'The All-India Progressive Writers Association: The European Phase', in *Marxist Influences and South Asian Literature*. Ed. Carlo Coppola in South Asia series occasional paper, No. 23. East Lansing, MI: Michigan State University, 1974.

Denning, Michael. *The Cultural Front: The Laboring of American Culture in the Twentieth-Century*. London and New York: Verso, 1997.

Eagleton, Terry. 'Nationalism: Irony and Commitment', in *Nationalism, Colonialism and Literature*. Ed. Seamus Deane. Minneapolis: Minnesota University Press, 1990.

'From the Postmodern to the Progressive: Questions' (1992). *Indian Literature*, 151–2.

Forbes, Geraldine. '*Women in Modern India*', in *New Cambridge History of India*. Cambridge: Cambridge University Press, 1996.

Gramsci, Antonio. *Selections from the Prison Notebooks*. Trans. Quentin Hoare and G. Nowell-Smith. New York: International Publishers, 1971.

Hajrah Begum. Interview on 1 September 1990. Oral History Archives. Nehru Memorial Museum and Library, New Delhi, 1990.

Jackson, Julian. *The Popular Front in France: Defending Democracy*. Cambridge: Cambridge University Press, 1988.

Kosambi, D.D. Exasperating Essays: exercises in the dialectical method. Calcutta: India Book Exchange, 1957.

Kumar, Radha. *The History of Doing: An Illustrated Account of Movements for Women's Rights and Feminism in India, 1800–1990*. London: Verso, 1993.

Lazarus, Neil. *Resistance in Postcolonial African Fiction*. New Haven: Yale University Press, 1990.

Lukacs, Georg. *The Meaning of Contemporary Realism*. London: Merlin Press, 1962.

Mahmuduzzafar. 'Intellectuals and cultural reaction', in *Marxist Cultural Movement in India: Chronicles and Documents*, Vol. 1. Ed. Sudhi Pradhan Calcutta: National Book Agency, 1979a.

Manto, Saadat Hasan. 'Taraqqi Pasand Socha Nahin Karte' [Progressives Don't Think] in *Mantonaama* [The Works of Manto]. Trans. and Ed. Devendra Issar. Delhi: Indraprastha Prakashan, 1996.

Mullen, Bill. *Popular Fronts: Chicago and African-American Cultural Politics, 1935–46*. Urbana: University of Illinois Press, 1999.

Nehru, Jawaharlal. 'A Tryst with Destiny', in *Nehru: The First Sixty Years*, Vol. 2. Ed. Dorothy Norman, New York: John Day, 1965.

Panikkar, K.N. 'Culture and consciousness in modern India: A historical perspective', in *Social Scientist* 18 (4), 1990 3–32.

Pradhan, Sudhi. (Ed.) *Marxist Cultural Movement in India: Chronicles and Documents*. 3 Vols. Calcutta: National Book Agency, 1979.

Premchand, Munshi. 'The nature and purpose of literature', in *Marxist Cultural Movement in India: Chronicles and Documents*, Vol. 1. Ed. Sudhi Pradhan. Calcutta: National Book Agency, 1979.

Rabinowitz, Paula. *Labor and Desire: Women's Revolutionary Fiction in Depression America*. Chapel Hill, NC: University of North Carolina Press, 1991.

Rai, Alok. 'The trauma of independence: some aspects of Progressive Hindi literature 1945–7', in *Inventing Boundaries: Gender, Politics and the Partition of India*. Ed. Mushirul Hasan. New Delhi: Oxford University Press, 2000.

Sarkar, Sumit. *Modern India: 1885–1947*. New Delhi: MacMillan, 1983.

Sharma, Ram Bilas. 'Report to the Sixth Session, All-India Progressive Writers Conference', in *Marxist Cultural Movement in India*, Vol. 3. Ed. Sudhi Pradhan. Calcutta: National Book Agency, 1979.

Siddiqui, Shakeel. 'Aaj bhi sulag rahen hain chah dashak purane Angarey' [They glow even today, those six decades old embers] in *Angarey*. Ed. Sajjad Zaheer. (Transliterated by Shakeel Siddiqui from the original, Lucknow: Nizami Press, 1932). Delhi: Parimal Prakashan, 1990.

Russell, Ralph. *How not to Write the History of Urdu Literature and Other Essays on Urdu and Islam*. New Delhi: Oxford University Press, 1999.

Tharu, Susie and K. Lalita. 'Introduction' in *Women Writing in India. Volume II: The Twentieth Century*. New York: Feminist Press, 1993.

Zaheer, Sajjad, 'Reminiscences', in *Marxist Cultural Movement in India*, Vol.1, Ed. Sudhi Pradhan. Trans. Khalique Naqvi. Calcutta: National Book Agency, 1979b.

————'A Note on the Progressive Writers Association', in *Marxist Cultural Movement in India*, Vol.1. Ed. Sudhi Pradhan. Calcutta: National Book Agency, 1979b.

————*Angarey*. (Transliterated by Shakeel Siddiqui from the original, Lucknow: Nizami Press, 1932). Delhi: Parimal Prakashan, 1990.

# Nation and Nationhood in Modern Sri Lankan Literature

CHELVA KANAGANAYAKAM

In the federal elections in Canada in 2004, the Bloc Quebecois—the French party in Quebec—won fifty-four out of the seventy-five available seats in the province, and the leader of the party, Gilles Duceppe, announced in his victory speech that 'Quebec forms a nation'.[1] The announcement drew attention to an issue that is deeply entrenched in Canadian politics, one that threatens to destabilize the idea of Canada as a unified nation. In the process of proclaiming what amounted to a secessionist statement, Duceppe implicitly pointed to all the contradictions that shape the national imaginary in Canada. Given the geography and demographics of the country, the problem of sovereignty manifests itself often in somewhat benign terms, but the fact remains that the country sanctions the presence of forces that have the potential to undermine its status as a nation. The possibility of separation is not taken lightly by Canada, but support for separation is not seen as tantamount to treason. Consequently, literature too is not overtly concerned with the politics of secession. Canada, however, continues to be an exception among countries that have to deal with secessionist claims. In different ways, the question of national unity arises in many other nations where the idea of the nation has come under considerable stress, including Sri Lanka, which is the concern of the present essays.

Despite all the limitations of Fredric Jameson's comment about Third World literature and national allegory, the reality is that postcolonial literature has a deep investment in the idea of a nation.[2] Nations, freed from or created by the Empire, have inspired and sustained the creative writing of postcolonial nations. If nation-building is not the major concern of so many recent authors, it is equally true that authors often work with assumptions that go hand-in-hand with the idea of a unified nation-state. Notions of land and space, history, tradition, culture, and ritual, for example, are shaped by and dependent on the fundamental principles that govern the distinctiveness of a nation. Regardless of regional, religious, or ethnic differences, literature assumes the presence of the salient features of citizenship and nationality. Hence the practice of foregrounding national literatures as a defining category in postcolonial studies. If literatures that come out of a particular nation cannot easily be replicated elsewhere, it is because authors have very different ways of locating the constitutive features of the nation to which they belong. While genre and narrative mode, for example, may cut across nations, the manner in which they are shaped has a great deal to do with the particularities of nation states.

Thus the relation between the postcolonial nation and its literature is clearly symbiotic. Even when the literature is openly critical of some of the framing principles of the nation, it endorses others in order to validate and implicitly accept the idea of nation. For example, in a text that is as openly critical of the nation as *The Trouble with Nigeria* (1983), Chinua Achebe speaks from the vantage point of a nation-state. The failures he records are set against the backdrop of a homogenous entity called the nation. Even in literature that has very little to do with politics, the nation is an implied presence. Realist texts, for instance, work with a community whose identity is framed and upheld by the nation. The nation is present not because writers make explicit reference to the political structures that define it but because they draw on conventions that are peculiar to the integrity of the state. Even something as inconsequential as a journey from one city to another often implies economic concerns that in turn reflect the preoccupations of the state. If 'The Drover's Wife' by Henry Lawson could only have been written in Australia and 'How My Brother Leon Brought Home a Wife' by Manuel Arguilla could have been written only in the Philippines, it is because the stories are underpinned by a number of social and economic concerns that in turn reflect the preoccupations of the nation. Jameson may have gone too far by insisting on the idea of allegory, but he certainly was right in identifying a metonymic function that forged a connection between literature and the state.

In Sri Lanka during the last two decades, and more specifically in the last few years, the idea of a nation has witnessed several challenges. Starting in the 1950s and gathering momentum in the early 1970s, one faction or another has challenged the idea of a unified nation. But it is only recently that there has been a national and international recognition of two 'distinct societies'—to use a term that is popular in Canadian politics. The peace process brokered by Norway and endorsed by several other nations implies more than an international will to put out fires. It amounts to saying that there is more than one national imaginary that needs to be accommodated within the nation-state. The peace process does not entertain the idea of separation, but it has, for the moment, not intervened in the anomalous situation of a nation-state allowing two mutually exclusive taxation systems and two visa systems. Thus, anyone travelling to the North of Sri Lanka is subject to another visa and to another taxation system.[3] The infrastructure that holds the system together is complex and often confusing, but despite all the challenges, the country continues to be both unified and divided. The Sri Lankan situation is unique in that two national imaginaries make up one nation, and the government has sovereignty over the entire island but does not control all the territory.

The process that led to the current state of affairs has had a long history, going back to the time of independence or even beyond.[4] There is, however, a major difference between the thinking that shapes federalist politics and that which informs secessionist claims. Until recently, the sustained opposition to a unified state appeared in the form of federalism. The position for federalism is: 'I want my share if we are to stay together.' With secession it is: 'I am different, even if we decide to stay together.' To some extent, the latter is true of the situation in Sri Lanka. The rise and consolidation of the Liberation Tigers of Tamil Eelam (LTTE) is the crucial defining moment in the idea of two nations.

At one level it is possible to argue that if the idea of a nation divides to create several nations or national imaginaries, then the literature would follow suit by dealing with different aspects of two or more nations. In short, one would expect the paradigm that applied to the unified nation-state to replicate itself in the new configuration. As allegiance shifts from one to the other, literature too should reflect that process. That scheme would explain the evolution of the literatures of, say, India, Pakistan, and Bangladesh. Until Independence, these three nations were part of British India. As Pakistan and later Bangladesh came into being, literature too became nation-centred. My argument is that such generalization does not hold true in the case of Sri Lanka. Here I draw specific attention to writing in English and in Tamil, although it is likely that literature in Sinhala would not be very different in its multiplicity. In Sri Lanka, the idea of a separatist nation has arrived at the expense of some of the cultural and social features that constitute a nation. In other words, there is at times a disparity between the claim of a new national identity and the conditions that reinforce that identity. In such a situation, the literature reinforces the hiatus between social conditions and the power structures.

The ethnic conflict in Sri Lanka has entailed, among other things, displacement of people on a large scale. The most visible of the displacement takes the form of diaspora and a scattering of people across the globe. But there is also an internal diaspora caused by people getting displaced by conditions of strife or by the forced occupation of security forces. Displacement of people from one village or city to another entails, inevitably, a regrouping of communities, of adjusting to different landscapes, of accepting new social and religious rituals. Class, caste, and gender, for instance, get reconstituted in new and often complex ways. Such internal diaspora also involves an economic cost as people leave behind their ancestral homes and land used for agriculture. The distinctiveness that drives the new national imaginary has also entailed, in Sri Lanka, a subversion of that very uniqueness. Communities that have, for centuries, lived in relative isolation and fostered conventions that are specific to them are now suddenly faced with the situation of having to share space with 'other' groups and adapt to new and, sometimes, unacceptable conventions. To take a specific example, some villages whose separateness has been underscored by a particular caste affiliation, are now compelled to live in close proximity to and interact with other castes. In such situations, ethnic loyalty alone does not override other cultural considerations. In an abstract sense, they now claim a sense of belonging on the strength of living in LTTE controlled areas; at the same time they experience a sense of the alienation of cultural and social displacement. While it is true that the conflict itself has been confined to certain areas and the effects have not been felt equally by all ethnic groups, even the most isolated areas of the country have been indirectly affected by the changes that occurred.

Thus the new configuration that has provided the basis for ethnic and even national identity has also disrupted the conventions within which that identity was formulated. Even relations within the family need to be restructured as landowners become workers and husbands and wives take on new roles. Rituals change as landscape and economic strength alters, with the consequence that old identities have to be jettisoned. By a curious irony, diasporic communities overseas, confronted with marginalization in their host countries, provide the economic strength to bolster an ethno-national identity in their home countries. As political structures get strengthened, the idea of nationhood takes firm roots, despite the fact that within the community itself there is no corresponding sense of consolidation. Of course, such ambiguity does not explain the positive energy that comes with territorial control, but a simple formulation that sees nationalism in relation to territorial control is hardly adequate or even accurate. Even the partial realization of a national dream becomes a deeply compromised affair, causing both a sense of belonging and otherness.

One also needs to keep in mind that a simple binary would not explain the whole process of rethinking the idea of a nation. The very recent division among the LTTE is a reminder that regional loyalties might well take precedence over ethnic ones. Although the conflict between the leadership of the LTTE and the Karuna group in the east has been largely discussed in relation to power structures, the fact is that the conflict points to primordial loyalties that are based on land and culture.[5] Although the conflict manifested itself as dissension among LTTE groups, the causes probably lie much deeper. Batticaloa, in hill country, remains an enclave of its own, with its unique cultural traditions, social rituals, and language practices. While a Tamil identity incorporates both the east and the north, where Tamils are concentrated, the differences between them are quite striking. In this instance the boundaries are much more difficult to define, but they are real, nonetheless. Historically, constituted identities do not always have the political power to morph into territorial claims, but they unsettle easy attempts to incorporate them into larger political or cultural structures.

Regardless of whether one celebrates or condemns the political decisions that constitute this new state of affairs, a two- or three-nation-state is in some ways a reality. It is real to the extent that a community of people have begun to think along such lines. And literature that grows out of this context plays an important role in drawing attention to the new ways in which one needs to conceptualize the current reality. To be specific, for people who live in the northern part of Sri Lanka, particularly the area that is administered by the LTTE, health care, security, agriculture, and a whole range of services are controlled by the LTTE. But their salaries may well be given by the Sri Lankan government, and they hold a Sri Lankan passport. Sovereignty is intact, but social cohesion has found a niche outside national unity. The integrity of Sri Lanka as a nation-state has been and will in all probability remain firm, but the legitimacy of separatist groups has altered the conceptualization of the national imaginary. On the one hand, the identity of Sri Lankans is predicated on their status as Sri Lankan nationals. On the other, their ethnic identity as Tamils is linked directly to the territorial control of the LTTE. And this state of affairs, inevitably, affects the literature that is produced.

In very broad terms, the literature produced locally is either in English or in the vernaculars, namely Sinhala or Tamil. In sheer quantity, Sinhala and Tamil literature outnumber the writing in English, although the latter has a greater reach and accesses an international readership. In addition, there is also a growing body of diasporic literature, both in English and the vernacular. About the vernaculars in the diaspora, little is known, but that too is an important aspect of this body of writing. In fact, in countries such as Canada and England, diasporic literature has flourished in ways that were totally unexpected. Any taxonomy has to recognize that these literatures occupy their own spaces while having some features in common. English writing, by comparison, is small, with a few writers in Canada, England, and Australia making up the major part of diasporic writing. The rest are located in Sri Lanka. While English writing is small in quantity, it occupies a special niche in its international reach and its influence.

I have argued elsewhere that there is a deep-seated anxiety among authors writing in English about the new political context.[6] A specific instance of this is Romesh Gunesekera's *Heaven's Edge* (2002), which frames its narrative within an allegorical structure in order to deliberately problematize the issue of representation. From a diasporic perspective, the anxiety might well be a result of recognizing that political divisions are not as clear-cut as they were when the idea of a unitary nation-state remained intact. A certain kind of humanism informs the text, which enables the narrator to critique the violence of conflict without engaging in the various ideological positions of the different factions. Along similar lines, Michael Ondaatje published *Anil's Ghost* in 2000, a novel that combines deep political engagement with aesthetic distance. The novel moves in and out of an allegorical structure, but what is most noticeable about it is its attempt to be objective and neutral. The author's decision to locate the narrative during a time when at least three groups—the Tamil separatists, the JVP, and the government—were involved in the conflict is in itself a strategy to remain neutral. The refusal to engage directly with political forces might well be a limitation in this body of writing, but there is clearly an unwillingness to take sides and espouse clear stances. It is possible to argue that those who write in English may well, in many cases, stand outside sectarian politics. Issues of class, language, and ethnic affiliation are often factors which explain why these writers may be less committed to radical stances than vernacular writers. But they too are aware of the indeterminacy of the context.

An interesting line of inquiry might well be the actual extent to which 'local' writers in English map the new political context. A point of comparison here would be the large number of novels that were written soon after the insurgency of 1971. In those texts, the moral and human issues did entail different stances, but the dominant ideological position worked with a particular version of the nation-state. The insurgency and separatism are, at some level, similar in that they contest a particular version of the nation. The current situation, however, leads to a very different kind of ambivalence. With the insurgency, the subjectivity of the authors amounted to an understanding of grief, loss, and misguided idealism, but there was no endorsement of the movement itself. Separatism in Sri Lanka is very different in its origins and evolution, and that is reflected in the literature as well. Of course, there are differences between, say, the work of Jean Arasanayagam and Carl Muller, or between Rajiva Wijesinha and Chandani Lokuge. But in all of them there is a consciousness and an anxiety about the problematic status of the nation. It is all too easy to claim that English writing is 'national' while vernacular writing is 'ethnic'. Such a formulation would be true to the extent that writing in English tends to be international in readership. Even writers who do not appear in the West tend to publish in India and in the process reach a wider South Asian audience. Diasporic writers are inevitably transnational. Notions of authorship tend to be configured differently when the conditions of literary production are dictated by publishing companies that think in international terms.

More importantly, those who write in English, even if they live in Sri Lanka, are located in cosmopolitan cities such as Kandy and Colombo. They belong to a class that moves easily among ethnic groups, and their fluency in English gives them access to a cultural nexus that celebrates hybridity rather than ethnic 'purity'. And there is, of course, the issue of language that is both a limitation and a source of empowerment. The language they use belongs to a tradition of writing that lends itself more easily to certain conceptual frames. Writing in Tamil, for example, reinforces 'Tamilness' in a way that is hardly possible in English. Whatever the causes, writing in English, even when it is most politically engaged, is firmly wedded to the notion of a unitary nation-state.

Shyam Selvadurai, whose work has been quite self-consciously 'ethnic' in many ways, has recently written an essay in the *New York Times* about his summer holidays in Canada. The essay entitled 'Summerscapes' is about visiting cottage country, a favourite pastime for Ontario residents who travel north on weekends and holidays to escape the city. For Selvadurai, the visit evokes memories of a home that was destroyed and he laments the injustice of not having a personal history to recall and celebrate. Strangely enough, his personal history is erased rather than reinforced by separatist claims. Being comfortably ethnic within the framework of the national is what he needs to affirm his personal identity, and that is no longer available in Sri Lanka. The essay ends with Selvadurai finding in cottage country markers of his previous visits and wonders whether in time, he too will be able to claim a history in cottage country:

With each year, I saw the progress of my entries from unfamiliar to familiar to be taken-for-granted; a growing knowledge of my landscape.
As I looked around the room, I found other evidence of my presence—a pair of fire-engine-red slippers, bought in Chinatown for $1 ... acid-washed jeans from my club days, turned into cutoffs, and then just abandoned ... One book held a photograph of me in my old favorite swimming trunks; on the back, a friend

had written 'f.y.i., Speedos went out in the 80's.' … I had been so caught up in the past, I had not realized that this Canadian holiday home held my history too.

In a very different way, the essay points to a crisis of sorts where national imaginaries have become more difficult to identify. Compare this with the stance in *Funny Boy* (1994) and the distinction becomes immediately apparent. The novel was published at a time when an oppositional stance was relevant. The irony is that the novel is a strong critique of the Sri Lankan government. Now, with the Tamils being much closer to regional autonomy, the author records his sense of permanent exile. Writers such as Selvadurai are uncomfortable in the various imaginaries that are flaunted in the present. Hybridity is often a casualty in such contexts. In the case of Selvadurai, there was no other way to configure the cultural and social costs of the new framework.

With vernacular writers, and I use writers in Tamil as a point of reference, the issues take a different form. Literature in Tamil is shaped by a very different set of conventions regarding authorship, audience, and conditions of production. It is more local in scope, and its readers expect a much closer engagement with issues of social and political identity. Being 'local' also accounts for the differences that one encounters between the writers from, say, Batticaloa as against the hill country. Even among the Jaffna-based writers who constitute the majority, there are significant differences, and they point to the problematic nature of literary production. The absence of homogeneity is more noticeable in the vernacular, with the consequence that approaches to the nation are predictably diverse.

There is, of course, a body of literature in Tamil that is clearly intended to be celebratory. In this literature the message is far more important than the artifice of the text. To say this is not to discount the significance of such literature, but to point out that it is created by conviction, by a deep-seated faith in the new configuration. Such writing is often endorsed or even facilitated by political forces. The ideological stance of this writing is never in doubt, but its challenge lies in the manner in which it celebrates nationhood in the absence of a territorial or political entity that can be called a nation. It is thus not surprising that some of them resort to originary myths, or historical narratives of conquest to reflect and legitimize the present. The nation is sometimes conceptualized in a manner that resembles a kingdom rather than a modern nation state. Tales of individual heroism are folded into a collective struggle for a Tamil identity. It is probably no accident that much of the literature that fall into this category tends to be poetry rather than fiction. Short poems lend themselves more readily to the expression of subjective, personal experiences that reiterate the glory of the present political order. Longer epic-like poems are equally effective in transforming the present into mythical narratives of celebration. Realist fiction would be more difficult to write along these lines since the tension between the two formulations of statehood would be difficult to avoid.

Equally interesting is the body of writing that has all the trappings of social realist literature, and often documents the collapse of a whole system of cultural values. This is a body of literature about sorrow and lamentation. Gender, age, land, ritual, sexuality, caste, and whole range of related issues are dealt with in these texts. A curious element of these texts is that the sense of loss does not necessarily entail a critique of the political system. Realist fiction that does not allude to politics at all is not necessarily evasive. It is often quite self-sufficient in itself, but its process of selecting contiguous features is such that political institutions do not enter the text.

There is, in such texts, no attempt to exonerate or blame those in power. There is a refusal to address the issue of who is to blame. The texts tend to avoid those markers that would identify the state apparatus as the guilty party. It is conceivable that such literature needs to be separated from that which was written by the previous generation of writers, whose social realism did not exclude the state. The paradox is that the literature records the collapse of values which were crucial to the identity of the ethnic group. It is for the continuity of such identification that secessionist claims were made and yet, in the interim, the literature is content with recording the loss rather than blaming one group or the other. This literature is about loss rather than blame; it is about portraying what has been lost rather than probing what has been gained. Consciously or otherwise, there is a hiatus between the literary world and the national imaginary.

The significance of this literature might well be that it reveals a dimension of secession that stands outside official narratives. It is not about how many died, or how many were displaced, or what kinds of rights were won as with what happens when the sense of community is disrupted, or when rituals fail, or when the relation with land and space gets strained. Official narratives might indicate how many were displaced, but literature provides a sense of how the displacement affects one's sense of rootedness. It is interesting how when a writer in English, such as Ondaatje, writes about state ideology without taking sides, and when a Tamil writer writes about domestic relations without any reference to those who wield power, they are both responding to a political situation that is both complex and fluid.

Diasporic literature occupies an interesting category altogether, partly because time and distance alter perspectives considerably. Faced with marginality in the host country, diasporic writers can be strongly—even idealistically—pro-secession, extolling the virtues of a new political order. As the same time, distance offers safety, and they can be critical or subversive, if necessary. At its best this literature records the crisis in culture as ethnic groups clash and fragile nations are born.

In a short poem by a diasporic writer, K.P. Aravindan (1999), there is a wonderful image of autumn and the gathering of fallen leaves. As the writer watches the scene, he is tempted into wondering where these various leaves belonged. As they are swept together and gathered they form an indistinguishable, but colorful mass, indicative of a new configuration, but the writer cannot help wondering about the loss of identity that enabled the new fusion. In these instances, the idea of a nation is made even more complex by the adopted land, which provides another home. If the wind in this poem is a trope for political change, then the poem drives home the hiatus between politics and identities based on nation states:

## Knowing

A wayward wind
in its embrace
at times brings fragrance
erratic force at others.

Whirling and rushing
across countries and continents
the indifferent wind
knows nothing.
Dead leaves
From trees and from the ground
gathered in its wake.

Together are plucked
green leaves
buds and blossoms.

Which belongs where?
Would the displaced
know their state? (35)

Timothy Brennan quite rightly points out that 'nations, then, are imaginary constructs that depend for their existence on an apparatus of cultural fictions in which imaginative literature plays a decisive role' (1990: 49). In the national imaginary of countries such as Sri Lanka, the relation between the two has become less transparent and certainly more ambiguous. With contemporary Sri Lankan literature, Jameson's notion of national allegory would hardly apply. We need a critical practice that would involve both the community and the nation without necessarily positing a traditional relation between the two.

## Notes

1. For a subsequent reiteration of his position, see http://www.mcgilldaily.com/view.php?aid=3431.

2. In a well-known essay, Jameson made the observation that 'all third-world texts are necessarily ... allegorical ... : they are to be read as what I will call national allegories ...' (1986: 69).

3. The destruction caused by the recent Tsunami further reiterates the complex intersections that make up the framework of the country. For example, countries that offered aid for rehabilitation of Tsunami victims had to take into account the absence of consensus about how the aid should be distributed. Some countries offered their assistance directly to the Sri Lankan government. Other nations, such as Canada, that did the same, were explicit about their desire to see that the benefits were evenly distributed. There were also nations that chose to deal independently with the government and the Tamil separatists. It is ironic that not even the magnitude of a Tsunami disaster could eclipse the deeply entrenched divisions in the country.

4. Nationalist historians tend to go back several centuries to the time of Sinhalese and Tamil kingdoms to legitimize the present state of affairs. A more pragmatic approach would begin with the year of Independence as a crucial moment in the opposition to a unified nation-state. However, until the late 1970s or even the early 1980s the idea of a distinctive society took the form of federalist politics. In practice, federalism adopted an oppositional stance, but it was really with the rise of militant separatist movements that the idea of two nations began to take root.

5. In the latter part of 2004, Karuna, the person in charge of LTTE affairs in the eastern part of Sri Lanka, openly expressed dissatisfaction with the manner in which the east has been discriminated against by the LTTE and opted for autonomy. A period of hostility followed and the 'revolt' was squashed by the LTTE.

6. An essay that deals with the notion of anxiety has appeared in the recent version of *Miscelanea* (2003).

## Works Cited

Achebe, Chinua. *The Trouble with Nigeria*. London: Heinemann, 1983.
Aravindan, K.P. *Kanavin Meethu*. Chennai: Ponni, 1999.

Arguilla, Manuel. 'How My Brother Leon Brought Home a Wife', in *How My Brother Leon Brought Home a Wife and Other Stories*. Westport, Conn: Greenwood Press, 1970.

Brennan, Timothy. 'The National Longing for Form', in *Nation and Narration*. Ed. Homi Bhabha. London: Routledge, 1990, 44–70.

Gunesekera, Romesh. *Heaven's Edge*. London: Bloomsbury, 2002.

Jameson, Fredric. 'Third-World Literature in an Era of Multinational Capitalism', in *Social Text*, 15 (Fall 1986), 65–88.

Kanaganayakam, Chelva. 'The Anxiety of Being Postcolonial', in *Miscelenea* 28, 2003.

Lawson, Henry. 'The Drover's Wife', in *The Penguin Henry Lawson Short Stories*. Ed. John Barnes. Victoria: Penguin, 1986, 19–26.

Ondaatje, Michael. *Anil's Ghost*. Toronto: McClelland and Stewart, 2000.

Selvadurai, Shyam. 'Summerscapes.' http://www.nytimes.com/2004/07/05/opinion/05selv.html.

————. *Funny Boy: A Novel in Six Stories*. Toronto: McClelland and Stewart, 1994.

# The Remains of Empire
## The Comic Melancholy of Clive James

BRUCE BENNETT

Since his arrival in London from Sydney in 1961 (ten years later than his decade-older friend and fellow writer Peter Porter) Clive James has travelled the world with astounding dash and has left records, not in bottles found on distant beaches but in hastily composed 'postcards' published in newspapers and then books by leading international publishers. The mood and manner are caught in *Flying Visits: Postcards from the Observer 1976–83*, which after appearing in the *Observer* were collected and published by Jonathan Cape in hardback in 1984 and by Picador in paperback in 1985. More rueful, less excitable than James, Porter writes in a poem called 'Anxiety's Air Miles' (Porter 1997: 19–20) of himself as a 'frequent flier' after he has 'ringed the globe five times'—a miniscule fraction of James's air travel. James' public life as writer, entertainer, and television celebrity might indicate a less reflective persona than we find in Porter's work, but I suggest in this essay that James's range and volume of work does not preclude depth and that the humorous, wise-cracking persona is complemented by a more serious (but not earnest) self who has reflected on the rise and fall of empires, and their legacies.

While Clive James can be accurately presented as an all-rounder in the cricketing sense that he bats, bowls, keeps wickets, and fields (often simultaneously), he himself prefers other sports for his metaphoric matrices, including surfing, skiing, and racing cars. In later middle-age, he has sportingly learnt the tango. James's *literary* sports include essays, poems, plays, songs, novels, and autobiography together with theatre, television, radio, and internet programmes. In a sense, his public life is a non-stop festival of words. In his 65th year, there were few signs of diminution in the kind of energy and ambition of earlier years. Perhaps he foresaw this period of his life in an early rock lyric called 'Senior Citizens', which he wrote for Pete Atkin. Here is one verse:

And there'll be time to try it all:
I'm sure the thrill will never pall
The sand will take so long to fall
The neck so slim, the glass so tall (James 2003: 322).

Among the various genres that Clive James's restless persona has occasionally inhabited are articles in newspapers and journals that most literary academics would give their eye-teeth to appear in, including the *New Yorker*, the *New York Review of Books*, the *London Review of Books*, the *Times Literary Supplement*, the *Atlantic Monthly*, the *New Statesman*, and the *Australian Review of Books*. The books on which his reputation as a literary critic, commentator, and reviewer chiefly depend are *The Metropolitan Critic* (1974), *At the Pillars of Hercules* (1979), *From the Land of Shadows* (1982), *Snakecharmers in Texas* (1988), *The Dreaming Swimmer* (1992), and *Even as We Speak* (2001). For many people, James is a television talking-head or is remembered chiefly as the *Observer*'s most brilliant, humorous, and widely read television critic when he wrote there in the 1970s and 1980s. His three volumes of autobiography beginning with *Unreliable Memoirs* (1980) have increased his fame as a witty and thoughtful raconteur of his own life. But James's literary critical essays and reviews preceded his other work and he has returned to this genre in recent years. His characteristic wit and humour is sometimes tempered, sometimes sharpened in these writings, in the service of a life-long attempt to understand empires and their consequences.

James's typical approach is not through theory; rather, he gleans knowledge and insight through the filter of opinion-making writers and intellectuals who represent aspects of the culture and society from which they have sprung. Such individuals include Gore Vidal, Philip Larkin, Alexander Solzhenitsyn, and Les Murray, through whose work James is able to explore both individual creativity and significant aspects of America, Britain, the Soviet Union, and Australia respectively. In each of them, and in other writers, he sees indications of the fate of nations, empires, and human imagination. In an essay called 'Unpatriotic Gore' James observes something Roman in his subject, Gore Vidal, and beyond the Roman empire the current American one which Vidal has so perceptively recognized and satirized:

Even early on [says James], he was already a Roman—he was the knowing voice piercing the mist at the baths, ridiculing the hypocrisies of a stifling hegemony. As the hegemony crumbled into an age of transition, he became more recognizably a Roman figure than ever, viewing the anabases of the new Caesars with an unfoolable eye (James 1979: 190).

James notes that Vidal has often been accurate in his prophecies: 'In 1968 he guessed Nixon would be the one. He knew that Kennedy's presidency was an irreversible disaster from the Bay of Pigs on ...' (191). More recent work by Vidal continues his deft use of historical precedent to represent and analyse political events in the world's most powerful empire. That he is far more politically savvy than Clive James is not to James's detriment: few could match Vidal's political knowledge and insight.

What value could Philip Larkin, the Englishman, have in a consideration of empires? Many commentators and critics have used Larkin as the base from which to mount a criticism of the 'middle England' he seems to represent. But James is cleverer and more sensitive to the poetry than that. In his ironically titled essay 'Don

Juan in Hull', first published in *Encounter*, James locates his subject in 'the old mercantile civilization which Larkin has been quietly celebrating most of his life, a civilization in which a place like Leeds or Hull ... counts as a capital city' (54). 'There is another and bigger life,' James insists, 'but Larkin doesn't underestimate this one for a minute' (James 1979). What is implied rather than stated by James is that these cities were active mercantile centres in the empire machine. There is nothing triumphalist or condescending in James' recognition of the 'little England' of the mid-twentieth century that Larkin represents, or its reduced horizons. Rather, like Porter in 'Seaside Resort' (Porter 1999: 198–200), James finds a pleasing melancholy in the limited world-view of a departed empire into which Larkin draws his readers. And Larkin's sense of missing out, as Don Juan never did, in the sexual stakes is also one of James' recurrent comic modes. The provincial view is of course what James thought he chose to leave behind in Australia in the early 1960s to become a self-styled 'metropolitan critic'. Yet he is attracted for a time by the siren song of desperation he hears through the Larkin persona, which reminds him of Leopardi—'disconsolate yet doomed to being beautiful' (James 1979: 59).

Clive James is not attracted with the same force as Peter Porter to 'deliquescent empires', such as Porter found in twentieth-century Vienna—the former centre of the Austro-Hungarian empire, now stripped of its possessions, and living on through the ghosts of its famous musicians, artists, and thinkers (Bennett 1991: 96–7). Yet the two Australians living in London, now part of Europe—which until the 2003 war on Iraq had seemed to deny most present-day imperial pretensions—both seem attracted to the remains of empire in the form of artistic figures who flourished in its heyday.

When James thinks about Britain, his adoptive country, he is more likely than Porter to defend its institutions, especially the monarchy, as a bastion against the new American empire. This tendency is evident in an essay called 'The Queen in California', which reports for the *Observer* on Queen Elizabeth's visit to the centre of America's entertainment industry in 1983 (James 1988:

225–36). James presents himself as ironic chronicler of a Royal tour that was almost washed out, both literally and figuratively. At one point in the essay James describes an 'entertainment' arranged by the American hosts:

> The Royals were seated with the British filmstar colony all along one side of a long table up on stage, like a Last Supper painted by Sir Joshua Reynolds. Before and below them stretched a sea of Americans all staring in their direction. It was a stiffening circumstance in which only Dudley Moore could possibly look cheerful, although Michael Caine was also trying hard (228).

Like David Frost before him, James is drawn to fame and glitter, but a residual sense of proportion and balance asserts itself as he reports on this out-of-proportion entertainment of an upstart American empire:

> The Entertainment had elephantiasis, like the evening in general. When Hollywood gets beyond energy without taste, it arrives at taste without proportion. Perry [Como] ruffled his hair to prove that it really grew on top of his head, even if it had started its life somewhere else. 'You obviously do *not* adore me', Frank [Sinatra] sang at the Queen, who if she didn't nod her head, didn't shake it either. The big night out was a downer, but it wasn't her fault. They had put her on display.
> In fact she had been had.
> The evening was a pay-off for Ronald Reagan's financial backers, who would never have met the stars if the stars had not come to meet the Queen. Buckingham Palace had been hustled into bankrolling the next campaign wagon (229).

The Queen is here given the role of dupe—a role played by many colonials through the history of Empire. Pope's *Dunciad* ends with universal darkness: James here uses his virtuosic comic talents to describe the skies swamping his event with rain, washing away difference, and significance.

James's position is unusual. He is an admirer and defender of the monarchy and of the present Royal Family and has been so since his leading role in the Footlights Revue in Cambridge, where he prevented any sketches about Prince Charles, who was then an undergraduate at Cambridge (Britain 1997: 117). Later, however, he wrote a mock epic verse play *Charles Charming's Challenges on the Pathway to the Throne* (1981), which also appeared as a double album featuring James himself, Pamela Stephenson, and Russell Davies.[1] Despite Philip Larkin's criticism of 'the corniness of his [James's] mocking the royals' (117), James's play was generally benign satire, with nothing like the savage attacks on Prince Charles by others in more recent years. James's subsequent espousal of the doomed marriage of Charles and Diana and his enthusiastic eulogy after her death revealed a recurrent strain of sentimentality in his nature.

A different kind of sentiment is evident in James's most successful novel, *The Silver Castle,* which is set in Bombay. The novel traces the rise of the protagonist Sanjay's fortunes from street child to Bollywood stunt-man and lover of a beautiful and famous film actress to his fall, both literal and metaphoric, back to the mean streets as a beggar. Sanjay's sentimental education is gained thanks to his luck, good looks, and astute self-management on the fringes of India's commercially successful film industry. Lacking any formal education, Sanjay exercises his considerable native intelligence in learning to read and speak like the Bollywood magazines. James's parody of these magazines and the industry that spawns them never descends to contempt for the romantic dreams they express—what he calls 'the democracy of longing'. Bollywood is no evil Empire.

Despite the corruption and cruelty it embodies, the Indian film industry offers to the public an escape and a relatively harmless focus for daydreams and desire. The popular, commercial culture it represents is not denied by James. Rather, it demonstrates a way in which previous exploitation of India by the British Empire and by powerful Western moguls can be reversed. The computer software industry is another avenue. James' compassionate portrayal of his Candide figure, Sanjay, in contemporary India evokes both laughter and tears. In the end, James tries to look beyond a natural scepticism to a hope that 'the new free enterprise society' may begin to show a 'trickle-down effect' to the poor.

Clive James's political inclinations have been what his Marxist critics would call 'bourgeois', but they are not necessarily blancmange. Ian Britain has summarized:

He has eschewed (at times trenchantly criticised) the extremes of the Thatcherite right, but he has also directed some of his most merciless satiric barbs at the British trade union and Labour party establishments ... Along with many other intellectuals disenchanted with Labour, James imagined he had found a political home for a while with the Social Democratic Party at the height of its short vogue in the early 1980s (117).

James's promotion of democracy has modest rather than utopian aims. In his view, 'democracy is even more important for what it prevents than for what it provides' (James 2001: xiii). What it prevents, in short, is a totalitarian state.

Although seldom openly political in his public appearances, James's autobiographical remarks in the Introduction to *Even As We Speak* indicate his opposition to totalitarian rule and the evil empires it has spawned:

The undoubted fact that democracy was currently making a murderous fool of itself couldn't make me forget that totalitarianism was still the enduring and implacable antagonist. I had opinions about what a democratic state should do in the circumstances—pull out of Vietnam, decommission the CIA, put Henry Kissinger on trial for sedition, stop subsidising the kind of dictators who exported their own economies to Switzerland—but it was part of my world view that a totalitarian view was unjustifiable in any circumstances (xiii).

We can see something of James's own evolution to this world-view in his various considerations of Nazi Germany and the Soviet Union. In particular, the writings of Soviet dissidents such as Solzhenitsyn, Mandelstam, and Zinoviev give form and detail to the horrors of Soviet suppression of the individual and convince James that the radical, left-wing views adopted by many opinion-makers in the universities were misguided. James is struck forcefully by his realization of the radical conservatism of Solzhenitsyn's critique of the Russian revolution:

> Solzhenitsyn … [traces] the Terror back to the revolution itself … It is the overwhelming tendency of Solzhenitsyn's work to suggest that the Russian revolution should never have happened (James 1982: 166).

In his early 1960s, James attempted to summarize an approach he derived from Karl Popper whom he described as 'the great deconstructor of Karl Marx's scientific pretensions':

> For a hundred and fifty years, left-wing analysis retained the impetus of Christian revelation. Even after the Soviet Union, its holy land, showed clear signs of coming to pieces, the Marxist heritage retained its prestige. In the Soviet bloc nobody with any sense believed any of it—direct experience had done its work—but in the West there was still a reputation for frivolity to be earned by not paying it sufficient respect (James 2001: xv).

If James seems something of the slow learner he accuses Australians generally of being when he turns to critiques of Soviet totalitarianism from as late as the 1980s, he nevertheless shows by then an impressive command of Soviet Russian literature and society, including a reading knowledge of Russian. Moreover, it is difficult to dodge his charge that literary and cultural critics in the universities were even slower to recognize that much of the ideological framework which had sustained them had been proved moribund in practice. While James is right, in my view, to be scathing about the 'waves of pseudo-scientific dogma that had taken over humane studies in the universities, most damagingly in the English faculty', he is more controversial in his attempt to trace this 'vacuous theorizing' and 'obscurantism' back to 'the French left, an obscurantism whose origins could in turn be traced back to the period of the Occupation, when there had been shamefully good reasons for intellectuals to hatch an impersonal language by which history would take responsibility for what they said' (xvi). A great deal better than a socialist paradise, he claims, is 'the bourgeois

democracy so despised by both extremes,' which 'proved, by its
power to defend itself, that it was capitalism's natural host' (xvii).
At such moments, it seems, James gets unusually close to soapbox
oratory, forgetting the critical obscurantism also emanating from
the right of the political spectrum. Nevertheless, the middling
position James occupies on the political spectrum is itself shown
to be difficult and contested territory.

How does Australia enter and make its mark in James'
international 'bourgeois democracy'? In part, James asserts that this
will occur through literary figures such as the poet Les Murray, who
gives readers and listeners a 'vernacular republic' within the world
of letters. (It helps the case, of course, that one of Murray's books
is called *The Vernacular Republic* (1982) and that James reviewed
it glowingly in the *New York Review of Books* (14 April 1983).)[2]
In James' commentary Murray plays the role of a large figure in a
national allegory of a country which seems no longer inclined to
'go on accepting the status of a second-hand country' (56). However,
much he might wish to call it something else, James expresses here
a post-colonial status for the country of his birth. However, James
is careful in his commentary to distance himself from Murray's wish
for an actual Australian republic, suggesting that there is nothing
'unimaginative about a wish to keep the monarchist tradition' (54).
(Japan is invoked by James in passing as an example in the Asia-
Pacific region of a continuing monarchy; he might have mentioned
Thailand. But both are 'home-grown'—not continuations of the
symbolism of a foreign empire. Supporters of the Australian
Republican Movement, such as myself, can equally invoke the
republics of India or Singapore.)

In James' dream-world of an empire of letters, outstanding
imaginative writers and other culture-makers are given a status and
value not accorded by the unregulated market place. National
broadcasters such as the American Broadcasting Company (ABC),
and British Broadcasting Company (BBC), are necessary partners
in this enterprise. But James wants to think about Australia in world
terms. In a *Times Literary Supplement* article called 'Les Murray
and his Master Spirits' (5 July 1996),[3] James praises Murray and

his 'forefathers' represented in the *New Oxford Book of Australian Verse,* such as A.D. Hope, Judith Wright, and Gwen Harwood, for playing their international role. 'A culture can never flourish,' he asserts, 'as a hedge against the world. It isn't a bastion for nationalism, it is an international passport' (225). James' is a serious and important voice in such essays, representing a sensible and informed point of view in the continuing struggle between local roots, provincialism, and emerging patterns of globalization.

That a new empire of letters is a dream does not deny its validity. James is interested in such dreams and the consequences they make possible. Behind the bluff suavity and witty one-liners, Clive James exhibits hints of what Ian Britain calls an 'awkward sage' (Britain 1997: 117). A self-described 'cultural reactionary', he also promotes the intelligent consideration of popular culture and a critical attitude to certain powerful media czars such as Rupert Murdoch.[4] James' version of bourgeois democracy is a troubled brew but more to his taste than the available alternatives. Debate, difference, and dissension within the bounds of rationality have their place on his menu; and it is interesting to find that his recent book of essays, *Even As We Speak,* is dedicated to the contentious journalist Christopher Hitchens 'in affectionate disagreement'. Clive James' contribution to intelligent discussion of literary and cultural studies, and to the cause of literature in the world, keeps a sense of humour and proportion, while it wrestles with ideas and issues, and empires come and go.

## Notes

1. The recording was by Arista Records.
2. The review was republished in *Snakecharmers in Texas; Essays 1980–87.* London: Jonathan Cape, 49–57.
3. The review was republished in *Even As We Speak,* 225–37.
4. For example, in *Even As We Speak* (254), James writes that Murdoch has cut himself off from Britain and Australia 'in pursuit of some dreary post-capitalist Utopia in which the hunger to acquire is a spiritual value …'.

## Works Cited

Bennett, Bruce. *Spirit in Exile: Peter Porter and his Poetry*. Melbourne: Oxford University Press, 1991.

Britain, Ian. *Once an Australian: Journeys with Barry Humphries, Clive James, Germaine Greer and Robert Hughes*. Melbourne: Oxford University Press, 1997.

James, Clive. *The Metropolitan Critic*. London: Faber and Faber, 1974.

———. *At the Pillars of Hercules: Critical Essays*. London: Faber and Faber, 1979.

———. *From the Land of Shadows*. London: Pan/Picador, 1982.

———. *Snakecharmers in Texas: Essays 1980–87*. London: Jonathan Cape, 1988.

———. *The Dreaming Swimmer: Non-Fiction 1987–1992*. London: Jonathan Cape, 1992.

———. *The Silver Castle*. London: Jonathan Cape, 1996.

———. *Even As We Speak*. London: Pan/Picador, 2001.

———. *The Book of My Enemy: Collected Verse 1958–2003*. London: Pan Macmillan/Picador, 2003.

Porter, Peter. *Collected Poems, Vol. 1: 1961–1981*. Oxford: Oxford University Press, 1999.

———. *Dragons in their Pleasant Palaces*. Oxford: Oxford University Press, 1997.

# 'A Construction from Spare Parts'
## Inventing National Identity in Singapore

EDDIE TAY

The literary history of Singapore is a history of encounters with the discursive formation of the nation. From its early incarnation in the form of experimentation with Engmalchin (a linguistic amalgamation of English, Malay, and Chinese) as examined by Anne Brewster in *Towards a Semiotic of Postcolonial Discourse* to the new generation of writers that includes Alfian Sa'at, Hwee Hwee Tan, and Lau Siew Mei, we are witness to writers who are involved in, to borrow a phrase from Benedict Anderson, imagining a community (Anderson 1991). As pointed out by Ban Kah Choon, Singapore's 'early years of independence after separation from Malaysia made the need for imaginative space ... all that more relevant' (Choon 1992: 11). However, unlike the works of Edwin Thumboo and his contemporaries, most notably Wang Gungwu and Ee Tiang Hong, in the works of the later generation of writers, nation and nationalism have come under persistent critique. By examining the poems of Edwin Thumboo and Alfian Sa'at, and specific moments in Hwee Hwee Tan's *Mammon Inc.* and Lau Siew Mei's *Playing Madame Mao*, this essay highlights instances where the nation and nationalism are articulated and critiqued in the literature of Singapore.

## Nation and Nationalism: The Case of the Merlion

> But this lion of the sea
> Salt-maned, scaly, wondrous of tail,
> Touched with power, insistent
> On this brief promontory ...
> Puzzles.
>
> Nothing, nothing in my days
> Foreshadowed this
> Half-beast, half-fish,
> This powerful creature of land and sea (Thumboo 1993: 80).

The poetry of Edwin Thumboo is particularly representative in terms of articulating the discursive formation of the nation; it has been said that 'he is the closest Singapore has to a poet laureate' (Lim 1994). As poet, academic, and university administrator, he is one of the few writers in Singapore who is able to lay claim to having shaped the literary consciousness of his generation and those that follow. His poem, *Ulysses by the Merlion* is much discussed, in part because it lays bare the mechanisms of how national identity is constructed. In the poem, the journey of Ulysses, hero of Homer's epic poem, is interrupted by his encounter with the Merlion. Ulysses, an experienced journeyman who 'sailed many waters, / Skirted islands of fire', is depicted as being perplexed and overwhelmed by the figure of the Merlion (Thumboo 1993: 80). This poem, more than any other literary work written by a Singaporean, has been subjected to intense scrutiny by many commentators.

The poem was first published in 1979, less than two decades after Singapore acquired national independence, when the nation's political elites faced the challenge of assimilating a community composed of several ethnicities into a cohesive society. A poem like this, some critics argue, articulates a national consciousness crucial to the formation of Singapore's national collective. Ee Tiang Hong writes of the poem in a celebratory tone, pointing out that 'Where [Thumboo's] voice in the earlier public poems was tentative ... it now had the force of conviction. Politics was now enmeshed with poetry' (Hong 1997). Others look at the poem with suspicion, arguing that *Ulysses by the Merlion* is an example of state propaganda disguised as poetry, that poetry in Singapore has become nothing less than a state apparatus with which to present to the populace a forced rhetoric of nationality. For John Kwan-Terry, 'The tone [of the poem] is eloquent, but the language is willed, and the images, particularly the icons of culture, are void of resonances' (Kwan-Terry 1991: 120). Not only is the language willed, one may even say that it is wilful in that the new is presented alongside epic narratives as ancient as those of Homer's as a strategy of national authentication.

Indeed, the poem places Ulysses by the Merlion, locating them on the same plane of mythic existence so as to legitimize the latter as a national symbol. In doing so, the poem conflates the discourse of nationalism alongside an uneasy alliance of the Homeric epic with the discourse of tourist consumption. The disjunctive status of Ulysses and the Merlion is all the more obvious by the fact that the former, derived from the Homeric tradition, possesses canonical stature while the latter is an invention by a government tourism board. The Merlion statue, with its head of a lion and body and tail of a fish, is a state-manufactured icon, created in 1972 by the then Singapore Tourism Promotion Board (now renamed Singapore Tourism Board) as part of a marketing strategy for the tourism industry. The head of the lion alludes to the thirteenth-century myth of how the island was named while the tail of the fish alludes to Singapore's beginnings as a fishing village (Yeoh 2003: 32). The reader's recognition of the Merlion as state-manufactured icon underpins the contrived and artificial attempt on the part of the poem to foster and affirm a national identity. As pointed out by Brenda Yeoh and T.C. Chang, 'there is an uneasiness borne of ambivalence towards the notion of the Merlion as national symbol' (40). However, one may regard *Ulysses by the Merlion* as representative of the national ethos, if only ironically: on the one hand, the Merlion is a contrived object manufactured for tourist consumption; on the other hand, it is 'a sign of its times, of globalizing logic and its banalities, and an ironically suitable symbol of Singapore' (42): 'They make, they serve, / They buy, they sell', and thus it comes as no surprise that 'This lion of the sea, / This image of themselves' receives the same treatment as well (Thumboo 1993: 80–1).

As a work located within a specific social-historical framework that articulates the anxieties of a particular community, *Ulysses by the Merlion* demonstrates some of the ambivalence and tensions that accompany the formation of a national identity. It is ironic that in a poem that makes explicit its nationalist agenda, the voice of the national bard is supplanted by the voice of Ulysses drawn from one of the central texts of the Western canon. Thumboo's poem is an instance of myth-making as to foster legitimacy upon the nationalist agenda, and this uneasy aligning of the Homeric epic with nationalism conflated with economic imperatives is not lost on the younger generation of writers. Thumboo's poem has sparked off a series of Merlion poems in Singaporean literature. They include Daren Shiau's *Merlion Speaks*, Felix Cheong's *The Obligatory Merlion Poem*, Alvin Pang's *Merlign*, and Alfian bin Sa'at's *The Merlion*. While each of these poems engages Thumboo's poem in dialogue in significantly different ways, it is Alfian bin Sa'at's *The Merlion* that is to be singled out as a polemical anti-nationalist poem that is not without its own irony.

Within the span of less than five years, the publication of his two poetry collections, *One Fierce Hour* and *A History of Amnesia*, his prize-winning short- story collection *Corridors*, along with the staging of his plays inflected with homosexual themes, Alfian has acquired a reputation as a anti-establishment writer. In *Singapore You Are Not My Country*, Alfian launches his polemic against the malleability of the nation towards the economic enterprise and the demands of modernization:

O Singapore your fair shores your garlands your GNP.
You are not a country you are a construction from spare parts.

You are not a campaign you are last year's posters.
You are not culture you are poems on the MRT (Alfian 1998: 41)

Alfian's poetry then, is a challenge against the all-too-transparent manufactured condition of Singapore that led to the writing of *Ulysses by the Merlion*. The *Merlion* may be regarded as a direct response to Thumboo's poem. In contrast to the mythic lyricism evidenced in Thumboo's poem, Alfian's riposte is delivered in everyday language via a staging of a dialogue between two people commenting on the Merlion. The tone is irreverent, describing the Merlion as a grotesque and limbless monstrosity. The Merlion, says the main speaker of the poem, is a mutant 'writhing in the water, / like some post-Chernobyl nightmare.' It is a dislocated being, 'marooned on this rough shore, / as if unsure of its rightful / harbour.' Unlike the enigmatic Sphinx whose lips 'are sealed / with self-knowledge,' the Merlion is a 'lesser brother' whose 'own jaws / clamp open in self-doubt' (21).

However, the poem undermines its staging of the improbability of the Merlion as a national symbol when the reader's attention shifts from the Merlion to the main speaker:

'And why does it keep spewing that way?
I mean, you know, I mean …'

'I know exactly what you mean,' I said,
Eyeing the blond highlights in your black hair
And your blue lenses the shadow of a foreign sky.
'It spews continually if only to ruffle
its own reflection in the water; such reminders
will only scare a creature so eager to reinvent itself.'

Another pause.

'Yes,' you finally replied, in that acquired accent of yours,
'Well, yes, but I still do wish it had paws' (22).

The irony of the poem is that the critique of the Merlion is articulated by someone who is equally eager to reinvent his or her identity; he or she is someone with 'blond highlights in ... black hair', 'blue [contact] lenses the shadow of a foreign sky', and who speaks with an 'acquired accent'. Just as the Merlion is said to be afraid of its own reflection, afraid to be reminded of its incongruous appearance (a limbless head of a lion with the body and tail of a fish), the same may be said of the speaker, who ruffles the image of the Merlion as he or she is afraid to be confronted with his or her own self-reflection. The self in the case of the speaker in Alfian's poem is othered in the process of disavowal. Just as Thumboo's *Ulysses by the Merlion* is fraught with ambivalence, the same is true of Alfian's *The Merlion*. The moment one presses for a nationalist agenda by constructing a national icon is the moment one inadvertently reveals the act of that construction as artifice; likewise, as Alfian's poem demonstrates, the moment one articulates scepticism towards the legitimacy of a national icon is the moment one would have to examine the condition of one's own identity-formation. If nationalism may be regarded as a form of political essentialism, then just as it is impossible to essentialize unproblematically, it is impossible to take on an anti-essentialist position with consistency. Both poems stage the impossibility of a pure essence with regard to the agenda of nationalism and its critique.

## Nation, Nationalism, and Essentialism

The poems of Thumboo and Alfian demonstrate how nationalism and its critique are articulated and contested; while their poems demonstrate the constructed, contested, and discursive nature of nationalism and its critique, the works of Hwee Hwee Tan and Lau Siew Mei focus our attention on the possibilities of a critique that goes beyond the national. It is useful to be reminded that Tan's *Mammon Inc.*, as a novel written by a Singaporean woman and published by an international conglomerate, is itself a global and transnational commodity. Indeed, both the novel and its author participate in the transnational thematic. The fact that Tan was raised in Singapore, lived in the Netherlands for a period of time, educated at Oxford University and later at New York University, and is now working as a journalist back in Singapore, testifies to the author's critique of nation and nationalism from a life-experience borne of the transnational. *Mammon Inc.* is a novel about an individual's encounter with globalization and how it necessitates a critique of nation and nationalism.

*Mammon Inc.* is a satire on how Singapore as an imagined community finds its identity to be constantly under erasure throughout the process of national formation. As Tan mentions in an interview, 'One of my theories about Singapore is that it's really trying to become a kind of franchise city of America.'[1] Singapore may certainly be regarded as a nation insofar as we recognize it possesses unique historical, cultural, and political features; however, Singaporeans as portrayed in the novel do not possess a deep awareness of the geopolitical and historical status of their nation. In this respect, *Mammon Inc.* is a critique of the cultural vacuity of Singaporeans in general, a cultural vacuity as a result of a nationalism that locates the beginnings of the nation via a myth of origins.

In her attempt to communicate with students from Oxford, Chiah Chen, the sister of the protagonist, attempts to engage their interest in Singaporean culture by explaining to them the significance of the miniature plastic Merlion statues she is giving out. She tells them of the thirteenth-century Malayan prince, Sang Nila Utama, who travelled by sea to the island where he encountered a lion. 'So Sang Nila Utama decided to call the island a new name, "Singa-pura", which means "Lion City". That's how my country got its name' (Tan 2002: 194). This unthinking appeal to an originary myth is problematic as the myth does not so much reflect historical truth as it does a modern attempt at utilizing historical myth in order to affirm Singapore as an imagined community. As mentioned earlier, the Merlion statue was commissioned by the then Singapore Tourism Promotion Board as a symbol of Singapore's identity. The iconicity of the Merlion statue enacts a violent shuttling between the sites of cultural (touristic) consumption and monumentality, between the historical and the contemporary, the mythic and the national.

Identity, and national identity no less, is never pure. As Ien Ang (2001) puts it in her preface to *On Not Speaking Chinese*, identity is always mistaken identity (viii). It is always other and never identical to itself. Identity involves recognition, but it inevitably suffers from mis-recognition. This is demonstrated in the situation of Tock Seng Edwards, Chiah Deng's previous boyfriend, who is treated like a foreigner in Singapore because of his skin colour:

> The durian seller stared at Tock Seng for a few moments.
> '*Wah*, your Chinese very good. Where did you learn how to speak such good Chinese?'
> '*Xin Jia Po*,' Tock Seng told him.
> 'You learn Chinese in Singapore? But where are you from?' he said.
> '*Xin Jia Po*,' Tock Seng said.
> 'Where are your parents from?' he said.
> '*Mei Guo*,' Tock Seng said. Then he added that he arrived in Singapore when he was one, and that he grew up in Singapore.
> 'Oh, you're from America. I like America. Sylvester Stallone' (Tan 2002: 48).

Despite the fact that Tock Seng has lived all his life in Singapore, he is regarded as an outsider and excluded from participation in the imagined community that defines national life.

In the novel, instances of mistaken identity constitute part of a larger critique of essentialism pertaining to national identities. The official ethnic categories in Singapore are Chinese, Malays, Indians, and others, the last usually referring to Eurasians. This constitution of ethnic identities under the aegis of nationalism leads to a predisposition to thinking about others in terms of stereotypes. Just as Tock Seng Edwards is mistaken for an American, Chiah Deng's parents are mistaken about Western culture. When Chiah Deng's parents first meet Steve, their immediate concern is whether Steve is HIV-positive. Their concept of Western culture is derived from popular culture:

'Yah, whenever I watch those Western movies on TV—they're only two hours long, but the men there always have sex at least three times in those two hours', my mother said. 'It's a miracle if they *don't* have Aids.'
'But that's just movies', my sister said in Chinese.
'Fiction. Made-up fantasies' (223).

Essentialism is a form of fetishism that allows no difference in identity, such that one believes that the durian is to tropical Singapore what Sylvester Stallone is to America.

If the above fictional examples seem like exaggerated caricatures of thinking via stereotypes under the aegis of nation formation and nationalism, the following example drawn from reality might suffice. In his letter to the forum section of *the Straits Times*, Singapore's major national newspaper, Abdul Shariff Aboo Kassim commiserates with the plight of the community of Bangladeshi construction workers in Singapore. He writes:

I am an Indian Singaporean with features and a physique resembling those of a Bangladeshi, so much so that Bangladeshis approach me and speak to me in Urdu. On countless occasions, people have called me 'Bhaia', a term commonly used to address Bangladeshis ... Going by my experience, life as a Bangladeshi in Singapore is tough (*Straits Times* 24 May 2005).

He goes on to recount his experiences of having been discriminated against as a resulted of being mis-identified:

I was taking a walk in my neighbourhood one day when, from a distance, a policeman called out to me: 'Hello!' 'Come here!' I walked towards him. He then asked: 'What you doing here? Where passport, work permit?' ... When I handed my identity card to him, he was taken aback. He was a lot more polite after that and explained that he was only doing routine checks. His exercise in damage control did not work because his actions in full view public view embarrassed me enough to ruin my day (Ibid.).

Other instances recounted include being given a scolding by a nurse at a private hospital for not responding immediately when she called his name. When she realized that he is a Singaporean, 'her standard of service went up several notches' (Ibid.). While this may be an isolated instance of a Singaporean Indian being mistaken for a Bangladeshi construction worker, one may surmise from this the extent of the discrimination faced by the community of Bangladeshi workers in Singapore. As the writer rightly notes, while he may be able to 'send feedback to the various businesses and organisations concerned about the incidents', the majority of the foreign workers may not be able to do so (Ibid.). Thus, there is a need for caution when it comes to identity formation under the aegis of nationalism as it fosters recognition and thinking about others and the self via stereotyping.

## Cultural Revolution of Singapore

Written in the tradition of magic realism associated with the novels of Milan Kundera, *Playing Madame Mao* differs vastly from *Mammon Inc.* While the latter examines the essentialist nature of nationalism, the former draws disturbing parallels between Singapore's political condition and China's Cultural Revolution as an act of critique. A former Singaporean who obtained Australian citizenship, Lau Siew Mei employs the transnational as a critique of the national: her novel, *Playing Madame Mao*, compares Singapore's political constitution to the excesses of the Cultural Revolution, playing with history to present a transgressive and at the same time, transformative vision of Singapore's political climate.

Indeed, the comparison with Kundera is not far-fetched; there is an instance in the novel where one of Kundera's novels, *Life is Elsewhere*, is mentioned, setting off common thematic resonances. Like Kundera's novel, *Playing Madame Mao* sets the personal against the political in contrapuntal balance, playing off a personal, intimate history of the self against the larger, impersonal, and often ruthless history of politics. Both novels suggest that, given the violence inflicted upon the fabric of the everyday life by what has been deemed as a political necessity, the personal has no choice but to be located elsewhere. As a result, life *is* elsewhere, it just is never where one happens to be. This novel, then, is motivated by a search for alternatives, for another national experience, another way of living. It is motivated by the suspension of reality for the universe of multiple possibilities. As the protagonist puts it,

At the end of dreaming, it is only a little room with cream walls that I wake up in. The curtains flap in the dust and smell of city living. It is a narrow area, and I am driven by desperation to look for a space beyond (Lau 2000: 22).

Composed of fragmented scenes and half-revealed imagery, *Playing Madame Mao* is a novel with multiple narrators and different levels of realities, ranging from the mythic to the historical to the contemporary. The novel presents a dystopian and phantasmagoric vision of Singapore. The plot revolves around the actual events of May 1987 in Singapore when a Marxist conspiracy was uncovered in Singapore, resulting in the arrest and detention without trial under the Internal Security Act of twenty-two people, some of whom were church leaders. They were alleged to have infiltrated and controlled Catholic and student groups with the aim of subverting the government. Subsequently, they were released on the condition that they would not in future participate in any political activity.

The Marxist conspiracy has its fictional parallels in the novel which begins with the arrest of Tang Na Juan, a polytechnic lecturer who wrote several articles attacking the government in a Catholic newsletter. His wife, Ching, trained as a Chinese opera actress, seeks a form of vicarious vengeance by playing Madame Mao:

With my husband taken from me, all I have left now is revenge. Hui has asked me to help him redraft the play. I will play a dominant role, going over each word, taking the actors through the rehearsals, making sure each intonation, each gesture, each movement, betrays a hidden intent: to satirise Them. My husband was arrested by a government of white clothes, led by a man I will call the Chairman (Ibid.).

The narrative at various moments subsumes character motivation and action under the swift, often dizzying transitions between different levels of reality. The novel is a labyrinth of mirrors: we are presented with an actress, Ching, who plays on stage the historical Chiang Ching who became Mao's third wife. Ching's best friend, a journalist by the name of Roxanne, is a mirror image of Roxane Witke, the American historian who went to China to study the plight of women under the Cultural Revolution. Witke eventually became the official biographer and confidante of the historical Chiang Ching. Ching's dissident husband, Tang Na Juan, has a historical counterpart in the person of Tang Na, a film critic and founding member of the communist-sponsored Art Society rumoured to be Chiang Ching's ex-husband (Witke 1977).

Playing Madame Mao is a carnivalesque disruption of history and the political status quo. It presents history and political reality not as finality but as a set of open-ended dynamic. For Bakhtin, the medieval carnival

offered a completely different, nonofficial, extraecclesiastical and extrapolitical aspect of the world, of man, and of human relations; [it builds a] second world and a second life outside officialdom, a world in which all medieval people participated more or less, in which they lived during a given time of the year (Bakhtin 1984: 5–6).

One may argue that Playing Madame Mao exemplifies Bakhtin's thesis that carnival in the modern world has migrated from the social sphere into the novel. The novelistic carnivelesque represents a suspension of authority, order, and hierarchy much in the same way as the medieval carnival does. In Playing Madame Mao, history is put into play by juxtaposing the Cultural Revolution with the events of the 1987 Marxist Conspiracy in Singapore; the novel creates numerous parallels between Mao and Lee Kuan Yew, then Prime Minister of Singapore. We are given descriptions of a Chairman whose 'hirsute attributes are rather diminished near the temples' (Lau 2000: 22). As in the carnival, where the rulers and the fools exchange places, the novel plays with the identity of Singapore's foremost figure of authority:

I think of making the Chairman appear like a figure in a Theatre of the Absurd. I write down his common nickname: Hairy. I pretend he is not the demigod he is in reality, presiding over our lives ... (23).

Even though his name is never mentioned in the novel, we know that the Chairman is the textual version of Lee Kuan Yew, who was known as Harry Lee when he was a student at Cambridge. The thematics of acting and staging are placed at the forefront. The protagonist is an actress based in Singapore, acting as Chiang Ching/Madame Mao because she wanted to seek vengeance for her husband. One is reminded that the historical Chiang Ching, Mao's third wife, was also an actress who played a key role as one of the members of the Gang of Four during the Cultural Revolution. At the height of her power, she played the role of a cultural commissar who supported, wrote, and staged works sympathetic to communist politics. Thus, in the novel, the theatre plays an important role in the doubled contexts of Singaporean politics and the Chinese Revolution. As Wei-Wei Yeo puts it:

The novel carries a political agenda, showing that with a culture of self-censorship and strict government control over all media agencies, information and opinions in the city are regulated, making their appearance like lines in a script. Thus the city *is* a stage, not simply *like* one, and the search for national identity is one of its most popular dramas [italics in original] (Yeo 2003: 248).

What is disturbing about the novel is that it suggests that Singapore's economic success and resultant progressive status from a third-world nation to first within a few decades is a consequence of nothing less than a cultural revolution of sorts. This revolution is brought about not by street demonstrations and open denunciations (though there are denunciations), but through careful social engineering and efficient administration utilizing policies and bureaucratic procedures with the consent of the populace. That there is a closure of ideological struggle is precisely what fosters the political legitimacy of the PAP. Several commentators have pointed this out, albeit the terms they used were different. In her paper aptly titled 'Politics in an Administrative State: Where has the Politics Gone?', Chan Heng Chee argues that post-1965, there 'has been the steady and systematic depoliticisation of a politically active and aggressive citizenry' (Chan 1975: 1–2). She points out that political debate in the public sphere has shifted away from ideological engagement towards matters of administrative bureaucracy.

The novel launches a powerful satire against Singaporean nationalism. Through the mirroring and counter-mirroring of political narratives, *Playing Madame Mao* presents a dystopian portrayal of Singaporean politics seen through the lenses of Mao's China, as seen through the eyes of Madame Mao, which is in turn seen through the eyes of an opera actress. Multiple realities and personalities collide to form a disorientation; yet it is a fruitful disorientation that serves to highlight the similarity of differences. It is tempting to think that the Cultural Revolution is a one-off affair in the history of politics, yet history, as the saying goes, repeats itself: 'Chairman Mao's ambitions are reminiscent of the overwhelming desire of the First Emperor of China to control time and in so doing, also history' (Lau 2000: 17). At the same time, the novel also suggests that in Singapore, economic progress is purchased at the expense of freedom of speech:

MIND YOUR OWN BUSINESS. It is written upon my forehead, everyone's forehead. The business of the state is not to concern me, only basic necessities like how to earn enough money to feed my belly and put a roof over my head. I am not to make comments on things I can have insufficient information on (20).

*Playing Madame Mao* interrupts and disrupts Singapore's political status quo through textual deployment. The text inserts feminist presences derived from a pastiche of strong women drawn from the recesses of Chinese history. Ching would 'learn to be a warrior woman. Like Hua Mu Lan' (140). She would also emulate the deeds of 'empresses and mother dowagers, and of the one empress in the long Chinese history who actually ascended the male-dominated throne, the Empress Wu Tse-tien' (140). This is where the novel's dialogic nature comes to the forefront. On the one hand, the novel comments on how blame for the excesses of the Cultural Revolution has been deflected from Mao and placed largely on the supposed ruthless ambition of the historical Chiang Ching; on the other hand, the novel utilizes descriptions of the excesses of the Chinese Cultural Revolution as a commentary on Singaporean politics.

## Conclusion

Nation and nationalism have come under persistent critique in the works of Singaporean writers. While Thumboo's *Ulysses by the Merlion* demonstrates some of the ambivalence and tensions that accompany the formation of a national identity, Alfian's *The Merlion* reminds us that the moment one articulates scepticism towards the legitimacy of an invented national icon is the moment one would have to examine the condition of one's own fluid (and to some extent, necessarily invented) self-identity. One may surmise that the novels of Hwee Hwee Tan and Lau Siew Mei, like Alfian's poem, are written out of a sense of alienation, of being out of place within the constrains of nation formation. As the protagonist of Tan's novel puts it, 'So that was my plight—to love the culture of a society that would never accept me. I longed to find some special place, a world where I would no longer feel alone and abandoned' (Tan 2002: 14). While *Mammon Inc.* demonstrates the dangers of relying on stereotypes under the sign of nationalism, *Playing Madame Mao* likens Singapore's political climate to that of the Chinese Cultural Revolution. Taken together, these texts place nationalism and the nation under critique, reminding us of the ambivalence, anxieties, and tensions of identity formation.

## Notes

1. Toh, Hsien Min. 'Mammon and the Discipline of Writing', in *Quarterly Literary Review Singapore*, Vol. 1, No. 1, October 2001. accessed 04 March 2004. (http://www.qlrs.com/issues/oct2001/interviews/hhtan.html)

## Works Cited

Abdul Shariff Aboo Kassim. 'Stop Discriminating against Foreign Workers', in *Straits Times*. 24 May 2005, H9.

Alfian bin Sa'at. *One Fierce Hour*. Singapore: Landmark Books, 1998.

Anderson, Benedict. *Imagined Communities: Reflections on the Origin and Spread of Nationalism*. Revised Edn. London: Verso, 1991.

Ang, Ien. *On Not Speaking Chinese: Living Between Asia and West*. London: Routledge, 2001.

Bakhtin, Mikhail Mikhailovich. *Rabelais and His World*. Trans. Hélène Iswolsky. Bloomington: Indiana University Press, 1984.

Ban, Kah Choon. 'Narrating Imagination', in *Imagining Singapore*. Eds Ban Kah Choon, Anne Pakir, and Tong Chee Kiong. Singapore: Times Academic Press, 1992, 9–25.

Chan, Heng Chee. *Politics in an Administrative State: Where Has the Politics Gone?*. Singapore : Institute of Southeast Asian Studies, 1975.

Hong Ee Tiang. *Responsibility and Commitment: The Poetry of Edwin Thumboo*. Ed. Leong Liew Geok. Singapore: Singapore University Press, 1997.

Kwan-Terry, John. 'Ulysses Circling the Merlion: The Invention of Identity in Singapore Poetry in English and Chinese', in *Perceiving Other Worlds*. Ed. Edwin Thumboo. Singapore: Times, 1991, 115–137.

Lau, Siew Mei. *Playing Madame Mao*. Australia: Brandl and Schlesinger, 2000.

Lim, Shirley Geok-lin. *Writing S. E. / Asia in English: Against the Grain, Focus on Asian English-Language Literature*. London: Skoob Books Publishing, 1994.

Tan, Hwee Hwee. *Mammon Inc.* London: Penguin, 2002.

Thumboo, Edwin. *A Third Map: New and Selected Poems*. Singapore: UniPress, 1993.

Toh, Hsien Min. 'Mammon and the Discipline of Writing', in *Quarterly Literary Review Singapore*, Vol. 1 (1), October 2001. accessed 4 March 2004. (http://www.qlrs.com/issues/oct2001/interviews/hhtan.html)

Witke, Roxane. *Comrade Chiang Ching*. London: Weidenfeld and Nicolson, 1977.

Yeo, Wei-Wei. 'City as Theatre: Singapore, State of Distraction', in *Postcolonial Urbanism: Southeast Asian Cities and Global Processes*. Eds Ryan Bishop, John Phillips, and Wei-Wei Yeo. London: Routledge, 2003, 245–64.

Yeoh, Brenda S.A. and T.C. Chang. 'The Rise of the Merlion: Monument and Myth in the Making of the Singapore Story', in *Theorizing the Southeast*

*Asian City as Text: Urban Landscapes, Cultural Documents, and Interpretative Experiences.* Eds Robbie B.H. Goh and Brenda S.H. Yeoh. Singapore: World Scientific Publishing, 2003, 29–50.

## Works Consulted

Alfian bin Sa'at. *A History of Amnesia.* Singapore: Ethos Books, 2001.

———. *Corridors: 12 Short Stories.* Singapore: SNP Editions, 1999.

Brewster, Anne. *Towards a Semiotic of Postcolonial Discourse: University Writing in Singapore and Malaysia.* Singapore: Heinemann, 1989.

Cheong, Felix. *I Watch the Stars Go Out.* Singapore: Ethos Books, 1999.

Kundera, Milan. *Life is Elsewhere.* Trans. Peter Kussi. London: Faber and Faber, 1986.

Pang, Alvin. *City of Rain.* Singapore: Ethos Books, 2003.

Shiau, Daren. *Peninsular: Archipelagos and Other Islands.* Singapore: Ethos Books, 2000.

# PART FOUR

Nations at Play

# Theatrical Representation and National Identity in Fiji

IAN GASKELL

Theatre is often described as being the most social of the arts. What that means, presumably, is that in addition to its practice of depicting imagined social collectives in action, theatre also, by means of the performance experience, actually constructs one out of its audience. This new collective is more than the simple physical phenomenon of individuals gathered together, laughing, weeping, and applauding as one. In their empathetic response, audiences identify with the imaginary. Through the workings of artistic convention, which ensures communication and which is predicated on consent, the mirror which theatre holds up to life simply reflects the predilections, the ideological image, of the audience gazing into it. And to the extent that the audience likes what it sees, it is, in a Lacanian sense, confirmed in its own apparently integrated communal identity. As a rhetorical practice, then, theatre attempts to call its audience into being, turning individual spectators into a collective and constituting them as a temporary community with a shared ideology and identity.

Kenneth Burke, who used the terminology of drama to develop his concepts, saw the end of rhetoric not as instrumental persuasion but as consubstantiality. His operative word was 'identification' (Burke 1969: 55). By identification, he means speaking empathetically, understanding that to influence a listener one needs to see things from his or her perspective. This suggests, of course, that dialectically creating identification, establishing affiliation and community, automatically requires the acknowledgement of division and difference—the 'other'. That acknowledgement can be inclusive or exclusive. I have stated elsewhere that if the audience is a microcosm of society, and if that society as a whole is ethnically and culturally diverse, then, by exploring, performing, and embracing difference 'theatre can function as a crucible, forging a new consciousness of social, and possibly national, identity'. Conversely, by playing to its own perceived community, excluding the others that compose a multiracial society, theatre serves to reinforce separateness (Gaskell 2002: 125).

Much of the theatre in Fiji, a country that is indeed ethnically diverse, takes the form of what is called 'cultural performance'. These, whether stemming from indigenous Fijian ceremony or Indo-Fijian classical or folk drama, are expressions of their respective communities. As such they are assertions of ethnic and cultural identity, which speak to their separate communities. The former, traditional Fijian ceremony, is central to all official state functions. In its confirmation of chiefs authority, its celebration of status quo, its strict protocols, and its careful arrangement of performer and participant-observer into an index of social hierarchy, indigenous ceremony asserts a conservative political ideology. It is exclusive. Performances derived from it are also the mainstay of folkloric presentations designed for the tourist industry. Indeed, such performances are perceived projections of the national identity. Performances of Indo-Fijian origin are not. They are 'other'. They play to their own community, one which is not promoted as part of the national image.

There are also forms of theatre, based on European models, which critically address social, economic, and political issues. Rather than simply exclude, these plays actually explore ethnic difference. One such play is Sudesh Mishra's remarkable drama

*Ferringhi* (2001). Physically staged through and around that instant symbol of Fijian culture, a circle of *kava* drinkers, the play is structured as a series of transforming revelations that recall the personal history of each member of that circle. These individual hallucinations conjured by the story teller, Ferringhi, together form a collective vision that is the nation's history. At one point, the fictive play-world reaches out to incorporate its audience. The character Puglu takes a *bilo* (serving cup) filled with an infusion of kava, Fiji's sacred, ceremonial drink, from the onstage *tanoa* (mixing bowl) and, leaving the playing space, offers it to several members of the audience in an act of communion. To each celebrant he recites the following:

> Drink deeply, my friend,
> For your personal thirst
> Is but a national thirst.
> What you sip in solitude,
> Sips the noisy multitude.
> Drink deeply, my friend (*Ferringhi*, Lila 2).

The thirst he speaks of is a shared, individual emptiness, a solitary yearning that communally represents a national need. The audience for whom any dramatist writes is an abstraction, the ideal spectator multiplied into a collective. So too a nation, a people, is a plurality of the person. It is, in the familiar definition, an 'abstract imagined community' constructed of individuals. Any theatre audience is, for the duration of performance at least, also a figurative community formed by a mutual experience. By using real kava in a ritual of communion, Mishra attempts to transcend the virtuality of his play-world and actualize a sense of solidarity and community. For this play written in seven *lila*s is a poetic account of a multiracial nation torn apart by ethnic division.

Just prior to Puglu's little ritual, Ferringhi, the story teller, has conjured a vision of the country as a tapestry of noise and colour made rich by its ethnic and cultural diversity:

The market was mackerelled with people. ... Bodies rubbed like chess pieces against each other: oiled bodies, bodies wearing cologne, tika, buddha balm, bodies squeezed into bermudas and dungarees or togaed in sarees, sulued bodies, brown, black, white, yellow bodies, bodies halting at the sight of spring onions, or falling at the feet of daruka, bodies giving darshun to the tutelary gods of bhindi, choraya, karamwa, bodies chatting over clubs of dalo, bodies prodding the joints of ginger, bodies embalmed in garlic, or grailing for food in a pursuit that dissolves differences (*Ferringhi*, Lila 2).

This vision of boisterous and exuberant harmony is shattered by the 1987 coup and the arrival of Major-General Rabuka's thugs:

And I see this gang coming towards the market out of nowhere. First, they like grey sandstorm, then they take shape. They have sticks and clubs and chains and knives; and they are beating and clubbing and looting and breaking—Ferringhi asks them 'why?' and the rioters in balaclavas respond in turn:

Seru:       Cause you never watch native rugby!
Rioter A:   Cause you never know native custom!
Rioter B:   Cause you on native land!
Rioter C:   Cause you go fish our native fish!
Rioter D:   Cause you never worship native Christ!
Seru:       Cause you go urinate on native Sunday!
Ferringhi says:
When they leave, the maarkit change; no colours, no forms, jus subdued voices in a smoked-out world. Nothing to see, nothing to locate. Once a carnival, now a world the tint of fear and resignation (*Ferringhi*, Lila 2).

The multiracial composition of Fiji has for many years proved a source of conflict. Recently, the debate on ethnic identity in Fiji entered a new phase. Early in July 2004, the high chief, Adi Litia Cakobau, presented a motion in the Senate to criminalize the use of the term 'Indo-Fijian'. Claiming that this self-redefinition was 'diluting the word "Fijian"' and deceiving the world, she said that 'a blatant lie is being subtly injected into the collective Fijian national and international consciousness.' She continued,

It is my inherited duty as a direct descendent of Ratu Seru Cakobau, the principal original recipient of our legal ethnic group identifier 'Fijian' to raise my concern on the subtle and devious means of psychological domination being systematically employed by social engineers of Indian origin to usurp the name 'Fijian' (*Fiji Times* 3 July 2004: 3).

Imposing her own homogenizing misrepresentation (and in words reminiscent of the thugs in Mishra's play), she collectively defined this alien 'other' in terms of the following cultural signifiers:

They are identified as Indians in all census counts. They are Indians in the Electoral Act. They have social, economic, political, ideological contact with India. Their political party receives cash and other forms of help from India…. They listen, speak, read, write and worship in Hindi. They eat Indian food, watch Indian movies and listen to Hindi music.

She also said 'her motives in making the statement were not racial or political' (*Fiji Times* 3 July 2004: 3).

Adi Litia's speech is 'nationalist' rhetoric. What is interesting here is that just as 'Indians' are characterized as a homogenous collective, so too are the indigenous Fijians themselves. But the indigenous Fijian society is not a cohesive one. George Speight used the same strategy in the 2000 coup, where he, too, spoke apparently for all Fijians. Terms like 'identity theft', 'displacement', and 'ethnocide' are part of this 'nationalist' rhetoric, where the idea of 'nationalism' designates not the assertion of a unified country but the project of a sub-nation asserting its own identity as the national image. For as much as the generation of fear about internal displacement and economic domination by the Indo-Fijian community is used as a rhetorical weapon, more telling is the idea that the distinctiveness of the indigenous Fijian culture, that image projected to the world, will be lost.

Much of the nationalist rhetoric reveals an almost obsessive anxiety about the international perception of Fiji. To use a social-psychological term, this 'perceived public persona' (how we think others view us) is a manifestation of a desire to assert uniqueness in the face of globalization—a distinctiveness projected through a range of cultural and ethnic markers that confer identity. This collective identity is sanctioned by those various government and public organizations that market Fiji as a tourist destination. In the brochures the 'friendly face of Fiji' (one of the marketing slogans), is decidedly not Indo-Fijian or for that matter, Chinese or mixed race. Illustrated with the white sandy beaches of the tourist resorts, the picturesque traditional villages and the happy natives with their famous smiles, the brochures of the Fiji Visitor's Bureau have marketed Fiji as 'the way the world should be'. Given the political, social, and economic problems of the country, this is not only a false assertion but it is also one predicated on excluding those cultures and ethnicities that don't conform to the approved national image. This image, this perceived public persona, is, of course, an abstraction, just as the nation itself is, to use a phrase dismissed by Paul James, 'a recently contrived, cultural *invention*' (James 1996: xiv).

The official national identity seems to be constructed from its own promotional material, or to put it unkindly, they've been reading their own reviews. To an extent, the desire for identity results in misrecognized unity, a distorted self-confirmation reflected in the mirror created by audience applause—an audience that often consists primarily of Australian tourists suffering from a shared delusion that they are participating in something authentic. In Althusserian terms, the image fostered by the various ideological state apparatuses in Fiji (for example, the Fiji Visitor's Bureau or the Fiji Arts Council) does indeed, in the well-known formulation, represent 'the imaginary relationship of individuals to their real conditions of existence' (Easthope 1991: 131). This ideology hails (interpellates) the decentred subject, providing a sense of unity, an identity, a place. Interpellation is a cornerstone of that species of rhetoric called constitutive, to differentiate it from the instrumental or purposive rhetoric described as words that sell cars (Charland 2001: 616). This kind of rhetoric is central to the nationalist endeavour—the calling into being of an audience already defined by the rhetoric itself, to constitute that audience as a collective and to differentiate it from the 'other'.

The word 'other' is actually an official designation in a country that categorizes its citizens by race. To cite *Ferringhi* again, Puglu conducts a self-interview playing both himself and the part of an irritated official:

*(impersonating an irritated official)* ... Put a tick in one of the boxes. Here let me do it for you. What are you: Fijian, Rotuman, European, part-European, Chinese, Indian or Other?
*(acting the role of the addressee)* Other.
*(as official)* What other?
*(as addressee)* Just other.
*(as official, losing his temper)* This woman here is Chinese, that man there is Fijian and I here am part-European. What are you?
*(as addressee)* Your others.
*(as official, to himself as he writes)* Indian (*Ferringhi*, Lila 2).

Mishra's point here is that while Indians are not officially 'other', they might as well be. The approved national image is a constitutive rhetorical construct, like the nationalist rhetoric that draws on it. As with George Speight's 'the Cause', the mantra that served as a rationale for the 2000 coup (that same murky phrase used by Othello to justify his murder of Desdemona), this nationalist rhetoric is an assemblage of vague associations. But by this rhetoric the indigenous Fijian is provided with, as Paul James would say, the 'structural subjectivities that ground national formation', namely:

... three categories of human existence and social relations—the body, space and time. ... The body relates to the nationalist emphasis upon organic metaphors such as 'the blood of the people'; space is relevant to the emphasis on territoriality; and time is important to the cultural themes of historicity, tradition and primordial roots (James 1996: xiv).

The Fijian ethos, that distinctiveness asserted through nationalist rhetoric, is constructed from these 'subjectivities'. In fact, as history shows, Fiji was never more than a geographical location inhabited by warring tribes of people who, to this day, do not speak the same native dialect nor share a particular physical resemblance from west to east. Fiji as an archipelago was ceded to Britain by a local chief (Cakobau) who, like his descendent, Adi Litia (and indeed like George Speight), took it upon himself to speak for all the indigenous inhabitants. The nation and its aristocracy were actually constructed by the British to accord with their ideas of governance.

Essentially speaking, the blood of the people is mixed, the space (ownership of the land) is contested, historicity is a melange of brief fact and sustained myth, with emphasis on the latter, and the primordial roots were a missionary fabrication, contrary to truth but taught for years, that the Fijians first came from Africa. Tradition, the basis for much that transpires in the country, is pretty much what happened yesterday. For example, the comparatively recent introduction of Christianity is accorded traditional status in ceremonies (Hereniko 1999: 156). Nevertheless, these three subjectivities—blood, space, and time—are fundamental to the construction of the Fijian identity. They are subsumed under the overarching concept of the *vanua*, a word that signifies the land, the people, and their culture (Ravuvu 1987: 14). The vanua is at the centre of Fijian ceremony.

Sadly, however, many of these ceremonies that mark various rites of passage and all significant social occasions have been eroded over time. The words for certain chants and other rituals are now lost. Certain elements like the *meke*, a form of dance theatre, have been decontextualized and commodified for tourist consumption. As the national image is reshaped for commercial purposes, cultural conservationists lament the debasement of the forms and the loss of Fijian identity that this entails. The theme of the sacred vanua and the commercialization of traditional culture is incorporated by Mishra into *Ferringhi*. Seru, who represents the Fijian perspective, sells to the colonial masters certain 'drilling rights' which happen to lie directly beneath their tanoa, the mixing bowl for the sacred, ceremonial kava infusion. Kava, hand-pounded from roots, is the most important spiritual element in Fijian ritual. The group is forced to relocate to a spot where a new tanoa, painted in psychedelic colours, rests on a large coca-cola mat. Crusher, the colonial, says,

It is indeed encouraging to see everyone living in peace and harmony in Fiji. Sometimes colonialism works, doesn't it? ...Of course the indigenous race must have, er, certain inalienable rights and privileges over the more recent immigrants. It is only fair. After all they were here first. It's common sense, isn't it? Like queuing for food. First come first served (*laughs*) (*Ferringhi*, Lila 3).

Seru, donning dark sunglasses, serves the flashy, pre-packaged, factory-made kava in silver bilos (serving cups usually made from coconut shells). But Ferringhi says, the kava 'lacks depth. The soul of the root is missing. Cosmetic kava.' Even Seru admits that 'the wood never go release its spirit' (*Ferringhi*, Lila 6). In an aside, he says,

> Does breadth of time
> Give depth of belonging?
> I've lost the rhyme;
> The land's not singing
> To me who claim it
> Over those whose hearts
> Have now rhymed it,
> Rhyme with them my heart.

Returning to the original tanoa, he says,

I was in the woods starved of light and, as I lay troubled under an umbrella tree, a leaf broke like surf on my face and I saw a star, and then another leaf broke, and I saw a clutch of stars, and so on it went till I was left with a constellation of stars and no longer knew the night. Once again, I was worm of soil and crab of ocean floor and the vanua was in me and I was in the vanua. (*to Ferringhi*) Vinaka Vakalevu, my Tusitala. (*to Crusher*) Our land won't play whore to your global economy. We gonna do our own thing, aren't we Tusitala? (*Ferringhi*, Lila 7)

This idea of maintaining traditional culture in a changing world and its significance in terms of Indigenous Fijian identity is raised as a thematic element and through formal innovation in the work of Fiji's first indigenous playwright, Jo Nacola. In a number of short plays, written some twenty years ago and collected under the title

*I Native No More*, Nacola expresses a distinctive Fijian sense of the world particularly in relation to the Indo-Fijian population and the latter's manifest success in commercial endeavour and adaptability to change. The concomitant failure by Fijians to excel in business and their attendant loss of self-esteem continues to exacerbate the racial disharmony in the country. Nacola addresses the issue more directly in *Gurudial and the Land*, a play that dramatizes the conflicting social perspectives of a traditional rural Fijian communal system and the globalized Indo-Fijian commercial orientation. The conflict is centred on the refusal by the Indian, Gurudial, to supply a steer for a community feast. He has done so in the past but has remained unpaid. The Fijians expect that, as an adopted member of their community, living on their land, Gurudial should share his comparative wealth as part of a system of reciprocal giving. He is 'their' Indian and as such is part of, and subject to the customary laws of the vanua, the Land in the play's title. The action moves through conflict, complete with racial stereotyping on both sides, towards a harmonious resolution, significantly, one that is achieved through the staging of a traditional Fijian ceremony. Having performed well in the ceremony, Gurudial is acknowledged as being part of the vanua. He has accepted their cultural traditions and they acknowledge his rightful place among them. He is paid for his steer, but the payment, like the steer, is treated as a gift.

In his well-constructed but somewhat melodramatic play, *Adhuuraa Sapnaa*, written in 1993 first in Fiji Hindi, Raymond Pillai provides a reverse perspective to Nacola's indigenous Fijian point of view. But here the intercultural difference between the races seems unbridgeable. Sambhu, a civil servant who has retired with his pretty young wife, Minla, to become a watermelon farmer, has little but contempt for his Fijian landlords, saying to his neighbour, Jona,

You people's God is for Sundays only. You have a Bible in your hand, you wear a coat and tie for two hours in church, and that's it. Then from Monday to Saturday, back to your old business—stealing, getting drunk, brawling and beating up your wife—

Jona, one of the landowners, retorts,

And you Indians? Every morning you wake up and do your puujaa, you don't eat meat or fish on Tuesdays and Fridays, you have prayer meetings and sing hymns till midnight. But you people steal too. Your women fight with their neighbours. And you men working in the fields, when you see any girl, you whistle and make cheeky remarks (*Adhuuraa Sapnaa*, 1.2).

Even more pointed are references to the intracultural differences between Hindus, Muslims, South Indians, Sikhs, and Gujaratis (Prasad 2001: 192). Giving his assessment of those who have not earned the moral right to a place in the land (and indirectly the reason for his own choice), Sambhu says,

The Bombaiyas didn't serve *girmit*. And we didn't do it either. True our elders did so, that's why they had the right to stay on in Fiji. But what right have we got? Until we pour out our sweat into this land, we can never claim we have any rights here (*Adhuuraa Sapnaa*, 1.3).

When his farm is sabotaged he is quick to blame the Fijians. Ironically, it is his Muslim farmhand, Jalil, who has done the damage at Minla's instigation. They are having an affair and she wants to migrate to Canada.

Presenting yet another perspective, that of the *kai loma* (the other), those like the playwright, himself, of mixed parentage, Larry Thomas has written a number of plays that address the problems of this somewhat marginalized segment of the population. In *The Anniversary Present*, which centres on the life of a mixed race family, Thomas deals directly with the issue of identity. 'Why do you call yourself part-European and not part Fijian?' asks one character. The answer, that it is a matter of status, produces the rejoinder that it makes no difference; they will always remain outsiders in the larger community. In *To Let You Know*, Thomas uses a multimedia style incorporating video images of life in Fiji interwoven with parallel, epistolary expressions of a Fijian and Indian each writing to their respective sons. The interracial conflict in the country and its potential for resolution is given visual expression in a particularly effective sequence in the play. As the Introduction to the play describes it,

A young Indian girl dressed in her sari performs a traditional, delicate dance to the rhythm of a *tabla*. Several sequences later a young Fijian warrior, costumed in grass skirt and war paint presents a spear dance to the beat of a *lali*. Finally, the two appear together, each doing his/her own choreography in the form of a cultural debate, the *tabla* and *lali* alternating and then playing together. As each dancer becomes more aggressive and insistent, they gradually adopt elements from each other's choreography and end by performing the same dance, a new one that harmoniously blends elements of both cultures—a joyful moment redolent with possibility and hope (Gaskell 2002: iv–v).

In representing difference, this and the other plays cited offer contrasting perspectives on identity. As drama, they are by definition dialectical, presenting conflicting views within their virtual worlds. They operate through dialogue; they are multivocal and inclusive in their exchange of ideas on race, as distinct from the univocalism inherent in traditional performance in Fiji. Dialectic is formed as the sum of the competing voices. But just as no one single voice in a play is that of the playwright—his voice is the sum of all the voices in the play—so, too, the various theatrical representations in this multiracial country together form an aggregate that constitutes a national identity.

## Works Cited

Burke, K. *A Rhetoric of Motives*. Berkeley: University of California Press, 1969.

Charland, M. 'Constitutive Rhetoric', in *Encyclopedia of Rhetoric*. Ed. Thomas Sloane. Oxford: Oxford University Press, 2001.

Easthope, Antony. *Literary into Cultural Studies*. London: Routledge, 1991.

*Fiji Times*, 3 July 2004, Suva.

Gaskell, Ian. 'The Hybidization of Traditional Performance in Contemporary Fijian Theatre', in *Multiculturalisme et Identité en Littérature et en Art*. Ed. Jean Bessière et Sylvie André. Paris: L'Harmattan, 2002.

————. 'Introduction', in *To Let You Know & Other Plays*. Larry Thomas. Suva: Pacific Writing Forum, 2002.

Hereniko, Vilsoni. 'Representations of Cultural Identities', in *Inside Out: Literature, Cultural Politics, and Identity in the New Pacific*. Eds Vilsoni Hereniko and Rob Wilson. Lanham: Rowman & Littlefield Publishers Inc., 1999.

James, Paul. *Nation Formation: Towards a Theory of Abstract Community*. London: Sage Publications, 1996.

Mishra, Sudesh. *Ferringhi* in *Beyond Ceremony: An Anthology of Drama from Fiji*. Ed. Ian Gaskell. Suva: Institute of Pacific Studies and Pacific Writing Forum, 2001.

Nacola, Jo. *I Native No More : Three Drama Sketches*. Suva: Mana Publications, 1976.

————. *Gurudial and Land* in *Beyond Ceremony: An Anthology of Drama from Fiji*. Ed. Ian Gaskell. Suva : Institute of Pacific Studies and Pacific Writing Forum, 2001.

Pillai, Raymond. *Adhuuraa Sapnaa* in *Beyond Ceremony: An Anthology of Drama from Fiji*. Ed. Ian Gaskell. Suva: Institute of Pacific Studies and Pacific Writing Forum, 2001.

Prasad, Mohit. 'Introduction', in *Adhuuraa Sapnaa* in *Beyond Ceremony: An Anthology of Drama from Fiji*. Ed. Ian Gaskell. Suva: Institute of Pacific Studies and Pacific Writing Forum, 2001.

Ravuvu, Asesela D. *The Fijian Ethos*. Suva: Institute of Pacific Studies of the University of the South Pacific, 1987.

Thomas, Larry. 'The Anniversary Present', in *To Let You Know & Other Plays*. Suva: Pacific Writing Forum, 2002.

# Performing the Nation
## Dave Carson and the Bengali Babu

POONAM TRIVEDI

Postcolonial studies have been slow to acknowledge the colonization of the performative sphere. The British Empire was serviced and sustained by a corresponding empire of entertainment. A cultural imperialism, in the form of a steady export from the West of elite and popular modes of entertainment, had as immutable an impact on Indian society as the political. Our own modes of performance were challenged, derided, and then, irrevocably changed or marked and hybridized. This essay is part of a larger project to document and analyse such developments in the performative sphere. While the influence in the highbrow literary sphere, for example, of Shakespeare on the growth of dramatic writing in the Indian languages, has been acknowledged, the evolution of the popular sphere of entertainment and its contamination by western practice has not been researched in any depth. This neglect of the popular and the public is surprising, because what and how we perform and 'play' is intimately connected with how we configure ourselves; that is, identity, role-playing, and performance are interdependent.

This essay will examine the work of one of the earliest and more remarkable of the visiting performers, Dave Carson, who in his repeated tours of India between 1861 and 1882(?) became not just the most popular but the most remembered of entertainers, whose songs and comic acts have become legendary, retaining a place in our theatrical and national memory. Dave Carson merits an extended discussion because he was that unusual kind of imperial showman who did not so much impose his mode of performance as refashioned his act so as to interact with his Indian audiences. He localized his songs and impersonations, his burlesques and pantomimes. He is thus credited with creating and putting into public circulation perhaps the most enduring, entertaining, but controversial character 'type' of the colonial period, 'the Bengalee Babu'. But what is less well known is that he also burlesqued and adapted that iconic canonical author, Shakespeare, and that he came as part of a black-faced minstrel group—which, literally, changes the complexion of his act and its reception. Issues of identity, representation, and colour, key issues of post-colonial inquiry, therefore become central to his playing and popularity.

To locate Dave Carson in the theatrical and cultural context of the India of the 1860s, we need to recall that theatre and theatre-going, as we know it today, developed under western influence. The earliest western or proscenium style modern theatres in India were established in the 1770s in Bombay and Calcutta by the English, but the next few longer-lasting theatres were set up with the active support and financial aid of the Indians. Were it not for Dwarakanath Tagore's substantial grant in the case of the Chowringee Theatre in Calcutta (1813), and Sunkersett Jeejeebhoy's gift of land and money for the Grant Road Theatre in Bombay (1846), these pioneering institutions may never have got started.[1] The players of the early theatres were all amateurs, but with the opening of the regular theatres, professional actors were commissioned to perform. The 1860s were a period of an increased influx of visiting companies. A steady flow of performing companies of actors, musicians, opera singers, acrobats, entertainers, circus artists, magicians, even dwarfs (including the legendary Tom Thumb), all visited the subcontinent as part of their world tour. India became a favoured halting point between

Europe and the Far East and Australia in the growing economy of entertainment.

The 1860s were also the period of the emergence of modern Indian theatre and its growth towards professionalization and commercialization. The impact of the visiting companies was seminal, and their manner as much as matter of performance was deeply influential. Vishu Das Bhave, the father of Marathi drama, for instance, performed his first play at the Grant Road Theatre because he was impressed with its 'order, the seating arrangements, the curtains, the scenery etc'.[2] and was not the least disconcerted by the fact that his gods and goddesses had to sit and battle in 'a most English looking parlour'.[3] The Parsi theatre companies, the earliest instance of modern professional theatre in India, were being formed in the 1860s, and show direct influence of the visiting companies: not only do they style themselves organizationally on the European model, themselves beginning to tour the subcontinent, but they adopt many of their artistic and presentational practices: like interspersing a farce between scenes or at the end of a serious play, or taking the liberty to adapt and change as canonical an author as Shakespeare, and interpolating a chorus line of dancing girls in every story. One of the earliest and more successful playing companies, of popular and not elite entertainment, was the San Francisco Minstrels led by Dave Carson, who made their first tour of India from 1861 to 1866. So successful was this tour that Carson returned to India several times with differing groups of artists—in the 1870s, every other year, holding a grand event in Bombay—and into the 1880s.

This was also the period of the emergence of new classes under the influence of colonialism and western education and their typification in the popular sphere, represented above all by the figure of the Bengali babu. The term 'babu' (Hindi), originally an honorific for an educated person, became narrowly associated with clerks who were employed by the English and was later used disparagingly to refer to the stereotypical qualities of a superficial westernization and obsequiousness increasingly associated with them. It was the beginning of a process which culminated in

Rudyard Kipling's satirical portrait of Hurree Chunder Mookherji in *Kim* (1901) and F. Anstey's caricature *Baboo Jabberjee* (1897), the most well-known responses to the new threat to and anxiety about the status quo that was presented by the English-educated Indian, particularly after the passing of the Indian Civil Services Act of 1861 which opened the door for recruitment of Indians as well to that elite ruling cadre. The significance of Carson's act is that he was the first to elucidate and perform on the public stage such class and character types as early as 1865.[4]

## Dave Carson and Black-face Minstrelsy

Dave Carson's life, as interesting as his work, represents in microcosm the diverse strands that went into creating our own colonial hybridities. Born an American in 1837, Carson left New York as a sixteen-year old in 1853 for Melbourne, Australia, where he began to perform solo and with groups in the gold-mining towns. He is first noted to be with the minstrel group, Totten's Harmoneons, then with the Ethiopian Serenaders. In 1856–7 he joined the party of Tom Brower, brother of Frank Brower (one of the original four of the Virginia Minstrels, the pioneering American minstrel group) to form 'The San Francisco Minstrels' who toured New South Wales, Victoria, South Australia, Queensland, Van Dieman's Land, and New Zealand. In 1861, the company split into two. One group left for Mauritius where, after playing at Port Louis, they were shipwrecked on the way to the Cape of Good Hope. The other group, organized by Dave Carson and consisting of Tom Brower, H.C. Campbell, J.O. Pierce, C.F. Palin, and the Leopold family, left Melbourne in August 1861 and after a voyage of fifty days arrived in Calcutta, and presented itself as the 'Original San Francisco Minstrels—a burlesque, opera, and ballet troupe'.[5] After a successful season in Calcutta, the company travelled up-country performing, as their advertisements proclaim, 'in all principle cities throughout India' (*The Times of India* [henceforth *TOI*], 28 February 1863). A rare surviving letter from Dave Carson written

from Lucknow, dated 9 March 1862, to the Editor of *Bell's Life in
Victoria*, gives valuable details of their tour:

Leaving Calcutta a month ago, we have played since at Cawnpore, where that
awful massacre took place in 1857. … We gave six concerts there. Since then we
have given eight performances at Lucknow. … The Theatre we perform in is a
splendid pile, and was once used as a harem by the King of Oudh. It has been
turned into a theatre by the officers of a regiment stopping here. We leave shortly
for Agra and Delhi; thence to Simla and probably to Cashmere.[6]

Other advertisements inform us that they travel via Raneegunj,
Benares, Allahabad, Meerut up to Punjab (Umballa), and the
Northwest Province (Lahore), returning to Calcutta by 22
November 1862 where they give a series of 'Farewell Concerts' prior
to their sailing for Madras around 23 January 1863, whence they
proceed to Bombay. Their debut concert in Bombay at the Theatre
Royal, Grant Road, is on 28 February 1863; they perform there
till 5 May 1863, leave for 'a little rest and quiet' (*TOI* 5 May 1863)
in Mahabaleshwar, visit Poona during the rainy season, and return
to Bombay at the start of the next cold season on 8 October 1863.
The company is hugely successful everywhere, so successful, in fact,
that they stay on in India for five years, repeating these tours starting
from Calcutta to the Upper Provinces during the summer, coming
down south to perform in Bombay till the early winter, and
returning to Calcutta for the festive season. They are finally reported
to leave India in May 1866. The company's unprecedented success
motivates them, or at least Dave Carson, the prime mover, to return
to the subcontinent frequently, becoming the only company to do
so. They return as 'Dave Carson's Minstrels' in 1869, and
subsequently, every other year, with new performers and even a
troupe of chorus girls till well into the 1880s. During this decade,
Carson establishes a more permanent foothold in Calcutta; he
becomes a lessee of the newly built Corinthian Theatre, and after
him, his wife is said to have run it for many years.[7]
　　Though the company as a whole merited its success, the lynchpin
of their popularity was Dave Carson, who was gifted with a quick

wit, acute powers of observation, the ability to adapt and improvise on local conditions, and the acting talent to mimic and impersonate. After their return from the first tour, the *New York Clipper* ran a feature on 25 May 1867 on the earliest minstrels in Australia in which Carson and his company had honourable mention:

in Calcutta ... they astonished the Hindus and Mohamedans not a little with the representations of the sports and pastimes of the Ethiopian race in the United States. ... [Their] tour of Hindustan ... where the audiences consisting of Parsees, Europeans, Hindoos, Musselmen [*sic*], and a host of natives from all parts of Asia greeted them at each performance with delight and hard silver, ... The San Francisco Minstrels were successful because Carson ... attained Hindostanese [*sic*] ... and the manner in which he mimicked and caricatured a certain class of the native people. ... Mr Carson wears some magnificent diamonds presented to him by a wealthy Parsee merchant of Bombay.[8]

At the end of their first season in Calcutta, the upper crust newspaper, *The Englishman,* sounded a prophetic note (4 February 1862):

We depart from rule in noticing the departure of the Minstrels who have largely contributed to the evening amusements of Calcutta through the cold season. The best test of their ability lies in the fact that their audiences have steadily increased in numbers. We have heard many speak of having listened to them a dozen times and on their two last appearances very many have been unable to get admission. So, if the strains of Calcutta approbation can be of service to them they should be well received upon their up country tour. [They] promise a better entertainment than could be afforded by any such company who have visited India, at any rate for some years past.

Such eulogy became frequent, almost predictable, as their tour progressed: the *TOI,* 3 March 1863, pronounced their first show in Bombay as a 'complete triumph'. On 12 March it noted how 'Dave Carson's "proficiency" in Hindustani is mirth moving to a degree, and the "notes" he has taken of the buggywallas and the "boys" make one's side to shake with laughter. All his characters are admirable and are played to perfection.' By the end of the month, letters were requesting items, for example, in *TOI*, 25 March 1863, which were especially composed for Bombay. On their return to Calcutta for their second season, *The Englishman* (28 November 1863) observed:

The San Francisco Minstrels possess the faculty rare among birds of passage of their genus in India of improving upon acquaintance... the interval has been improved by them as was evidenced by the increased precision and better style of their concerted pieces. It is impossible for Dave Carson to stretch his facial muscles beyond their old limit, but he has not studied the language in vain, and last night he passed in Hindustani with full honours and put into most effective practice his researches in politics.

By the time they left India in 1866, the San Francisco Minstrels and Dave Carson had more than proved themselves, as is confirmed by a leader in *The Englishman* (10 March 1866):

The success of Dave Carson is quite a legitimate one. He is by no means an ordinary 'Brudder Bones' ... he possesses considerable powers of observation, a vein of true comic conception and gifts of mimicry [of] ... unlimited range.... But by far the greatest merit he has displayed has been the courage and skill with which he has determined to amuse Anglo-Indians with the world around them, and to prove to them that human life will everywhere afford ample material for genuine humour.

Carson's subsequent visits were enthusiastically received by packed houses; as he himself said at the start of the 1876 season, 'It seemed as if he was coming back to the bosom of his family' (*The Englishman* 27 November 1876). And as *The Statesman* (27 November 1876) noted, 'A very large audience assembled ... to welcome back that old favourite and able caterer for public amusement. Dave must have been highly gratified when he stepped forward to make his bow to witness a house crammed from the floor to ceiling.' References to Dave Carson in memoirs and accounts of this period too, repeatedly term him 'Prince of Entertainers' (H. Hobbs),[9] 'The Star' of the 'most spectacular' of the shows

(Teresa Albuquerque)[10] and an 'excellent farceur' (Kumudini Arvind Mehta).[11] Such evidence is ample proof of the extraordinary achievement and impact of Dave Carson's act. What was the secret of his success? What attraction did this American/Australian company singing and performing blackface Negro skits and ditties hold for Indians and expatriate English a century and half ago?

The stage act of Dave Carson and his San Francisco Minstrels was entirely determined by the conventions of the minstrel show, a musical entertainment in which white actors 'blacked-up' and performed as negroes, and whose popularity quickly spread across America and Europe and then to the colonies from the 1840s till the 1880s when it was overtaken by the vaudeville.[12] As explained in *The Oxford Companion to American Theatre*, the typical minstrel show consisted of three parts: the first comprised songs and dances with humorous exchanges between the company seated in a semi-circle, with the interlocutor in the centre, and the tambo and bones players at the ends. The second part was a free wheeling olio of variety acts and comic sketches and included a 'stump speech' which mocked the do-gooders of high society. The third section incorporated a farce and burlesque, usually on plantation life, and the show ended with rousing songs and dances.

The programmes of the San Francisco Minstrels as advertised in Calcutta and Bombay, particularly in the early part of their initial tour, show all the staple ingredients of the standard minstrel show: overtures, harmonic singing, solo songs which included well-known pieces of the minstrel repertoire, like 'Merry is the Minstrel's life', 'Brudder Bones', 'They have sold me down the River' (from *Uncle Tom's Cabin*) in the first part; followed by concertina and piano duets, typical stump speeches like 'Aunty Smith on Women's Rights' and impersonations as a 'Blue Tail Fly' in the second. This was followed by burlesque sketches from 'Ethiopian' (black life) operas like 'We're a Band of Brothers' and 'Grand Plantation Jubilee', in the final part. The items on offer changed twice a week and the final burlesque often incorporated, following the mid-nineteenth century fashion, mandatory travesties entitled 'Shakespearean Readings' with Carson cast as the 'Juvenile Tragedian'.

## Localizing the Minstrelsy

But the company was not confined to the traditional black-face minstrel show. The popular and non-formal nature of the minstrel conventions lent themselves to adaptation. In Australia, the San Francisco Minstrels had created localized pieces like the 'Bushranger' songs (which they also performed in India). So it was only a matter of time before they improvised on the Indian context. By the time they returned to Calcutta from their first round tour of the subcontinent in November 1862, Dave Carson was being praised, as noted earlier, for his command over Hindustani and Indian politics. Reviews of their return shows in Bombay in late 1863 note songs adapted by a transposition of a few words in Hindustani, for example, 'I am going to Charleston' became 'Hum Jata Charleston', and 'Hold your Horses' became 'Hold your Ghoras'. Advertisements were punctuated by Hindustani words, for example 'Dekho! Dekho!! Dekho!!!', 'Burra Khabar', and 'Ram, Ram, G'. Localized new songs, for example, on eminent Parsee gentlemen, Jeejeebhoy and Cowasjee, and a skit, 'The Indigo Planter', were immediate hits. By the following season, December 1864, the localizing prowess of the Minstrels had taken off. Not just the language but also the personages of the bazaar were appropriated into the show to cater to the local taste. As the *Bengal Harkaru* noted in its review of 17 December 1864, 'Their tour through the country has only afforded them an opportunity for adding new characters and jokes to their repertoire.' 'New Characters from the Indian bazaar!' trumpeted their advertisements. The celebrated 'new original song' 'The Bengalee Baboo', was the first presentation on 16 December 1864. On 19 December, they had a 'Hindustanee Nautch', 20 December saw 'The Delhi Mummy', and on 27 December, Othello was transformed into 'Othello Sahib Bahadoor'. On 6 April 1865, at the start of their second tour in Bombay, the *TOI* observed that 'their entertainments have become peculiarly adapted to this country, as they are interspersed with local allusions and characteristic sayings that are daily met with throughout India.' 1865 was the beginning of a series of new topical hits in the shape of songs, caricatures, and impersonations: 'Old Bill Biley and the Indian Navy' was presented on 2 January, 'The Dak Gharree' on 9 January, 'The Calcutta Police Court' on 3 February, 'The Bombay Police Court' on 20 April, 'Curry Bart' on 25 April, 'Bombay in July' on 5 May, 'Davejee Carsonbhoy's Dream', and 'Tight Little Island' (on Bombay) on 17 May, and somewhere in between, a courtship song-cum-skit with a 'Portuguese [this is, Goan] Girl'. Carson also improvised stump speeches on leading issues of the day, viz. Mutlah shares, tea plantations, Income Tax, and the Extravagance of the Government, etc.

It is more than evident that such pervasive localizing and interaction with the audience was a major cause of the continuing popularity of the San Francisco Minstrels. Visiting entertainers, and even the minstrel show, were not new to the metropolitan cities of India. But they almost always stuck to their tried-and-tested shows. The Christy Minstrels, an even more reputed group, whose visit during 1863–5 overlapped with that of the San Francisco Minstrels, did not receive the rave reception that Dave Carson came to command. That they were compelled to add a token localization, a song and dance, 'The Bombay Share Mania', and a character, the 'Bombay Post Office Peon', to their last few shows, clearly to garner a repeat audience, reveals the popular pull of localized entertainment. While the details of most of these songs and skits do not survive, their very titles, gleaned through newspaper advertisements, and reviews and letters (for all minstrel groups used the urban print media very effectively) give a feel of the evolving nature of their repertoire. In his later tours Carson continued to add to his repertoire with songs like 'Maree Jan' (3 August 1869), 'Khoob-Thatta' (17 August 1869), 'Mozuffernuggar' (23 April 1869), 'The Calcutta Palki Wallahs' (27 November 1876), 'Four Aryan Brethren' (19 December 1876), and 'Calcutta Four in Hand' (30 December 1876). The quintessential burlesque of the minstrel show too was Indianized and the Christmas pantomime was entitled 'The Headless Chowkidar' (22 December 1876). And by 1877, Carson was advertising as many as eight impersonations out of which three were Indian, one German, and another Yankee.

Carson's strategy was different from the usual visiting entertainers: right from the beginning, he systematically refashioned and localized their 'darkey acts' to communicate directly with his audience, which could not have comprised only Europeans. There persists a view among Indian theatre historians, which needs reinvestigating, that early English theatre in India was witnessed almost exclusively by Europeans and that the Indian presence was tokenist and elite. While this may have been so at the very start of western theatre in India during the 1770s, by the 1830s, as mentioned at the start of this essay, Indians were crucial in more ways than one to the survival of theatre in India. While there were differences in the composition of the audiences in Bombay and Calcutta—Bombay always had more Indians, with a fair sprinkling of Parsees, intermingling socially with the English, than Calcutta which was governed in most aspects by the hierarchy set by the Viceroy—there is considerable evidence from letters to newspapers, and some memoirs, that theatre audiences in the mid- and late nineteenth century comprised a mix of Europeans and English-educated Indians, with the numbers of the latter on the increase. Dave Carson's act therefore had to target its audiences accordingly. An advertisement of 10 August 1869 provides proof of such targeting: it boldly announced that 'Baboo Davee Kar-Sen takes this opportunity of informing his Aryan Brethren residing at Entally, Ballygunge, Boitakanee, Mocheekhola, Chitpore, Seetapore, and China Bazaar, that he will introduce on this occasion his most intimate friend, RAM JAM THUNDA GHOSE, B.A., THE ORIGINAL BENGALEE BABOO'. Carson transformed not just the foolish stage Negro into an Asiatic, but also the traditional audiences for such shows.

Carson had a gift, we are told, for picking up the local note, both musical and topical. He would take old Indian melodies, sung by ayahs, nautchwallas, and other itinerant musicians, and incorporate them into his repertoire with witty words to boot.[13] After a few months of travel in the subcontinent, he picked up some Hindustani that he deployed very effectively to satirize the foibles of his audience. Robert C. Toll in his foundational book on the minstrel show,

*Blacking Up,* notes how the original (American) San Francisco Minstrels were known in minstrel history as the 'unrivalled masters of the spontaneous ad lib'[14] and Carson, their Australian/Indian avatar, more than lived up to it. Improvisation was in his blood and audiences would wait and watch who or what will be the target of his barbs at every performance. His chief innovation, however, was his impersonations of the regional character. Since Calcutta and Bombay were the main centres of entertainment, it is his creations of the Bengali Babu and the Parsi Mashr for which he is still remembered today. Though the Bengali Babu as a sociological type originated some time earlier in the century,[15] it was Dave Carson's singular contribution to treat this and other impersonations with a serio-comic effusion and to put them into circulation in the popular domain throughout the country.

The Bengali Babu, the Parsi Mashr, and Anne Maria D'Cruze as an Indo-Portuguese (a less well remembered but equally significant impersonation) represent communities that came into prominence with colonialism and the growth of urban India. It is Carson's perspective deriving from the inherent oppositional and subversive roots of the black minstrel show which sensitized him to pick up, formulate, and perform these types for the first time, types which were to constitute the nation to be, and which were to people the nation's imagination.

As D.E. Wacha reminisces in *Shells from the Sands of Bombay* (1920), a rare memoir of western India:

It was that humorist, Dave Carson, who really made the Grant Road Theatre famous among the play going folk of Bombay and for years altogether attracted thousands to the house ... [He] knew how to catch his audience, especially with local topics of interest and many a topical song. He was protean in many respects and was never more happy than when he donned the garb of the Parsi mashr of the period and made love to 'Rati Madam'. The house used to go into roars of laughter at both his sallies of wit and his songs. He was a gifted actor and on the boards of the Grant Road Theater played many parts which those who heard him could even recall today with the greatest pleasure. But the skit with which Dave Carson's name will be remembered is his caricature of the Bengalee Baboo in the famous song of the same name. Even today the Indian bands ... play this tune ... at Hindu weddings or at the doors of the Parsis on their New Year's Day.[16]

If there was some sense of discomfiture at this lampooning of the natives by a white, albeit in a comic form, a look at exactly what constituted his act would help give a more nuanced understanding of his popularity. A few fragments of his songs and some descriptions of his act have survived. Early in his tour, in March 1863, he adapted one of the classic minstrel songs sung by every group, 'The Whole Hog or None', to address Bombay's audience with wit and punch:

As a place of generous people, Bombay it has the name,
One may do good and get surprised to find it fame
With its 'Jeejeebhoys' and 'Sassoons' and others of that run,
How many years have been bound to go 'The Whole Hog or None'.

There is Cowasjee Jehangir thinks his money is but trash,
On many institutions he spent a lot of cash,
He ought to be made a baronet for all the Good he's done;
And his motto it should be, to go 'The Whole Hog or None'.[17]

This combination of irony and praise, of the sly hit wrapped in a compliment, was Carson's métier. His caricatures managed to be inoffensive. Carson further introduced a song on the 'Scenes in the Bombay Police Court', developed a 'New Local Burlesques Speech Opera: Bubble And Squeak Or Bombay In July' with a song 'I'm a jolly old Broker', advertised on 5 August 1865 *TOI*, and another in May 1865, 'Tight Little Island', devoted to the various reclamation schemes which were being made to extend the tight little island space of Bombay.

But it is in his impersonation of the Parsi gent that he shows his genius: the *TOI* (19 May 1865) recounts how Dave Carson's

'getup' as a Parsee, Davejee Carsonbhoy, took everybody by surprise. All who had seen the 'Bengalee Baboo', naturally expected a faithful representation of a

Parsee, but they were hardly prepared to find the character so faithfully represented as it was.

And again on 6 June 1865, the *TOI* noted:

With the peculiar turban of the race inclining at the same angle with the nose—white collar-less body coat, red silk trousers, white stockings and shoes with the toes turned up like the prows of a Venetian gondola, Dave has the true Parsee cast of features—sloping forehead—long full nose, on an elongated face—full lips, large mouth, with chin slightly receding —long neck and shoulders falling.

As 'Davejee Carsonbhoy', Dave Carson would sing of the 'Bombay of his Dreams of 1872', and then try to make love according to the dictates of 'Rati Madam', another of his musical inventions satirizing the bold Parsi woman with her tight skirts and independent mind.

Carson also Indianized the mandatory drag act of the minstrel show: his 'Zuleika, the Pearl of Punjab', was the nautch girl incarnate, and together with Brower as the Rajah and Pierce as the subservient 'surrengee wallah', it became one of the oft-repeated acts. And it was not only the natives who were his targets: the English were not spared either. He devised a popular song, 'Curry Bart', which poked fun at the then Governor of Bombay, Sir Bartle Frere. Every class and type and every place was subject to his stinging hits, for example, in the songs 'Delhi Mummy' and 'Dustoorjis'. Yet, such stereotyping and mockery would not merit serious attention if it were not so stupendously popular. His satire went beyond mere snobbish ridicule. As *The Englishman* of 19 December 1864 observed: 'the local hits were capital and well appreciated ... the Bengalee Baboo was an impersonation of native character something above mere mimicry and the nautch in which fair Zuleika was the prominent actress might be called perfectly ear-splitting.' *The Bengal Harkaru* said on Carson's return to Calcutta in March 1865:

it is useless to criticize this actor. His Bengalee Baboo and nautch girl are worthy to rank with Lord Dundreary. Anything more true, and at the same time more irresistibly comic and absurd it is impossible to conceive. His jokes are entirely his own, and are screaming. The whole … was such a success. In his memoir, Harry Hobbs, an army man and man about town in Calcutta, observes: There must have been something more than snobbish humour about Dave Carson, his 'Bengali Baboo', 'Mari Jan', and japes about a Bengali taking singing lessons from an English woman, but jibbing at 'Sol Lah', seem to have taken root in the minds of so many thereby proving that he was an artist.[18] Carson did not, however, rest content on his laurels; he continually added to his improvisations, showing his Bengalee Baboo in a new light every season: the Baboo receiving his first dancing lesson (14 February 1865), going to college in Radha Bazaar (11 December 1876), and the Baboo in England (19 December 1876).

A surviving verse of this song, 'The Bengalee Baboo', shows Carson's skill in a humorous use of Hindustani and his ability to sharply etch a character; it further reveals an unexpected sympathy underneath the stereotyping, a sympathy with the subordinated position of the colonized in the reference to the 'islave' (slave) which the Baboo swears he will not become:

I very good Bengalee Baboo
In Calcutta I long time stop;
Ramchund Tunda Ghosh my name,
Very good Hindu, smoke my hooka,
Eat my dal bhat every day,
Night come I make plenty pooja
Here is the nautchwalla tom tom play.
Kooch parwa nahi good time coming
Babu never make islave.[19]

A double irony is at work here. The Bengali babu was derided in Bengali society for his slavish Anglophilia. Carson's song, even while it makes fun of the babu's philistinism—the smoking, eating, and nautch—celebrates it by adding a note of defiance 'Kooch parwa nahi' (I don't give a damn) and thus gives the babu a voice rejecting his moralizing Bengali superiors, which goes on to assert that the babu will, in fact, never be enslaved. From his outsider positions of an American and a black-faced artist, Carson acquired the freedom to critique colonial society. He exploited the traditions of minstrelsy where, in an inversion of middle-class norms, there was often a celebration of food and drink. He also used the double-edged ironies built into many minstrel songs and dances which were imitations by white artists in the black-face of Negro burlesque imitations of white practices.[20]

Carson not only created and performed these character types but he also played them off each other. At his benefit night on 3 June 1865 in Bombay, while doing the Bengalee Baboo number, he interpolated some swipes at the Parsee character. On being asked by his musical tutor what he thought of Bombay and the Parsees, the Bengali Baboo replies 'Oh! Parsees very niche people—Oh! Parsees too goods people—Oh! But (Tapping his cranium, and in a confidential and self-sufficient tone) got no intellect; not like one first class Bengalee gentleman.' At the end of his first tour *The Englishman* (10 March 1866) acknowledged his achievement in its usual ponderous fashion:

His representation of the Bengalee Baboo is a finished portrait ... Not less happy are the sketches of Anglo-Indian and Portuguese life. We have no reason to believe such representations have ever been attempted before, and if there be anything discreditable to us in the fact that an American artist (we use the word advisedly) should be the first to point out to us the materials for humorous creation lying immediate around us, we must not the less give credit to whom the credit is due.

In the context of colonialism, this regular playing of 'native' character types by a white entertainer, who localized more than half his programme, was paradoxically to bestow a public respectability on them even as they were being satirized; natives were positioned centre-stage in theatricals which started out as designed for the whites. This comic centring becomes a significant acknowledgement and recognition of their positions and identities. As Homi Bhabha (1994) has pointed out, 'mimicry must continually produce its slippage, its excess, its difference.'[21] Since audiences found his show side-splitting and returned in droves to watch him, can we venture to say that Dave Carson taught us to laugh at ourselves?

## The Babu in Bengali Literary and Theatrical History

Yet, in what becomes a postcolonial paradox, the 'Inimitable Dave', as the papers were wont to call him, has been singled out in Bengali theatre history and made notorious as the 'Englishman' who only mocked and ridiculed the Bengalis in his infamous song and impersonation. (On the contrary, the Parsees, equally ribbed by Carson, seemed to have lapped up all the attention. They seem to have registered no complaints, either then or subsequently, against Carson's impersonations.) Sumanta Banerjee (1989), culture historian, seems to endorse this view, even though, as he himself has shown, the babu as a figure of fun had been around for a few years in Bengali prose prior to Carson. He names Bhabanicharan Bandyopadhyay's *Naba Babu Bilas* (1825) as the first extended piece on the Bengali babu as the spoilt offspring of a parvenu, a new class which amassed great wealth through contact and service with the English.[22] The Bengalis themselves were deeply critical of this new class. Bankim Chandra Chattopadhyay's stronger satirical piece 'Baboo' (1874) expanded the category of the babu to include characteristics of clerks, teachers, banians, lawyers, magistrates, editors, even audiences at the theatres—all those classes which had emerged to service the English administration and had acquired, in a facile fashion, some of its tastes and habits. Another harder hitting long poem 'Bangalir Babu' by a woman writer, Mokshodayani Mokhopadhyay, published in 1882, sums up this socio-cultural formation acutely:

> Alas, there goes our Bengali babu!
> He slaves away from ten till four,
> Carrying his servitude like a pedlar's wares.
> A lawyer or magistrate, or perhaps a schoolmaster,
> A subjudge, clerk, or overseer:
> The bigger the job, the greater his pride;

The babu thinks he's walking on air.
Red in the face from the day's hard labour,
He downs pegs of whiskey to relax when he's home.
He's transported with pride at the thought of his rank.
But faced with a sahib, he trembles in fear!
Then he's obsequious, he mouths English phrases,
His own tongue disgusts him, he heaps it with curses.
The babu's learnt English, he swells with conceit
And goes off in haste to deliver a speech. ...[23]

As Sumanta Banerjee admits, 'the babu in fact had been a perennial butt of ridicule in the farces written by the "bhadraloks" all through the nineteenth century. The class composition of the babu had changed through the years, but certain characteristics had remained common.'[24]

Is then the persisting umbrage and a sense of injury against Dave Carson's milder satire on the 'Bengalee Baboo', almost innocuous in comparison, indicative of a racial and a colonial recoil? Has Carson's satire stuck in the Bengali cultural memory because it was created by a white person? Or was it that the public space of the stage where Carson's Bengalee Baboo was physically 'em-body-ed' made it seen and heard to be more openly transgressive than the caricatures by the Bengalis themselves which remained locked within the leaves of a book? The 'liveness' of performance has a disturbing and disruptive immediacy beyond other genres of literary creation and this was further borne out by the story of the proscribed performance of another theatrical rendering of the Young Bengal figure, similar to the Bengali babu, in Michael Madhusudan's *Ekei ki Baley Sabhyata?*[25] (1860). Even though this farce was written for and published by the Belgachhia theatre and its patron Rajas, it was not allowed a public performance because some of the Young Bengal class took exception to its satire. Carson's caricature of the 'Bengalee Baboo', unlike those in Bengali prose and poetry, inhabited the volatile space of the public stage, with its shifting lines of being and becoming. It was repeatedly praised for its truthfulness to form: 'Carson's Bengalee Baboo ... in its comical and truthful delineation ... [is] a true photographic likeness of this great Bengali butt' (*TOI*, 17 April 1865) 'whose "jocatives" ... and thin varnish of western civilisation which coats over the semi-barbarianism of the baboo caste' (*TOI*, 6 June 1865) 'is a finished portrait, and ... far from exaggeration ... [we] appreciate the care and delicacy with which each tone and gesture were imitated' (*The Englishman*, 10 March 1866). It was perhaps too true to be good! It instigated Ardhendu Sekhar Mustafi, a versatile actor of the period, to perform a repartee against Carson's act in the form of a pantomime in which he dared to ridicule the typical English Sahib,[26] again in the mixed English-Hindustani lingo of the time which Carson had cleverly appropriated. Of all these variants on the Bengali babu, however, it is Carson's caricature, performed for over twenty years, which remains inscribed, and controversialized—catalyzing subversive humour against the English—in Bengali theatre history.

## White Skin, Black Mask, Black Skin

Yet this is not all. Carson would remain a minor figure in the empire of entertainment if it were not for the very 'hue', the colour of the company, which, I would like to argue, helped win him popular support. It was not just the forms and conventions of the minstrel show which Carson adapted so deftly and which won him his audience but also the intrinsic skin colour of the minstrel, the blackface. Skin colour in the original minstrel show was not just a simple semiotic issue: it 'allowed the white to psychologically black out the realities of black life', functioning as a salve to the white American conscience.[27] Theatre historians have argued that it was a 'non-threatening way to cope with racism', that the ethnic stereotyping made the foreign immigrants, like the Irish and the Germans, more understandable and less threatening if laughed at. And Negroes themselves used this mask of the 'grinning blackface' after the Civil War to garner attention for themselves.[28]

In the Indian context, and in the light of Dave Carson's phenomenal success, another dimension of meaning is given to 'blackface'; it facilitates rather than blocks communication. Elsewhere, I have argued that Indians, a predominantly dark-hued race, whose major gods are dark-coloured, do not traditionally have a negative or discriminatory attitude towards the colour black. Conversely, they are subliminally drawn towards those of dark hue, seen for instance in the fact that *Othello* continues to be the most frequently performed Shakespeare play in India.[29] Dave Carson's darkened skin, it may be argued, made him seem like one of us, facilitating and making more palatable his stinging jibes against us. This susceptibility to his skin colour also helps put into perspective a significant incident highlighting this politics of the performance of colour, which was triggered off by a fracas over double-booked seats that took place towards the end of his first tour in Bombay.

The San Francisco Minstrels' shows were so much in demand that complaints of seats being misappropriated were frequent. As a matter of record, they were the ones to introduce colour-coded and numbered seats in Indian theatres. On 13 May 1865, a Parsee gentleman, already ensconced in the Grant Road Theatre Royal, found his seat being claimed by a white man. He refused to budge, even after being offered a box by Carson and being told that the white man was the chief magistrate. The white man and his larger party were then accommodated in more than one box, but a slew of letters on both sides of the issue appeared over the next few days in the *TOI* revealing how the drama off-stage had served to stoke simmering undercurrents of the social and racial situation. The Parsee justifies his action, but is upset at Dave Carson's seeming deference to the white man: '[I] would have given up [my seat] had he [the magistrate] asked me,' he says. And he adds, 'I am surprised to learn that he [Dave Carson] is tainted with the idea that black skin should bow to the white one...' (*TOI*, 15 May 1865). Carson's riposte a day later underlines how colour and caricature were interpellated: 'Your correspondent raises the question of colour, I like this! Don't I wear a black skin from choice? Don't you all come to see our black skins and especially my cavernous red mouth...?' (*TOI*, 17 May 1865).

Keeping in mind the fact that Dave Carson was a visiting showman who needed to keep on the right side of the city authorities, what the episode unravels is that the Indian seems to have been taken in by Dave's consummate act and blackface persona; that somewhere he may have begun to believe that Carson was one with the Indians, and hence he experiences a dislocating sense of shock when he finds Carson seeming to defer to the burra sahib. Who then is the 'real' black man, the aggrieved Parsee, or the blackface performer whose colour may not be even skin deep, but who within the liminal space of the stage is able to transmute his whiteness so convincingly that when the mask slips, it shocks! Black-face American minstrelsy, transplanted in Australia and transmuted in India, with its inherent 'Whim, Wit, Waggery' (*The Englishman*, 13 January 1862), or what Carson in his bilingual word-play called 'muskerry' (Hindi *maskhari* = drollery) was able to speak to audiences in a more meaningful and enduring way than most other travelling visitations of the empire of entertainment. Thus, the performative zone through its power of transformation, where identities form and un-form, where actors and characters slip in and out of roles, where the fictive becomes real and the real turns fictive, can unpick and lay bare, and make bold to enact, the shifting truths which lie beneath colour, representation, and identity.

## Notes

1. See my Introduction to *India's Shakespeare: Translation, Interpretation and Performance*. Ed. Poonam Trivedi and Dennis Bartholomeusz. Newark: University of Delaware Press, 2005.
2. Bhave, Vishnu Das. *Natya Kavita Sangraha*. Poona: n.p., 1885, 7–8.
3. *The Bombay Telegraph and Courier* 12 March 1853, Rev. of *Raja Gopichand*.
4. Anindyo Roy's *Civility, Literature and Culture in British India 1822–1922* (London: Routledge 2005), which explores the imposition of a normative code of manners and behaviour—'civilty'—as part of the Imperial control, discusses Kipling and Anstey's 'Babu' figures but does not mention Carson's earlier creation.

5. The original, that is, founding company of this name was founded in San Francisco in 1850 by Charley Backus, Billy Birch, and others and moved to New York in 1865. It was the city's longest lived minstrel company until it was absorbed in the Haverly Mastodons in 1883. Dave Carson's company styled themselves on the more famous original. See *The Oxford Companion to American Theatre*. Second Edn. Ed. Gerald Bordman. New York: Oxford University Press, 1992.

6. I am indebted to Richard Waterhouse, University of Sydney, for this and other information about Carson in Australia.

7. Major Hobbs, H. *Indian Dust Devils*. Calcutta: H. Hobbs and Co., 1937, 110.

8. Courtesy Richard Waterhouse.

9. H. Hobbs, op. cit., 109.

10. Albuquerque, Teresa. *Urbs Prima In India: An Epoch in the History of Bombay 1840–1865*. New Delhi: Promilla and Co, 1985, 92.

11. Mehta, Kumudini Arvind. 'English Drama on the Bombay Stage in the late Eighteenth and the Nineteenth Century', PhD thesis. University of Bombay, 1960, 168.

12. For the history of the minstrel show, its evolution and its spread across the globe, see Waterhouse, Richard. *From Minstrel Show to Vaudeville: The Australian Popular Stage 1788-1914*. Kensington: New South Wales University Press, 1990.

13. H. Hobbs, op. cit., 111.

14. Toll, Robert C. *Blacking Up. The Minstrel Show in Nineteenth Century America*. New York: Oxford University Press, 1974, 150.

15. See Banerjee, Sumanta. *The Parlour and the Streets: Elite and Popular Culture in Nineteenth Century Calcutta*. Calcutta: Seagull Books, 1989 for a history and discussion of the babu as a social and literary type.

16. Wacha, D.E. *Shells from the Sands of Bombay: Being My Recollections and Reminiscences 1860–1875*. Bombay: Bombay Chronicle Press, 1920, 350–1.

17. Teresa Albuquerque, op. cit., 92.

18. H. Hobbs, op. cit., 110.

19. As recalled by D.E.Wacha, op. cit., 352.

20. See Richard Waterhouse, op. cit., 6 and 4, on the 'cakewalk', a dance in which 'the minstrels were imitating the slaves, who were parodying their masters'.

21. Bhabha, Homi K. *The Location of Culture*. London: Routledge, 1994, 86.

22. Sumanta Banerjee, op.cit., p.180.

23. Mukhopadhyay, Mokshodayani. 'Bangalir Babu', in *Women Writing in India 600 B.C to the Present*, Vol. 1, Eds Susie Tharu and K. Lalita. Delhi: Oxford University Press, 1993, 219. I am indebted to Meenakshi Mukherji for helping me to locate this piece.

24. Sumanta Banerjee, op. cit., 180.

25. Sumanta Banerjee, op. cit., 182.

26. This was titled 'Mustafi Sahab ka Pucca Tamasha' directly lampooning Carson's 'I am a Pucca Bengali Baboo', and was in the form of a *kobir ladai*, a popular repartee. The details of this song are compiled from Das Gupta, Hemendra Nath. *The Indian Stage*, Vols I & II. Delhi: Munshiram Manoharlal, rpt. 2002, 203, and from the research of Minoti Chatterji.

Hum bara sahab hai duniya mein
None can be compared hamara saat
Mr Mustaphi name hamara
Chatgaon mera ache bilat.
Rom-ti-tom-ti-tom

Lord of all hai ham
Chunagali mera mokam
Coat pini pantaloon pini,
Pini mera trousers;
Every two years new suit pini
Direct from chandni bazaar
Rom-ti-tom-ti-tom

Chingrifish and kancha kela,
The only hazree once I eat;
Charpai is my palang posh,
Morah is my royal seat.
Dirty nigger hate hamara
Vadda maayla ache, chho, chho, chho!
Rom-ti-tom-ti-tom.

27. *The History of North American Theatre: From Pre-Columbian Times to the Present*. Eds Felicia Hardison Londre and Daniel J. Watermeier New York: Continuum, 1998, 142.

28. Robert C. Toll, op. cit., 272.
29. 'Colour and Class Constructs in Indian re-visions of *Othello*', paper presented at the Fourth International Seminar on 'Shakespeare and Class', Shakespeare Society of India, Delhi University, South Campus, 6–8 March 2003.

# Changing Nations
## British and Spanish Postcolonial Films

ISABEL SANTAOLALLA

'A nation is nothing without the stories it tells itself about itself,' Nuria Triana-Toribio remarks in the introduction to her book on Spanish national cinema (2003: 6). And, since nations are intimately tied up with narrative acts, the cinema, probably the most powerful narrative machine of the twentieth century, is ideally placed to mediate national imaginaries and identities.

What follows offers some reflections on one of the many possible ways in which this function may be performed, in particular on the ways in which, through the presence of the postcolonial 'other' and specific mechanisms of space construction, the cinema can undermine the conventional 'us' *vs* 'them', 'here' *vs* 'there' dichotomies, and thereby challenge the more stable and prescriptive notions of national identity. I shall illustrate this argument by referring mainly to one Spanish film, *Flowers from Another World / Flores de otro mundo* (Iciar Bollain 1999), and, in less detail, to a British one, *Playing Away* (Horace Ové 1986), two texts that allow meditation on the changing discourse of identity in the European cinema.

Notions of European identity have become increasingly contested during the latter third of the twentieth and beginning of the twenty-first centuries. This is partly down to the pressure from Eastern European states for membership of the European Union following the break up of the Soviet Union, the asylum 'crisis' arising from the Balkan conflicts of the 1990s, and the steadily growing increase of immigration into Western Europe, even into countries, like Spain and Italy, that had traditionally been the source, rather than the destination of migrants.

In the cultural sphere, the competing discourses initiated by the above-mentioned changes have led to demands for a more fluid concept of 'Europeanness', which more often than not have been greeted by the political elites of many European nation states— and especially Brussels, as the centre of the legislative machinery of the European Union—with normative views of European identity.

Against this background, reflection here on the situation in Spanish cinema could be of interest, for two reasons in particular. First, because the transition, in Spain, from dictatorship to democracy after 1975 has led to vigorous debate on the meaning of nationhood in a country marked by regional and cultural differences (Spain is divided up into seventeen autonomous regions, and has four official languages), reflecting, perhaps in an intensive way, similar patterns across Europe. And second, because the rise in the number of immigrants to Spain in the last two decades— above all from Africa, Spanish America, and Eastern Europe—is now steadily bringing it in line with other European countries with high levels of immigration. The suddenness of the phenomenon has caught many by surprise, and is making a considerable impact on social and economic structures, as well as on the country's collective imaginary. Spanish cinema has only recently begun to reflect on the country's changing ethnic landscape and the new stories emerging from it. For their part, countries like the UK, Germany, and France already have a long history of the representation of ethnic minorities in their cinemas and terms like 'Black British cinema', 'cinéma de banlieu', and 'cinéma beur', have long been in circulation.

*Flowers from Another World* touches on a key phenomenon of modernity: the relentless migration from rural to urban spaces (see

Nair 2001). The film invites reflection on the notions of 'transculturalization' and 'deterritoralization', in ways that tie in interestingly with thoughts developed by, say, Wolfgan Welsch and John Tomlinson. Welsch's work on 'transculturality', for instance, views cultures as entangled networks, hybrid in the presence of 'other' cultures within one's 'own' culture (1999). Connected to this is the concept of 'deterritorialization', that is, the notion that identity may be disengaged from land or region. As borders reveal their permeability and temporal fragility, the experience of place as a basic referent of identity is also destabilized (Tomlinson, via García Canclini, defines deterritorialization as 'loss of the 'natural' relationship of culture to geographical and social territories' [1999: 107]).

*Flowers from Another World* is a film that, though seasoned with heart-warming humour, is also characterized by elegiac elements associated with its central drama: that of a village on the Spanish central Castilian plain steadily depleted of its human population and in desperate need of nubile women whose marriages to the local bachelors would regenerate and ensure the survival of the community.

In this film time is, as in Lefebvre's phrase, 'aprehended within space' (2000: 95). The ubiquitous road in *Flowers* acquires symbolic value as an expression not only of spatial relations between objects, places, and people, but also—since it is the image with which the film begins and ends—of ominous temporality. Bollain herself underlines the manifold significance of 'space' in her film: 'The pan shots [of the landscape] keep giving us the sense of time passing and they also remind us where we are, the surroundings in which the characters move. The landscape and the village that the pans show are almost like another character in *Flowers from Another World*. It [sic] witnesses the evolution of three couples and at the same time it influences each relationship (...)' (La Iguana 1999).

The opening sequence of *Flowers from Another World*—a shot of a windswept, barren land suddenly roused from its lethargy by a speeding coach full of loud, vivacious women—establishes at the outset the film's defining features: the pervasive influence of landscape, and constant spatial negotiation. Having accepted the invitation as guests of honour at a party for bachelors in the remote village of Santa Eulalia, on the arid Castilian plain, a group of assorted women is welcomed by the local female-starved men and a cheering crowd of onlookers.

This incident in fact replicates the real-life parties organized in the 1980s by various villages across Spain, following the example of San Juan de Plan, in the Aragonese Pyrenees. Having seen on the village bar TV William Wellman's *Westward the Women* (1951)—in which a group of women from the North American East is transported by Robert Taylor to the West to be the wives of single pioneers—the locals were inspired by the film to halt the process of depopulation by issuing an open invitation to women throughout the country to a village party to meet the local men, and hopefully, marry, settle down, and raise a family.

There is a beautiful symmetry in the way in which Bollain's film is sparked by real-life events that were themselves prompted by another film. *Flowers from Another World* and *Westward the Women* each tells the story of a journey undertaken by women in search of husbands; in both, the female caravanserai is led by a male go-between; in both, too, the group of daring women leave their familiar surroundings and are seen crossing a desolate landscape, in search of a better life in a rugged, forsaken spot. But these broad similarities are matched by striking differences. *Westward the Women* is, after all, a variant of the popular epic genre—literary as well as filmic—of the American Frontier, and, as such, focuses on the hardships of the journey itself, ending with the arrival of the heroic women to the, as yet, undomesticated land that will thereafter become their new home. In the film's final sequence, the camera chooses to record the moment from a distanced, though unstable, position on the ground, and not— as might have been expected, having followed their plight for weeks—from the women's perspective. Eschewing subjective shots from the point of view of the women, *Westward the Women* seems concerned more with documenting the 'birth of a community', and less with the anxieties and aspirations of individual lives. The nervousness or apprehension, as well as eventually the excitement, of the suitors and their brides, are recorded in a succession of alternating shots of the men and women seen from ground level. The formality of the occasion is further stressed through the muted welcome of men too long unused to female company to know at first how to formulate their vocal greeting. They help the women down from the wagons and, only after a shaved and groomed Robert Taylor—the women's handsome and grumpy guide—enters the frame, smiling and relaxed, do the male hosts begin to unbend, rushing after the female arrivals to release their finally uninhibited sentiments.

*Flowers from Another World* starts where *Westward the Women* ends: the arrival of the coach in the village marks not the closure, but the beginning of these other women's heroic adventure. The formal overlap with the Hollywood forerunner is obvious, but so too are the differences, above all the fact that, right from the start, the camera here accompanies the women, and records the encounter with the men—with the whole village, in fact—through a series of subjective shot/countershot exchanges, allowing the women to share control of the look. As the locals and the outsiders nervously examine one another through the coach windows, the negotiation between the two worlds (male/female, here/there) is visually conveyed economically and effectively. The women are escorted down from the coach that has brought them from their various places of origin, and, following their welcome by a rural guard of honour, continue their adventurous 'crossing' first through the streets of the village, then through the narrow archway that allows them entry to the town hall and finally through the even narrower corridor formed by two lines of rose-brandishing men. In this opening sequence, then, the group of outsiders is not only allowed entry to the spiritual centre of this community, but is welcomed in a way that is not all that remote from parallel situations in myths and legends, where the arrival of a young outsider brings the hope of a new life to a troubled and endangered kingdom. After all, these women can save this depleted village from total disappearance.

In contrast to the silence in *Westward the Women*, there is music and cheering here. The sequence, additionally, echoes scenes from one of the most well-known Spanish films, *Welcome Mr Marshall / Bienvenido Mr Marshall* (Luis García Berlanga 1952), a satirical comedy about the inhabitants of a Castilian village who organize an Andalusian-style welcome for the *americanos*, the USA Marshall plan envoys who in the early 1950s were supposedly coming to Spain to bring economic aid to help in the reconstruction of the country. The women's arrival in *Flowers* recalls the scene in *Welcome Mr Marshall* in which the villagers rehearse the arrival of the Americans: details like crowded balconies shot from the street, the musical procession, the cheering, and the welcoming banners seem like deliberate gestures towards it. The allusion perhaps warns that the superficial trappings of the festive welcome—as in its famous precedent—offer no guarantees of lasting happiness, thereby preparing the audience for disillusionment and the return to the grimmer, more tedious realities of village life.

From this point on, *Flowers from Another World* concentrates on the parallel narratives of two women—Patricia and Marirrosi— as well as, eventually, on a later arrival in the village, Milady. Patricia (Lissette Mejía) is a Dominican mother-of-two who finds, in the introverted, mother-dominated Damián (Luis Tosar), the 'passport' to Spanish nationality, and a secure home for herself and her two young children. Marirrosi (Elena Irureta), a financially-independent nurse from Bilbao, seeks a partner who will offer the emotional fulfilment that neither her work nor her adolescent son can provide; she appears to find this in Alfonso (Chete Lera), a polite refugee from city-life who has opted for the tranquility of the countryside, and who dedicates himself to the cultivation of his greenhouse plants and exotic flowers. When, a few days later, Milady (Marilin Torres)—a stunning twenty-year old mulatta from Havana—is brought to the village by the boastful builder Carmelo (José Sancho) from one of his sex-trips to Cuba, the trio of heroines is complete. The film rewards the courage of these women by granting them privileged screen space, and by very often aligning its gaze with theirs. This is particularly true of Patricia and Milady: in the aftermath of the *fiesta*, the narrative becomes more interested in the plight of the two Caribbean women than in the story of

Marirrosi and Alfonso. And this, according to Bollain herself, is because 'everyone knows a Marirrosi, everyone knows an Alfonso, as it is an everyday and conventional tale' (Bollain and Llamazares 2000: 59).

Some reviews of the film have delighted in recognizing the familiar elements of Spanish culture. The *Diario de Burgos* reviewer, for instance, emphasizing the importance of its setting, praised the film's accurate representation of the real, authentic Spain: 'I found something that is truly *ours*. From the Spanish land, from *our* countryside, from our people. I bumped into the pillars of *our* culture, the roots of *our* customs, and the noblest instincts of human nature, not to mention the different temperaments that add colour to every nook and cranny of *our* country' (Alonso 1999: 36; my emphasis). Yet, the greater attention given by the film to stories involving the Caribbean women has tended to produce reviews that describe the film as a clash between two different worlds: the warm exuberance of the Caribbean mulattas and the cold sobriety of their Castilian hosts. The scriptwriter himself, Julio Llamazares, has discussed the film in similar terms: 'This film goes against nature. Like its theme, using forceps to insert some women who are the essence of life, warmth and vitality into a world that is very closed and on the point of extinction' (Bollain and Llamazares 2000: 47).

The encounter produces shocks on both sides, something illustrated most vividly by Milady's arrival in the village. Milady's self-assured but puzzled look on first acquaintance with the 'natives' as she enters the spiritual centre of the community—the square with its bar and village fountain—re-enacts in inverted form the arrival of the Spanish conquistadors in the 'new world'. Moreover, her tall, slender body functions here as the flagpole around which the colours and symbols of imperial power—her patterned lycra leggings—are wrapped and deployed to mark the act of colonization. The irony, of course, is double-edged, as Milady's body is inscribed not with the Cuban flag, but with the stars and stripes of Old Glory, an indirect allusion to Spain's loss of Cuba to the US, as well as to US expansionism in general, and perhaps even to Cuba's own insidious colonization by the US today.

Significantly, this sort of reverse colonization takes place not in the urban spaces usually associated with immigrant life and postcolonial, multi-ethnic encounters, but in the very heart of (pen)insular Spain, contravening practices, elsewhere as much as in Spanish cinema, that have tended to privilege the city—because of its heterogeneous nature—as a stage for the dramatization of contemporary stories of immigration, or for the encounter between old and emergent versions of ethnicity. Thus, Spanish films like *Down and Out / En la puta calle* (Enrique Gabriel 1996), *Things I Left Behind in Habana / Cosas que dejé en La Habana* (Manuel Gutiérrez Aragón 1998), or the more recent *The Suit / El traje* (Alberto Rodríguez 2002), connect with, say, British films like *My Beautiful Laundrette* (Stephen Frears 1985), *Sammy and Rosie Get Laid* (Stephen Frears 1987), *Young Soul Rebels* (Isaac Julien 1991), or *Wild West* (David Attwood 1993).

*Flowers*, though, is nearest in this respect to films like *Bhaji on the Beach* (Gurinder Chadha 1994) and *Playing Away* (Horace Ové 1986), which are structured around the idea of a journey into the furthest reaches of a traditional—respectively popular and rural—English culture.[1] The 'crossings' in *Playing Away* and in *Flowers* are comparable and, in fact, both films share many structural and even stylistic similarities, above all in the *mise-en-scène*.

In Ové's film, the East Anglian village of Sneddington is holding a fund-raising week in aid of Third World charities. To round off the activities, a team of West Indians from the multi-ethnic London borough of Brixton is invited down for a cricket match. The journey from city to village, organized by the team's captain Willie Boy (Norman Beaton), is seen by most of the group as an unwelcome chore and an eccentric adventure. As in *Flowers from Another World*, the camera alternates between interior, almost claustrophobic, shots of the group inside the van and medium or long shots of the vehicle making its way in the middle of the expanse of rural landscape— here not the barren land seen in *Flores*, but the green, pleasant countryside which has become the iconic image of traditional England. In both films, the exterior long shots—sometimes bird's eye shots—emphasize the smallness of the vehicle as it penetrates more and more deeply this unfamiliar world, almost suggesting the danger of being absorbed and effaced by this alien territory.

The journey that Willie Boy and his team undergo reveals the complexities of the juxtaposition of two cultures condemned to establish a dialogue, even if the result is as incongruous as the trombone and cymbals version of the calypso song 'Island in the Sun' with which the inhabitants of Sneddington welcome the Brixton party.

When the team—called, appropriately, 'The Conquistadors'— enters the innermost sanctuary of the Empire, the culture-clash is inevitable and the encounter becomes almost uncanny. As in *Flowers from Another World*, the visitors are merrily welcomed and allowed entry to the spiritual centre of the village, greeted with music and speeches. Flags also play a significant role here, functioning as ironic reminders of an overseas imperial past, and of current 'colonization' of the metropolis by its former subjects. Milady's irreverent display of the US flag leggings in *Flowers* ties in with Willie Boy's offering to the inhabitants of Sneddington of a small Jamaican flag pennant peering out of a battered Tesco supermarket carrier bag, a moment also used by the film to emphasize the fact that conflicting forces and differences exist not only *between* communities, but *within* each community. As Willie Boy offers the white hosts the Jamaican flag as a present from the whole team, one of the West Indian players mutters, with contained anger, 'I'm no fucking Jamaican!'. Similarly, the bus load of women in *Flowers from Another World* is not a monolithic whole. Although clearly united in their objective, differences between them ocassionally become evident, as when one of the Spanish women points at a group of Caribbean immigrants sitting at the back of the bus and whispers to her fellow nationals: 'They are all over the place now! Pamplona is full of them!' Thus, although mostly aligning their perspective with the West Indian and female outsiders respectively, the films do not romanticize them, and often make room for the display of the tensions and shortcomings of both groups.

*Playing Away* also exposes the limitations of national stereotypes through humour. Caribbeans are shown to be predictably afflicted by a chronic lack of organization, as a conversation between Willie Boy and Boots makes clear (Willie Boy: 'Why is it that everytime we have a game to play we are so damned disorganised?' / Boots: 'Listen man, we are not the M.C.C., you know?'). And British eccentricity, for its part, is satirized through all the arrangements made for the 'Third World Week' by a well-meaning but patronizing gentry. When viewed from the outsider's perspective, English village pub culture, the beautiful countryside, bicycles, charity events and vicarage tea parties with cucumber sandwiches become denaturalized and strange.

Similarly, *Flowers from Another World* frustrates expectations of the familiar (the Spanish village and its inhabitants) and the unfamiliar (the Caribbean mulattas). Here, as in Freud's notion of the 'uncanny', the familiar and the unfamiliar—the *heimlich* and the *unheimlich*—inhabit the same space, a terrain of ambiguity in which opposites may coincide (Freud 1985). On closer scrutiny, then, conventional associations of meaning attached to the dichotomies 'here/there', 'us/them' are undermined through mechanisms of construction related to character and setting. The apparent opposites established on the arrival of the coach progressively dissolve. The film steadily reveals a whole series of links and overlaps, as well as differences, between individuals, groups, and their settings. Characters, for instance, are not easily placed; rather, they relate to one another in varied ways, a process that inhibits rigid categorization, for example, in the case of the women characters and their various allegiances or groupings:

| | | |
|---|---|---|
| Patricia and Marirrosi (arrive together in bus) | // | Milady (arrives on her own) |
| Milady and Patricia (black and foreign) | // | Marirrosi (white and Spanish) |
| Patricia and Marirrosi (single mothers) | // | Milady (childless) |
| Milady and Patricia (move to village) | // | Marirrosi (remains in Bilbao) |
| Patricia (stays in village) | // | Marirrosi and Milady (abandon village) |

Similarly, the film frustrates our initial expectations about what is familiar and unfamiliar in its use of space, particularly the village and its surroundings. In legends and myths, as, say, in anthopological, literary and legal discourses, a shared set of meanings traditionally associates the spaces a community inhabits with notions of protectiveness and security. In contrast to the wilderness, villages—and, above all, their houses—epitomize shelter, intimacy, and warmth. They are, as Bachelard puts it, the 'centre', the place that protects the individual's daydreaming (1964: 6). In *Flowers from Another World*, however, Santa Eulalia and the fields around it are portrayed, more often than not, as inhospitable, unforgiving, and hard. Although the banner that welcomes the women at the beginning of the film reads 'Welcome. Make yourselves at home,' there is very little in the village—and indeed in its houses—that suggests the idea of homeliness. Upon arrival, Milady asks Patricia: 'Tell me. Is this place always so ugly?' According to Iciar Bollain, this was a sought-after effect: 'We always thought that the landscape had to be rather rough, not gentle but harsh. Actually, in landscape terms, the film does not pay tribute to Cantalojas, where the film was shot, a place that is much more beautiful and varied than the way it is shown in the film' (Bollain, in La Iguana 1999).

The three houses that appear in *Flowers from Another World* all fail to convey the traditionally positive associations of the home. Although their shape, decor, and provision of homely comforts set them apart, their narrative and symbolic value is shared: they become visual expressions of their inhabitants' feelings of estrangement and alienation. The houses transmit an uncanny feeling of disquiet (clashing colours in Damián's mother's house), chill (Carmelo's house's cold colour-scheme and metal and glass decoration), or precariousness (Alfonso's house, which is still under construction). These houses become claustrophobic environments, where the prevalence of witch-like mothers denies the newlyweds any privacy, where sex-fixated men demand continuous availability from their women, and where, above all, their inhabitants are imbued with melancholy and loneliness.

It is not surprising, then, that characters seek release from these spatial constraints. And, while many scenes rely on indoor, claustrophobic settings to mark the characters' entrapment, the film also abounds in areas of liminality, seemingly offering the possibility of the negotiation of space: thus, the road connects the 'here and the there', and Alfonso's glasshouse is halfway between the indoor and outdoor worlds. Yet, objects that should theoretically help to overcome spatial isolation, like telephones and vehicles, provide only momentary relief. Milady's phone calls to her family and her Italian boyfriend, for instance, only increase the pain of separation. And the pain of distance is even more poignantly revealed when Patricia is visited for the day by friends from Madrid. As they reach the back entrance of the house, the few yards that separate them from Patricia, who welcomes them from inside the house, become almost insurmountable, as they wade through hay and cow dung. Daisi's complaint—'I'm covered in shit'—and Patricia's reply—'I warned you to look down'—point not only literally to the ground, but also perhaps to the migrant's need to kowtow and lower expectations on arrival at their newly adopted surroundings. This most symbolic crossing of the threshold and Daisi's subsequent conversation on her mobile phone with somebody in Madrid, while having lunch in Patricia's dining room, acutely express the metaphorical distance between 'here' and 'there', and, most interestingly, defines the 'here' (the familiar—for Patricia, Damián, and for the spectators who are by now identified with their story), not as an empowering, but as a disempowering space: 'But, listen, I am *here*![silence] I told you I *couldn't* [silence] But the point is that I *cannot* do that [silence] But I told you that I was coming *here*, that I was going to be away, that I was not going to be in Madrid [silence] But how can that be if I am not *there*? I am *here*, sweetheart!'

Similarly, the many vehicles used by characters at various moments—coaches, cars, motorbikes, tractors, and lorries—are ultimately ineffectual, often used even to emphasize the characters' progressive entrapment, rather than the potential for liberation. When Milady hitchhikes her way to Valencia on a lorry, all we see of her flight is a brief shot of her dancing in a dark and crowded disco. Furthermore, the film's refusal to allow the characters to step out of their physical constraints is even more sharply focused in the scene in which she escapes with Oscar (Rubén Ochandiano). Although the narrative offers Milady the opportunity of leaving Santa Eulalia, the scene is shot in a way that emphasizes only the difficulties lying ahead: Milady is seated low; she opens the window as if in need of fresh air; and the car and road disappear in the distance, seemingly devoured by the mountains. Although Milady subsequently leaves Oscar as well, we only catch sight of her sneaking out of their hotel room. We never succeed in observing her in the open air, or in Valencia, or in her dream paradise, Milan. The urban 'promised lands' are repeatedly mentioned but never visualized. Iciar Bollain comments that although scenes of Milady and the lorry driver were shot on the coast near Valencia, she finally decided not to include them in the final cut:

For instance, when Milady reaches Valencia—shot but never seen in the film— she eats king prawns and *paella* at a kiosk, with the beach in the background, and she's accompanied by the lorry driver, who's extremely amusing. They even swim with their clothes on. That was a flash of light and colour in the middle of the film, and after much thought, we decided we shouldn't ever leave the village (Bollain and Llamazares 2000: 63).

Although in principle offering the possibility of a successful negotiation between the 'here' and the 'there', roads in the film either restore characters to their point of departure (Patricia, above all, but also Milady in her several attempts at flight) or lead to dead ends and sadness (as in the cases of Marirrosi and Milady). Furthermore, although numerous shots of a road disappearing on the horizon seem to hold out the promise of transition, they also paradoxically mark the distance between the two worlds. The women are even denied momentary relief from the constraints of their oppressive homes in open spaces, such as when Patricia and her friends take a walk along the road outside the village, where they are reduced to sexist stereotype by the occupants of a speedy van, who address them as '*chochos!*' (pussies), a 'compliment' that persuades them to interrupt their momentary outdoor excursion, driving them indoors once more.

Trapped in this pattern of claustrophobic repetitions are, above all, the men in the village who, more than anybody else, lead lives blighted by their heritage and surroundings. Alfonso ends up on his own, having proved unable—unlike in his greenhouse—to create a space in which Marirrosi's and his own hopes can flourish, perhaps precisely because he is intoxicated by the feeling of sheltered independence provided by his own glasshouse—his withdrawal into village life. Carmelo, for his part, is last seen eating his Christmas dinner in the cold and lonely atmosphere of his *unheimlich* home. Only Damián is granted an opportunity—despite the many difficulties—to break free, with Patricia, from this pattern of loneliness.

The film marks the passage of time and, towards the end, we see the men at the bar organizing another bachelor party. At the end, the road again locks the narrative into a cyclical structure that, although offering the possibility of renewed hope, returns characters and spectators alike almost to where they were at the opening of the film. The last sequence is actually both similar to and dissimilar from the one at the beginning. The group of—by now multi-ethnic—children clearly symbolize the potential for regeneration and integration. But perhaps most telling in this scene is the position of the camera: while in the opening of the film the camera identified itself mainly with the 'outsider' women (although occasionally adopting the viewpoint of the locals), it remains emphatically distanced here, denying access to either the world inside the bus or, most significantly, the by now theoretically familiar inhabitants and locations in the village. *Flowers from Another World* ends up constructing Santa Eulalia, its surrounding landscape and its inhabitants, as another 'Other', equally, if not more, unfamiliar than the women who come from beyond.

In this way, by rethinking the Self in terms of the Other, hitherto stable and unified notions of identity are irrevocably altered. While, on paper, most of the women are citizens of the Third World while the men belong to the First—peasants, but Spaniards all the same—the latter know that they have become marginal in the 'new' modernized Spain. In this sense, the film—like *Playing Away, Bhaji on the Beach,* and others—shows the Other to be not 'out there', in the beyond, but woven into the local fabric, helping generate new citizenship, in imaginative as well as in literal ways.

## Note

1.    For an analysis of these two films see Santaolalla 2000.

## Works Cited

*Books and Articles*
Alonso, Carlos. 'Genuinamente nuestro', in *Diario de Burgos,* 2 June 1999.
Bachelard, Gaston (1958). *The Poetics of Space.* Boston: Beacon Press, 1964.
Bollain, Iciar and Julio Llamazares. *Cine y literatura. Reflexiones a partir de 'Flores de otro mundo'.* Madrid: Páginas de Espuma, 2000.
Freud, Sigmund (1919). 'The Uncanny', in *Art and Literature.* Harmondsworth: Penguin, 1985, 336–76.
La Iguana. '*Flores de otro mundo* pressbook', 1999. http://www.la-iguana.com/ HTML/principal.htm. accessed 23 April 2003.
Lefebvre, Henry (1991). *The Production of Space.* Trans. D. Nicholson-Smith. Oxford and Malden, Mass.: Blackwell, 2000.
Nair, Parvati. 'In Modernity's Wake: Transculturality, Deterritorialization and the Question of Community', in Iciar Bollain's *Flores de otro mundo (Flowers from Another World)', Post Script,* 21: 2, 2001, 38–49.
Santaolalla, Isabel. 'Cinematic Journeys to Insular England', in *Shifting Continents/Colliding Cultures. Diaspora Writing of the Indian Subcontinent.* Eds Ralph J. Crane and Radhika Mohanram. Atlanta, Amsterdam: Rodopi, 2000, 217–24.
Tomlinson, John. *Globalization and Culture.* Oxford: Polity Press, 1999.
Triana-Toribio, Nuria. *Spanish National Cinema.* London: Routledge, 2003.
Welsch, Wolfgan. *Transculturality: The Puzzling Form of Cultures Today.* Ed. Mike Featherstone and Schott Lash. London: Sage, 1999, 194–213.

*Films*
*Bhaji on the Beach* (Gurinder Chadha, UK, 1994)

*Down and Out / En la puta calle* (Enrique Gabriel, Spain, 1996)

*Flowers from Another World / Flores de otro mundo* (Iciar Bollain, Spain, 1999)

*My Beautiful Laundrette* (Stephen Frears, UK, 1985)

*Playing Away* (Horace Ové, UK, 1986)

*Sammy and Rosie Get Laid* (Stephen Frears, UK, 1987)

*The Suit, / El traje* (Alberto Rodríguez, Spain, 2002)

*Things I Left Behind in Habana / Cosas que dejé en la Habana* (Manuel Gutiérrez Aragón, Spain, 1998)

*Welcome Mr Marshall / Bienvenido Mr Marshall* (Luis García Berlanga, Spain, 1952)

*Westward the Women* (William Wellman, USA, 1951)

*Wild West* (David Attwood, UK, 1993)

*Young Soul Rebels* (Isaac Julien, UK, 1991)

# Cricket and West Indian Writing

## KATHLEEN FIRTH

Ashutosh Gowariker's Hindi film *Lagaan* (2001), with its story of a victorious 'battle without bloodshed'[1] against the British overlords in India, reawakened a curiosity I have long had about the game of cricket and its passionate following by colonized peoples. For here was a game central to the British Public School ethos, the system that produced a class of Englishmen largely possessed of elitist views of culture and chauvinist attitudes.

It was through recurrent references in the early fiction of Trinidadian writer, V.S. Naipaul, that my attention was first drawn to the prominence of the game in the lives of West Indians: the slum kids in *Miguel Street* (1971) playing cricket in the road with a make-shift bat and tatty ball that counts for 'six and out' if hit into a certain Miss Hilton's yard, which they dare not enter (24); or the hilarious episode when Hat, the street's spokesman, takes thirteen slum boys to a big match and commands them all to pee at the same time against the railings before the players enter the field so as not to bother him during the game (156). Never having been to a real match before, the boy narrator is caught by Hat's enthusiasm:

Hat taught me many things that afternoon. From the way he pronounced them, I learned about the beauty of cricketers' names; and he gave me all his own excitement at watching a cricket match (154).

Hat's surrogate-father role for the slum kids is rendered plausibly throughout the *Miguel Street* sketches; yet what disturbed me in this episode was Hat going crazy and screaming out 'White people is God, you hear!' when a Trinidadian cricketer 'reached his 150' (155). For all his excitement, why should Hat pay tribute to the colonial master at the climax of the last day of the match between Trinidad and Jamaica? The brown boy narrator is seemingly not perturbed by the remark, and Naipaul takes it no further; but as I have argued elsewhere, notwithstanding the fact that all Naipaul's themes are present in embryonic form from the outset, he was not overtly concerned with issues of race and class in his earliest works of fiction (Firth 1987: 104–5).

It was in his first work of non-fiction, *The Middle Passage* (Naipaul 1962), where Naipaul would incorporate cricket into his generally caustic appraisal of West Indian society, especially when his native island was the object of his disdain: West Indian cricket, he affirmed, was the only activity which allowed the individual Trinidadian to 'stand out and be measured against international standards' and thus become a 'hero-figure' in the eyes of his fellows. Beyond cricket, he went on, there was a dearth of motivating factors to succeed, for Trinidad was a society that 'demanded no skills and offered no rewards to merit' (44). Thus, if it was not the team spirit but rather the individual performance the crowds turned out to see and applaud, that is to say, the hero's panache counting more than the overall cricketing skills on display, it would follow for Naipaul that many were the stories of individual failures, just as his earlier works of fiction had been bent on showing satirical portrayals of his hapless countrymen.

Naipaul does indeed refer to a failed cricketer's story in *The Middle Passage* (45), namely: *Moon on a Rainbow Shawl* (1957), by the Trinidadian actor-playwright Errol John. John (1924–88) was the son of one of those cricketing 'hero-figures', but he was a writer with a proper understanding of the causes for failure, not to mention a compassion which Naipaul lacked. The play is set in a seedy Trinidadian barrack yard and reflects the futile lives of the yard's dispossessed dwellers. The main storyline concerns Charlie

Adams, a character with a past of local cricketing fame who is now a broken man, the victim of island-club prejudice. Charlie tells a young boy admirer that the reason he had not been chosen to tour England with the West Indian team was because he had once protested against the shabby treatment dealt to the players from the lowest classes, the blackest men, by the whiter-skinned club committees:

In them days, The Savannah Club crowd was running almost everything. People like me had to lump it or leave it (…). In them times so when we went Barbados or Jamaica to play cricket, they used to treat us like hogs, boy. When we went on tours they put we in any ole kind of boarding-house. The best hotels was for them and the half-scald members of the team. So in twenty-seven, when we was on tour in Jamaica, I cause a stink, boy. I had had enough of them dirty little boarding-house rooms. I said either they treat me decent or they send me back. The stink I made got into the newspapers. They didn't send me back. But that was the last intercolony series I ever play. They broke me, boy (John 1957: 62).

Another black writer, Michael Anthony, takes the reader into the world of the child through the eyes of young narrators; thus there seems to be nowhere in his stories a concern for the racial or socio-political issues that engage many Caribbean authors. Anthony's work conveys, rather, a genuine love and appreciation for his island home, where cricket, played by boys and girls alike, is a fun, part of the process of growing up. His stories are deceptively simple, leading certain critics to ask what, if any, is their point. Others, however, have recognized Anthony's brilliant evocation of place and mood, and the subtlety with which life's little dramas are brought to the attention of the reader (Cumber Dance 1986: 23–4). In the title story of the collection entitled *Cricket in the Road* (Michael Anthony 1973), for example, the boy narrator projects his fear of tropical storms onto the game itself. He and a couple of street kids play cricket every afternoon after school, even though storms in the rainy season will oblige them to suspend the game and scurry indoors, the narrator to hide in panic under his bed. During one afternoon's play, a storm breaks when it's the narrator's turn to bat, but on returning to the street some hours later the others think it's only fair, given that a new game is starting, to toss a coin to decide who should bat first. The narrator loses the toss and then, in a fit of rage comparable to the tropical storm's, throws their bat and ball away into impenetrable undergrowth, thereby putting an end to cricket in the road for several weeks to come. Yet it is cricket that enables Anthony to bestow an atmosphere of reconciliation and atonement on the story's ending, when the friends, having acquired another bat, invite the narrator to play first batsman in a new game. What we now witness, however, is a batsman transformed into an embarrassed child with tears in his eyes. He confesses: 'And I cried as though it were raining and I was afraid' (43).

The story is characteristically Anthony in the way he expresses and discovers himself in writings which are obviously autobiographical. Characteristic too is Anthony's paradoxical approach: his are very simple, albeit well-structured stories, in which, on the other hand, he always manages to arouse the reader's interest in other issues that sometimes seem more important than the ones that are resolved in the narration. And this apparently unsophisticated rendering of a story accounts for certain critics' frustration with Anthony, that 'So What?' response to his work I referred to earlier. I have suggested, however, that the point to be taken in this piece is the child's embarrassed and repentant acknowledgement of the fear of his own fear, a soul-destroying fear generating in the child a reaction not only capable of alienating his friends but also of betraying cricket's ethical code of 'fair play'.

C.L.R. James' *Beyond a Boundary* (1963) reassures me that my conclusions regarding this story are not at all far-fetched, while it serves to refute Naipaul's dismissal of Trinidad's cricketers in *The Middle Passage*. For among many other things, *Beyond a Boundary* is about cricket and, especially, James' reverence for the game. First published in 1963 and never out of print since then, *Beyond a Boundary* is celebrated by cricket lovers worldwide as a masterpiece and has even been described as 'the most important sports book of our time' (Warren Sussman qtd in Haigh 2003: 145). The idea of 'fair play' permeates the work, beginning when James reminisces on playing for his school team and acquiring a certain code of ethics, already hinted at by Michael Anthony and scorned by Naipaul. James writes:

We learned to play with the team, which meant subordinating your personal inclinations, and even interests, to the good of the whole. We kept a stiff upper lip in that we did not complain about ill-fortune. We did not denounce failures, but 'Well tried' or 'Hard luck', came easily to our lips. We were generous to opponents and congratulated them on victories, even when we knew they did not deserve it (25).

As well as cricket, *Beyond a Boundary* is a book about literature, philosophy, politics, art, society, all of these issues approached from the perspective of a postcolonial writer who had assimilated the public-school code, which, though seemingly paradoxical, became the 'moral framework of [his] existence' (26). But because *Beyond a Boundary* is written by perhaps the most outstanding mind among the many outstanding minds to have been produced by the Anglophone Caribbean, the remainder of this essay will endeavour to engage with certain cultural influences that created CLR James and with the responses of his exceptional intelligence to those influences.

Born Cyril Lionel Robert James in Tunapuna, Trinidad, in 1901, James was to take first place competing for an island scholarship to attend Queen's Royal College, one of a network of schools modelled on the English public-school system, offering a classical education and producing a class destined to serve as administrators of colonial rule under the British and later take over the reins of power after independence. James's father was a respected, disciplined schoolmaster of the black middle-class, his mother a Wesleyan convent-educated girl who despised carnival and calypso and adored English novels—'and as soon as she put them down I picked them up', writes James (16). Grandfather Josh, James' 'spiritual grandfather', was 'a card' (12) and very popular with everybody, even his white superiors on the sugar estates, despite his obstinate refusal to tell how he repaired machinery when the white engineers failed. On one occasion he virtually saved a sugar estate from economic collapse but still refused to disclose how his empirical know-how had been used in the engine room: 'Why should I tell them?' he asked his admiring grandson, 'They were white men with all their M.I.C.E and R.I.C.E. and all their big degrees, and it was their business to fix it. I had to fix it for them' (15). Another colourful relative, Cousin Nancy, remembers stories of her days as a house slave; and there were several aunts with two of whom James spent many years of his childhood and youth, elderly maiden aunts who survived on sewing and needlework, making them 'primmer and sharper than ever' in his eyes (8); and there was Aunt Judith, 'the English Puritan incarnate' (11), fulfilling her Christian duty right up to the day she collapsed and dropped down dead, having prepared and served a 'great spread' of a meal, as expected, for a crowd of her son's friends who had been invited to Trinidad's Tunapuna club to play a festive cricket match (11–12).

Further family anecdotes and the presence of cricket in their lives—after all the family house was located behind the Tunapuna Cricket Club—led James to surmise that his cultural inheritance was in fact Puritanism and cricket, an inheritance that was to be consolidated in the public-school classrooms and on the public-school playing fields. Yet for all his love of the English classics and his devotion to the game—throughout his childhood and youth James read and re-read *Vanity Fair* some twenty times, he tells us, and took cricket-score clippings from all the English magazines available (*passim*)—James became aware at an early age that all these influences survived in a colony whose existence was guaranteed by the crudest of racist and imperialist attitudes. He was disgusted to realize that much of the adulation showered upon him as a brilliant scholarship winner was because colonial society had been conditioned to accept the inferiority of the black man, and now his own brilliant achievements had placed him at the centre of attention. Whence the acknowledgement of a spiritual grandfather in Josh, though Josh himself never revealed any racial or national consciousness; whence also the duality of the young James' attitude to life. 'Two people lived in me', he writes, 'one the rebel against all family and school discipline and order; the other a Puritan who would have cut off a finger sooner than do anything contrary to the ethics of the game.'(28).

Disturbed by the society in which he lived, James's initial response was to rebel against family expectations of a school system that set the seal on him as a future candidate for the colony's Legislative Council. He shirked his scholastic responsibilities, shaming his parents and causing anxiety for all the teachers in the family, who feared for their own careers if James was expelled from the Queen's Royal College. He was punished by not being allowed to play cricket; so he lied, devised ruses, borrowed, or stole money to get on the cricket pitch for a half-hour or so after school and on Saturdays.

Though James was in later years to come to understand the 'catastrophe' he had threatened to bring on his very respectable family, they need not have worried. Along with the English classics, the young boy was getting an education he would never regret, and developing an attitude to the established order through cricket, which game he initially perceived as a great social leveller. National and racial issues were never bought up at school: 'In our little Eden [they] never bothered us' (30); yet he would come to the realization that freedom from prejudice existed only within the boundaries of 'little Eden' and its playing fields, and then only for the players.

One telling experience occurred when he decided to join the war effort and see the world. This was in 1918, the last year of the First World War and his final year at school. Though rumour had it that the recruiting body known as the Merchants' Contingent only took on white or brown young men from the upper classes, a verily undaunted James went along to the recruiting office. He was not only tall and fit, but well-known by now as an up-and-coming cricketer, not to mention his keeping goal for his prestigious public school in the first-class football league. When his turn to be interviewed arrived he walked towards the examiner's desk: '[The merchant] took one look at me', he recalls, 'saw my dark skin and, shaking his head vigorously, motioned me violently away' (31). James was not unduly disturbed, however, despite the shame and anger on the part of his schoolmasters back in 'little Eden'. He writes that the insult to his dignity didn't last for long 'because for so many years these crude intrusions from the world which surrounded us had been excluded' (31).

Perhaps the cruellest lesson, the one which jolted him into a proper understanding of what awaited him after Queens Royal College (QRC) days, was learnt from his closest friend within the boundary. He was a frail white boy with whom James shared a passion for Dickens and whose physical handicap—'he was a left-hander' (31)—James shielded on the cricket pitch. The boy left to study in England, but when he returned to Trinidad and they met up again, they only shared feelings of awkwardness and guilt:

… something had gone wrong with us. … The school-tie can be transplanted, but except on annual sporting occasions the old school-tie cannot be. It is a bond of school only on the surface. The link is between family and friends, between members of the class or caste (32).

Cricket and the urge to write and get published eventually took James to England. The vehicle was an invitation from Learie Constantine, the famous Caribbean cricketer then playing for the Lancashire league, who offered James his home in Nelson with the request for collaboration in writing his autobiography. Although the two men had much cricket in common, the chapter dedicated to Constantine in *Beyond a Boundary* reveals that at first it was Constantine's national and racial views that had an impact on James, rather than the other way round. Nor was it James who took radical politics to Nelson, but rather Nelson, a small Lancashire town known as 'little Moscow' and a stronghold of the Independent Labour Party, which first exposed James to Marxism (Haigh 2003: 47). Through meeting lowly workers and cultivated working-class men and women like Harry and Elizabeth Spencer, who ran a teashop and bakery and possessed an impressive number of books and records (Harry financed a trip to Paris libraries for James when he needed material for his work on Toussaint L'Ouverture), James' colonially-conditioned mind was opened up to new horizons by life in working-class Nelson. For one thing, he realized that the darker races were not the only victims of master-class exploitation, and for another, that Britain's 'intellectual life was not confined to the capital and the universities', as one British intellectual was to concur (Ward 1980).

After Learie Constantine introduced him to the *Manchester Guardian's* sports editor, James was taken on board as cricket correspondent; he was to write little fiction thereafter. He had been writing short stories and a novel whilst he was a teacher in Trinidad as well as helping Alfred Mendes to pioneer indigenous writing through their short-lived magazine, *Trinidad* (1929–30), and had arrived in Nelson in 1932 with a few of the stories and the novel, which was to become the first novel by a West Indian published in Britain. *Minty Alley* was the only novel he was ever to produce, appearing in 1936 to good reviews, although its big success did not come until it was first reprinted in 1960. It was said that the novel 'states in the clearest possible way the basic problem in the Caribbean: the problem between the West Indian intellectual and the uneducated'—to which James retorted: '... when I wrote it I hadn't the faintest idea I was doing that. I wrote it at the rate of a chapter a day practising my art' (qtd Hamilton 1980).

Notwithstanding the disclaimer, a political conscience had been developing in James from his early QRC days, when, as we have seen, he began to gain an insight into the established order's disregard for the lesser breeds, although it was certainly only after his Nelson reawakening to the dynamics of socialism (not to mention his renewed self-confidence as the *Guardian's* respected cricket correspondent) that James' opus became prompted by an eagerness to express his views on significant socio-political issues rather than by the desire to entertain. He was now a fervent believer in the classless society of Marx and Engels, and in cricket he had found a 'metaphor for colonialism', especially in the symbolism that West Indian teams were led always by members of the local white autarchy (Haigh 2003: 150).

At the end of the decade he produced *The Black Jacobins* (1938), the history of the only successful slave revolution under its leader Toussaint L'Ouverture in the French colony of San

Domingo in 1798, which led to the founding of Haiti. James chose the subject, he said, because 'he was tired of hearing and reading about blacks having things done to them and wanted to show them in the saddle' (qtd Hamilton 1980). Indeed, in answer to the accusation that he had never written in depth about the dictatorships that had ruled Haiti since Tousssaint's time, he responded that that was a matter for later historians, for his job had been 'to dig up the other side of the story' (qtd Davis 1986).

Needless to say cricket's ethical code would continue to influence James' world view permanently. His rejection of Stalinism is characteristic: 'I realised the Stalinists were the greatest liars and corruptors of history there ever were,' he proclaimed about the decade in which Stalinist mythology dominated the left (qtd Arlott 1989). Thereafter he was keen to meet prominent Trotskyists, eventually meeting the leader himself in Mexico in 1938 to discuss world revolution ... and cricket! But James, though remaining a committed Marxist to the end, became disaffected when he realized that the movement was not only indifferent to race and cleaved to an elitist ideology—'my politics cannot be governed by any system. I take the game as it comes' (qtd Porter 1986)—but also because Trotsky dismissed sport as a distraction from the class struggle (Haigh 2003: 149). Later he was to fall out with Eric Williams, the first Prime Minister of independent Trinidad, with whom he was invited to collaborate in the 1960s. James dissented from the political direction post-colonial Trinidad was taking and abhorred the little faith Williams was showing in the people who had brought him to power. Sadly for James, his native island reflected the general problem of the Caribbean: in his view, despite independence, the islands remained colonial regimes. Nor did his opinions soften over time: in an interview he gave in 1980 he continued to dismiss the Caribbean leaders as 'Just holding on for what the imperialists left' (qtd Mike Phillips 1980).

James died in London in 1989. He had written relentlessly about the injustices of the world, witnessed throughout personal experiences in his native Caribbean, Europe, Africa, and the US. Yet he was to remain an incurable optimist to the end: 'I'm optimistic because I simply cannot believe that those who promote democracy will be defeated,' he claimed not long before his death (qtd Davis 1986). This statement surely testifies to a lasting faith in and reverence for the game of cricket which, to James's mind, as another black writer from the Caribbean has written eulogistically, meant 'much more than a sport: it exemplifie[d] all that is decent and positive in human achievement' (Caryl Phillips 1986).

## Note

1.   Blurb from DVD version of *Lagaan*. Aamir Khan Productions Pvt Ltd, 2001.

## Works Cited

Anthony, Michael. *Cricket in the Road*. Heinemann Caribbean Writers Series, London, 1973.

Arlott, John. 'Behind the Marxist Crease', in *Guardian,* 1 June 1989.

Cumber Dance, Daryl. 'Michael Anthony', *Fifty Caribbean Writers: A Bio-bibliographical Critical Sourcebook*. New York: Greenwood Press, 1986, 19–25.

Davis, Clive. 'In praise of cricket and revolution', in *Guardian*, 17 February 1986.

Errol, John. *Moon on a Rainbow Shawl*. London: Faber and Faber, 1957.

Firth, Kathleen. 'Aspects of V.S. Naipaul's Caribbean Fiction'. Unpublished PhD thesis presented at Barcelona University, Spain, 1987.

Gowariker, Ashutosh. *Lagaan*, DVD version Aamir Khan Productions Pvt. Ltd., distributed by Columbia Tristar Home Entertainment and SRC, Madrid, 2001.

Haigh, Gideon. 'C.L.R. James', *New Writing 12*. Eds Diran Adebayo, Blake Morrison and Jane Rogers. London: Picador, 2003, 144–56.

Hamilton, Alex. 'The cricketing Marxist and the tests still to come', in *Guardian,* 25 June 1980.

James, C.L.R. *Minty Alley*. Republished 1971. London: New Beacon Books, 1936.

_____. *The Black Jacobins: Toussaint L'Ouverture and the San Domingo Revolution*. Republished 1963. New York: Vintage Books, 1939.

_____. *Beyond a Boundary*. Republished 1993. Durham: Duke University Press, 1963.

Naipaul, V.S. *Miguel Street.* Republished 1971. Middlesex: Penguin, 1959.

_____. *The Middle Passage: Impressions of Five Societies—British, French and Dutch—in the West Indies and South America.* Republished 1977. Middlesex: Penguin, 1962.

Phillips, Caryl. 'The absolute all-rounder', in *Guardian,* 28 November 1986.

Phillips, Mike. 'The Caribbean Mind', in *Time Out,* 11 July 1980.

Porter, Henry. 'Reasons to be cheerful', in *the Sunday Times,* 2 March 1986.

Ward, Colin. 'The scholarship boy who travelled', in *the Times Educational Supplement,* 27 June 1980.

# Notes on Contributors

**John Clement Ball** holds a doctorate from the University of Toronto and teaches postcolonial literature in the Department of English at the University of New Brunswick, Fredericton, Canada. He is co-editor of the journal *Studies in Canadian Literature* and the author of *Imagining London: Postcolonial Fiction and the Transnational Metropolis* (University of Toronto Press 2004) and *Satire and the Postcolonial Novel: V.S. Naipaul, Chinua Achebe, Salman Rushdie* (Routledge 2003).

**Bruce Bennett** is Emeritus Professor in the School of Humanities and Social Sciences, University of New South Wales at the Australian Defence Force Academy in Canberra. He is a Board Member of the Australia-India Council, and is on the executive of the Australian Academy of the Humanities. He has written or edited *Spirit in Exile* (1991), *An Australian Compass* (1991), *The Oxford Literary History of Australia* (1998), *Crossing Cultures* (1996), *Australian Short Fiction: A History* (2002), and *Homing In* (2006).

**Homi K. Bhabha** is Anne F. Rothenberg Professor of the Humanities, Department of English, Harvard University; Director of the Humanities Center at Harvard; and Distinguished Visiting Professor in the Humanities at University College, London. He is the author of *The Location of Culture* (Routledge 1994, 2004) and editor of the essay collection *Nation and Narration* (Routledge 1990). Bhabha's new book, *A Global Measure*, will be published by Harvard University Press.

**Shirley Chew** is Emeritus Professor of Commonwealth and Postcolonial Literatures at the University of Leeds. She is the founding editor of *Moving Worlds: A Journal of Transcultural Writings*. Her work in progress includes the *Blackwell History of Postcolonial Literatures*. Her review of Vikram Seth's *An Equal Music* was published in *The Times Literary Supplement* (2 April 1999).

**Austin Clarke,** Caribbean-Canadian novelist, is the author of nine novels, including *The Survivors of the Crossing* (1964), *Amongst Thistles and Thorns* (1965), *The Toronto Trilogy* (rpt. 1998); three books of memoirs, including *Growing Up Stupid Under the Union Jack* (1980); and five short story collections. For his novel *The Polished Hoe* (2002), he won the Giller Prize and the Commonwealth Writers Prize. Clarke has played an important role in the Civil Rights movement in Canada, and in the black cultural movement in North America.

**Geoffrey V. Davis** is Professor of English in Aachen University in Germany. He read Modern Languages at Oxford, wrote his doctorate on East German literature and his postdoctoral thesis on South African writing. His recent publications include *Voices of Justice and Reason: Apartheid and Beyond in South African Literature* (Amsterdam 2003) and a co-edited collection, *Staging New Britain: Aspects of Black and South Asian British Theatre Practice* (Brussels 2006).

**Kathleen Firth** is a Senior Lecturer in Postcolonial Studies at Barcelona University, her main research interests being Canadian, West Indian and Indian literatures. Her publications include K. Firth and F. Hand, *India: Fifty Years after Independence: Images in Literature, Film and the Media* (Leeds: Peepal Press 2001). She is at present preparing a volume on Indian writing in English for Spanish university students.

**Ian Gaskell**, theatre director and designer, is Professor of Theatre Arts at the University of the South Pacific, Fiji. He has been undertaking research with the Wan Smolbag Theatre Company of Vanuatu for several years in assessing the educational effectiveness of community theatre. He has published papers on several playwrights of the region, and edited *Beyond Ceremony: An Anthology of Drama from Fiji* (2001).

**Gerald Gaylard** is a senior lecturer in the English Department at the University of the Witwatersrand. His most recent publications are a special edition of 'Scrutiny 2' devoted to the work of Ivan Vladislavic (2006) and *After Colonialism: African Postmodernism and Magical Realism* (Wits Press 2006). He works in the fields of postcolonialism, postmodernism, and African studies, against a backdrop of realism and romanticism, and is currently interested in ecocriticism.

**Priyamvada Gopal** is Senior Lecturer in the Faculty of English, Cambridge University, and Fellow of Churchill College there. Her *Literary Radicalism in India: Gender, Nation and the Transition to Independence* (of which her contribution here forms a part) was published in 2005.

**Sukeshi Kamra** is an Associate Professor in the English Department, Carleton University, Canada. She is the author of *Bearing Witness: Partition, Independence, End of the Raj* (University of Calgary Press 2002) and is currently working on a book-length study of the formation of the nationalist public sphere in colonial India. She teaches courses in South Asian culture and postcolonial theory.

**Chelva Kanaganayakam** is Professor of English at the University of Toronto. He is the author of *Counterrealism and Indo-Anglian Fiction* (2002), *Dark Antonyms and Paradise: The Poetry of Rienzi*

*Crusz* (1997), *Configurations of Exile: South Asian Writers and Their World* (1995), and *Structures of Negation: The Writings of Zulfikar Ghose* (1993). He has also edited *Moveable Margins: The Shifting Spaces of Canadian Literature* (2005) and *Lutesong and Lament: Tamil Writing from Sri Lanka* (2001).

**Meenakshi Mukherjee** is a literary critic based in Hyderabad. Her books include *The Twice Born Fiction* (1971), *Realism and Reality: Novel and Society in India* (1986) and *The Perishable Empire* (2000). She has taught in several universities in India, the last and longest spell being in Jawaharlal Nehru University, New Delhi.

**Isabel Santaolalla** teaches at Roehampton University, London. She has published on postcolonial literature, cultural studies and film, and on the representation of ethnicity and gender in both Anglophone and Hispanic cultures. She is the editor of '*New' Exoticism: Changing Patterns in the Construction of Otherness* (2000), and co-editor of *Luis Buñuel: New Readings* (2004) and *The Transnational in Iberian and Latin American Cinemas* (2007). She is the author of *Los 'Otros'. Etnicidad y 'raza' en el cine español contemporáneo* (2005).

**John Scheckter** is Professor of English at Long Island University, New York. He is the author of a thematic study, *The Australian Novel 1830–1980* (1999), and numerous examinations of Australian, American, and Canadian fiction and autobiography. He is a founding member and past president of the American Association of Australian Literary Studies. His current research is in the seventeenth-century origins of imperial vision.

**Vikram Seth,** poet and novelist, has published three volumes of poems: *Mappings* (1980), *The Humble Administrator's Garden* (1985), and *All You Who Sleep Tonight* (1990); three novels: *The Golden Gate* (in verse, 1986), *A Suitable Boy* (1993), and *An Equal Music* (1999); a travel book, *From Heaven Lake* (1983); a book in verse for children, *Beastly Tales* (1992); a book of translations, *Three Chinese Poets* (1992); and a libretto, *Arion and the Dolphin* (1994). His most recent book, *Two Lives* (2005), is a biography.

**Eddie Tay** is Honorary Assistant Professor at the School of English, University of Hong Kong. His articles on transnational Anglophone literatures of Singapore and Malaysia have appeared in *Textual Practice* and *Southeast Asian Review of English*. He is also the author of two volumes of poetry, *Remnants* (2001) and *A Lover's Soliloquy* (2005), and has appeared at various international literary festivals.

**Harish Trivedi** is Professor of English at the University of Delhi and has been a visiting professor at the universities of Chicago and London. He is the author of *Colonial Transactions: English Literature and India* (1993; rpt. 1995), and has co-edited *Literature and Nation: Britain and India 1800–1990* (2000), *Post-colonial Translation: Theory and Practice* (London 1999), and *Interrogating Post-colonialism: Theory, Text and Context* (1996; rpt. 2000).

**Poonam Trivedi,** Reader in English at Indraprastha College, University of Delhi, received her doctorate from the Shakespeare Institute, University of Birmingham. She has co-edited a collection of essays, *India's Shakespeare: Translation, Interpretation and Performance* (2005), authored a CD-ROM 'King Lear *in India*' (2006) and published on women in Shakespeare, Shakespeare performance in India, and Indian theatre.

# Index